The
Backyard
Birdhouse
Book

Building
Nestboxes
and Creating
Natural Habitats

The Backyard Birdhouse Book

Building Nestboxes and Creating Natural Habitats

René and Christyna M. Laubach

STOREY BOOKS

North Adams, Massachusetts 01247

*The mission of Storey Communications is to serve our customers
by publishing practical information that encourages
personal independence in harmony with the environment.*

Edited by Deborah Burns and Marie Salter
Cover design by Barbara Werden and Meredith Maker
Cover: Eastern Bluebird © Jeremy Woodhouse, New England Stock Photography;
background habitat photos © A. Blake Gardner
Text design and production by Mark Tomasi
Production assistance by Susan Bernier and Jen Rork
Internal photo credits may be found on page 195
Watercolor illustrations by Brigita Fuhrmann
Indexed by Nan Badgett/Word•a•bil•i•ty

Storey Books are available for special premium and promotional uses and for customized
editions. For further information, please call Storey's Custom Publishing Department at
1-800-793-9396.

Printed in the United States by Banta Book Group, Menasha, WI.
10 9 8 7 6 5 4 3 2

Library of Congress Cataloging-in-Publication Data

Laubach, René.
    The backyard birdhouse book : building nestboxes and creating natural habitats
/ René and Christyna M. Laubach.
    p. cm.
        Includes bibliographical references and index.
        ISBN 1-58017-172-9 (hc). — ISBN 1-58017-104-4 (pbk)
1. Birdhouses—Design and construction. 2. Birds—Nests. 3. Cavity-nesting birds. 4. Bird
attracting. I. Laubach, Christyna M. II. Title.
QL676.5 .L37 1999
598.156'4—ddc21   98-35972
                                                                        CIP

Contents

To mamusia, tatus i Ani,

and to Elmer Mellen

Foreword

A survey conducted by the U.S. Department of the Interior in 1991 determined that more than 60 million people engage in residential bird feeding. More recently, statistics have shown that bird-watching, after hiking and backpacking, is the fastest growing form of outdoor recreation in the United States. These powerful figures reveal the infatuation that Americans have with birds. Indeed, people love birds! They love to find and identify them, watch them, photograph them, count them, read about them, feed them, and construct homes for them. To address this last point, René and Christyna Laubach created *The Backyard Birdhouse Book* — a resource that should prove invaluable to anyone interested in enticing cavity-nesting birds onto their property, or in possibly trying to enhance larger landscapes for the benefit of cavity-nesting bird species.

The Backyard Birdhouse Book describes North America's cavity-nesting birds within the context of the ever-changing landscape that has characterized so much of the continent since the arrival of the Pilgrims in the 1600s. From the ancestral clearing of forests for farming and building materials, to the more recent removal of dead trees and snags from suburban woodlands for perceived aesthetic and silviculture benefits, bird species that require cavities for nesting have been put upon. When human-induced nest-cavity shortages are compounded by pressures brought about by alien nest-site competitiors such as European Starlings and House Sparrows, and predation by domestic animals such as house cats, the value of encouraging and properly managing cavity-nesting birds becomes obvious.

Fortunately, it has been clearly proven that "backyard bird conservation" can make a difference. As stellar examples, witness the spectacular increases enjoyed by Wood Duck and Eastern Bluebird populations in eastern North America during the past quarter century, both largely attributable to aggressive cavity-nestbox erection programs on the species' behalf. Time will tell if similarly dedicated efforts can help restore dwindling American Kestrel and red-headed woodpecker populations in regions of the country where these species appear to be declining.

By integrating a pleasing blend of avian natural history with useful ecological management suggestions, the Laubachs have produced a blueprint for anyone seriously interested in wishing to attract cavity-nesting bird species to their dooryard. A broad variety of nestbox construction options and techniques for discouraging predators mirror the similarly broad range of nesting behaviors employed by cavity-nesting birds in different parts of the country. The thoughtful reader should be able to integrate these variations to suit the particular site where cavity nestboxes are being deployed. At the same time that guidelines are offered for the homeowner wishing to attract cavity-nesting birds to the backyard, *The Backyard Birdhouse Book* also offers broader perspectives on techniques and methodologies that bird clubs, scout troops, garden clubs, and Audubon chapters might usefully employ in attempting to restore or increase healthy cavity-nesting bird populations over larger landscape areas.

With this carefully researched, handsomely illustrated, and easy-to-use guide as a reference, both suburban and rural residents alike now have a compendium of meticulously compiled information at their fingertips that should make it possible for people living almost anywhere in North America to provide appropriate housing for cavity-nesting birds.

— Wayne R. Petersen
Field Ornithologist, Massachusetts Audubon Society
Vice President, American Birding Association

Preface

Once you have witnessed a successful nesting, your enthusiasm for birds and nestboxes will increase exponentially. This book is an outgrowth of our love and interest in birds. We have spent countless hours birding, in many far-flung locales, and enjoying every single minute. Seeing the whole life process, from the birds returning in spring to the fledging of young, thrills us to this day no matter how many times we have observed it. Watching this occur in a nestbox that you have built and placed makes the experience particularly meaningful.

We have organized this book to be user friendly. Questions, problems, solutions, and special insights are given to maximize the likelihood of success as you begin working with nestboxes. Remember, though, that attracting birds to a nestbox can be a bit like making a piecrust: We all start with the same basic recipe, but some of us have greater skill than others do. If at first you don't succeed, try again! For easy reference, we have capitalized only the species names of birds featured in this text.

The book begins with an introduction to cavity nesting. We explain why birds use cavities and the difference between primary and secondary cavity nesters. We also answer the question, "Why erect nestboxes?" To get started with your nestbox project, you must first appraise the habitat in your area and find out what birds are present. Once you know this, you'll be better able to choose the appropriate box to build. The first chapter guides you through this process.

We also share keys to birding success. Box design and location must be carefully considered, as well as when to make the box available to birds and how and when to monitor. We answer common hows, whys, and what-ifs, to inform you about these important issues.

The second chapter profiles 27 cavity nesters. Even if you decide not to build a nestbox, this chapter offers valuable information on common cavity nesters, including bird size, nest construction, incubation period, age at fledging, food choices, competitors, parasites and predators, type of habitat required, and life history. The more you know about the birds you are trying to attract, the better.

In the third chapter, we provide detailed step-by-step directions for building eight nestboxes. Whether a novice or an experienced woodworker, you'll find all the information you'll need to make a suitable box for the species you want to attract. This chapter lists all the materials and tools needed to construct a particular box, discusses how to select the proper screws and bolts, and provides detailed cutting and assembly instructions. If you follow these directions, you *will* build a nestbox. Illustrations will guide your work.

When your nestbox is complete, you'll need to mount it in an appropriate location and consider whether you'll need a predator guard. Several mounting options and tried-and-true predator guards are presented in the fourth chapter. Predator guards are a simple way to safeguard nestbox residents and are highly recommended.

In an effort to help birds and increase the likelihood of your success in attracting the desired species to your nestbox, we have included a special chapter on landscaping a habitat. The habitat needs of birds can be very specific. Used in conjunction with the habitat information provided in the profiles chapter, this section will help you make your property more desirable to birds. By implementing some of the simple adjustments we suggest, it's possible that the number of birds visiting your property will double.

The book's final chapter is devoted to conservation opportunities. Whether you choose to participate by yourself or with a friend or family member, all are rewarding ways to spend time enjoying nature and to increase your knowledge of birds.

Writing this book has been a wonderful opportunity for us to share our love of birds with others. It has given us many happy and memorable hours together. May all of you have good success with your cavity nesters and, likewise, experience the joys of the world around us.

— *René and Christyna Laubach*

Acknowledgments

We would like to thank Henrietta (Ani) Zielinski, for her help with our initial literature search; Gabe Hoebel-Russell, who kept us up-to-date via the Internet; David Clapp of the Massachusetts Audubon Society's South Shore Wildlife Sanctuaries, for information about their successful martin gourd nesting efforts; Elmer Mellen, for inspiration and his many insights into the science and art of bluebird trail management; and Kathy Winstanley, for taking publicity photos for us. Thanks also to Dan and Mary Galusha, for allowing their bluebird trail to be photographed.

We would also like to thank the staff of Storey Books, particularly Deborah Balmuth, Deborah Burns, and Marie Salter, for asking us to put these thoughts on paper and for working with us to make this book a reality.

Fundamentals of Nesting

Of the approximately 650 different species of breeding birds found in North America, only 86 nest in cavities. Natural cavities are found in nature for a variety of reasons. Woodpeckers, also called primary cavity nesters because they excavate their own nest sites, are the principal architects of many cavities. These birds excavate a new hole each breeding season. Abandoned after their initial use, the holes are then occupied and used by other species, including wrens, bluebirds, flycatchers, and swallows. The species that rely on pre-existing holes are termed secondary cavity nesters.

Other manufacturers of cavities include high winds, lightning strikes, ice storms, insects, and fungal infections, as well as a host of plant diseases. Together, these provide an endless supply of broken limbs and dead standing trees. Limbs that are broken or a tree split by lightning may be invaded by a fungus. Over time, the heartwood rots. A natural cavity may result, and birds may claim the hole for a nesting site. The decaying wood also makes it easier for some birds, such as chickadees, to excavate cavities of their own.

Problems arise, however, since few humans see the value of these dead trees. Many are cut for firewood or removed for aesthetic reasons. Broken limbs are frequently cut off because the tree has an unsightly and unbalanced appearance. Potential nest sites are thereby eliminated.

Reasons for Cavity Nesting

Why do some birds choose to nest in cavities? Compared to open nests, such as the ones robins construct, cavities provide better protection, from not only the elements but also predators, for nestlings and adults. Residents of cavities are shielded from rain and snow, along with cold temperatures, that early arrivals could encounter in spring. Cavities also provide a haven from the temperature extremes of midsummer. Avian predators such as crows and jays are usually foiled by the small entrance hole and have less accessibility to the young. Cavity nesters are also rarely victims of cowbird parasitism. This all translates into greater nesting success. Studies have found that cavity

◄ Primary cavity nesters, such as this red-headed woodpecker, provide important nests sites for many secondary cavity-nesting species.

Nestling survival rates are generally lower for open-nesting birds, like this American Robin, than for cavity nesters.

nesters experience a 60 to 80 percent fledging success, whereas open nesters have only a 20 to 40 percent success rate. In addition, open nesters tend to fledge, or leave the nest for the first time, at 9 to 11 days, whereas cavity nesters tend to fledge at an average of 16 to 22 days. By extending the brooding period, the young birds leaving the cavity nest are larger, stronger, and better able to fly than those individuals in open nests. This also contributes to the overall higher survival rate of the cavity nesters' young.

If cavities are such good places to nest, then, why don't all birds use them? Birds need certain physical and behavioral adaptations in order to use cavities. Cavity-nesting birds must have strong feet in order to cling to the vertical face of the tree or nestbox. They must also be behaviorally suited to entering and exploring small, dark spaces. Most, if not all, open-nesting birds will not explore dark holes or even crevices. Suitable cavities are always in demand, and there are more potential tenants than cavities. Frequently, aggressive competition results between prospective tenants. This is one reason why it is fairly easy to attract a cavity-nesting bird to a nestbox, provided that you place it in the proper habitat.

Need for Nest Sites

Each year thousands of acres of suitable wildlife habitat are being destroyed, primarily for use in residential development and intensive agriculture. In the late 1800s, the eastern half of North America was mostly small farms. These farms had a number of woodlots full of old trees, where cavity-nesting birds could rear their young. Even timber fence posts used to delineate fields and pastures provided potential nest sites.

Natural cavities, such as this one occupied by a family of House Wrens, are often in short supply.

Today, woodlots are being cleared, and timber posts are being replaced by more durable structures. The patchy, grassy areas of old fields, which in the past provided foraging areas for bluebirds and other species, are being plowed under in order to make room for monocultural row crops such as corn. And with the intensification of monoculture farming, pesticides and herbicides have been applied more intensively. This practice affects birds both directly and indirectly, often killing the bird and always contaminating its insect prey.

Also, greenhouse gases (including carbon dioxide, methane, nitrous oxide, and chlorofluorocarbons [CFCs]) emitted from vehicles and industry are involved in climatic changes. In the near future, possibly as soon as 25 to 50 years from now, some parts of North America could experience unusually cold winters with above-average snowfalls, while other parts of the country see significant shifts in overall climatic conditions and droughts. These changes will have an effect on all birds and other life forms, not only the cavity nesters.

Aggressive Undesirables and Others

Many cavity-nesting birds lose their nest sites to more aggressive birds. Two species in particular have had an impact: the House Sparrow and the European Starling. The House Sparrow, not a sparrow but a weaver finch, was introduced into the United States in 1851 and 1852. Within six decades, it had succeeded in overrunning the entire country. With its sharp bill, it can pierce the skull of nestlings and adults. The European Starling, on the other hand, was introduced into Central Park in 1890. From those first 100 individuals, the starling population now numbers more than 200 million! Starlings will kill or evict young birds from their cavity nest. They are a direct threat to woodpeckers,

House Sparrows and some other introduced species pose a threat to native cavity-nesting birds.

especially the downy, hairy, Red-bellied, and red-headed woodpeckers, as well as the Northern Flicker. If these species are negatively affected, then the number of cavities made anew each year will decline, which in turn will have a direct influence on secondary cavity-nesting birds. The increased populations of house cats and, in some cities, squirrels add to the hardships experienced by cavity-nesting birds. Birds, after all, play a vital role in our environment. They consume vast numbers of insects, along with literally thousands of pounds (kilograms) of weed seeds a year. If it were not for birds, these seeds would become fodder for insects and small mammals. Birds help keep these populations in check.

How We Can Help

For a number of decades, wildlife biologists, ornithologists, and interested individuals have erected nestboxes for cavity-nesting birds. Many success stories have been entered into the annals of conservation. For example, about 100 years ago Wood Duck populations in North America were extremely low. Excessive lumbering along rivers decreased the available nest sites. In addition excessive shooting at twilight, when ducks returned to their roosts, affected the population adversely. Nestbox programs that were started in the 1930s and continue today are credited with helping the Wood Duck rebound.

In many areas, nestbox programs in part have brought back Wood Duck populations from near extinction during the 1930s.

Bluebirds have experienced a similar success story. A properly constructed nestbox placed in a suitable habitat can indeed be a remedy for the decreasing availability of nest sites faced by cavity-nesting birds.

Attracting birds is a challenge: Much remains unknown about some of the most common species. Yet watching birds select a nest site, build a nest, and raise young can be a fascinating and exciting experience. It is a wonderful opportunity to observe and enjoy nature. It can also provide immense satisfaction to nestbox owners, who are doing their part to help restore the natural balance that humanity disturbed. Placing and maintaining nestboxes could be considered a method of enhancing an existing habitat. It does not, however, eliminate the need for preserving and managing wildlife habitats or conserving dead trees.

Location, Location, Location!

Both your geographic location and the placement of your nestboxes will determine what birds you will attract. Chickadees, House Sparrows, and starlings appear to be adapted to a wide range of nesting situations. The latter two species, however, are undesirable tenants: They can and do inflict a toll on native birds such as chickadees and bluebirds. Provided that the habitat is appropriate, House Wrens can be fairly easily enticed to nest in urban settings. Most suburbs have a good mixture of trees, shrubs, and lawn, which can attract a wide variety of birds such as the Tree and Violet-green Swallows, Purple Martin, Bewick's Wren, Tufted Titmouse, and Northern Flicker. Country settings can interest species such as bluebirds, Carolina Wrens, Wood Ducks, and barn swallows. Still, not all are present across North America. Knowing what species are present will help you decide what bird to attract. This will also be a deciding factor in the type of box you build or purchase, and where you place it.

Placing a Nestbox in the Proper Habitat

Before you place a nestbox, consider whether you have the proper habitat for the type of bird you are trying to attract. If your nest site is near a park or a woodlot with big trees, you will probably have an easy time attracting woodpeckers, chickadees, nuthatches, and Tufted Titmice. These birds can be lured to nestboxes in shaded areas, because they ordinarily nest in woodlands and along woodland edges. Many birds, in fact, prefer to nest along the edges of habitats: dunes that abut beaches, cliffs, the edges of ponds or rivers, forest edges near meadows, and the shrubby borders in yards.

Knowing habitat needs will assist you in placing your nestboxes in the appropriate sites. Not all cavity nesters will accept housing placed in the middle of a yard or meadow, away from the protective cover of woods and underbrush. Chickadees will not nest in a field the way bluebirds or swallows will. Keep in mind that most woodland species favor having shrubs near the nestbox that they can use as perches as they travel in and out. And remember that birds need to find food in the area of the nestbox. If the proper food is not available, they will travel to places where it can be found. If this is the case, chances are good that they will not nest in your box. Doing your homework, learning what birds exist in your area during the breeding season, and assessing your habitat can result in luring the desired species to the area where you place the box.

Like other cavity nesters, bluebirds benefit from properly constructed nestboxes placed in suitable habitats. Here, Eastern Bluebirds have taken up residence in a Peterson box (see design on p. 135).

Choosing What Species to Attract

Attracting *any* native species to your nestbox should be considered a success. This is accomplished by determining what species are present, knowing their individual requirements (such as food, water, and housing), and knowing if the area you are considering meets the species' requirements. Luck also plays a role. All native birds have their charm and beauty. Each has a special niche in its ecosystem. Given the current losses of nest sites, the production of fledging young should be an occasion for celebration.

The birds listed in this book are excellent candidates for nestboxes. Each will benefit from your placing boxes in the appropriate habitat. Each will also provide you with unique insights into the private lives of our avian neighbors. In some cases, very little is known about a species. If you have successfully attracted one of these to your nestbox, the information you gather during the breeding season can actually add data to our understanding of that species.

Keys to Birding Success:
Box Design and Location

The nestboxes described in this book are relatively easy to build. Most will attract a variety of birds, although some are specific to one species. Whether you are an experienced woodworker or a novice, read and study the directions for assembling the box you have chosen to build, and the accompanying drawings. If you decide to purchase a box instead, our directions and illustrations can tell you if the box you plan to buy is built correctly, or if you should make modifications.

Think Like a Bird

Good nestboxes should be of sturdy construction and made from at least ¾-inch (1.9 cm) thick untreated lumber. Be sure to keep the rough surface of the wood on the inside of the nestbox. The natural cavities that birds use for nest sites have a rough-surface interior that provides plenty of footholds, which are especially handy for young birds. The nestbox that you make or buy should mirror these natural cavities. If the box is deep and smooth, footholds must be added. Cutting a series of horizontal grooves (kerfs) into the wood below the entrance can make it easier for the young birds to fledge.

The roofs of nestboxes should be sloping and extend beyond the sides of the box. Depending on the design, the roof should extend 2 to 5 inches (5.1 to 12.7 cm) beyond the front of the box. This will exclude any driving rain, wind, and sun, and will help deter predators. Generally, the sides of the box should extend at least ¼ inch (.6 cm) beyond the floor to allow water to drip off.

Access to the box should be easy, to facilitate nest inspection and maintenance. The best-designed boxes have a roof that detaches for inspection and a side panel that pivots out for cleaning. Box sides should have ventilation holes or spaces, and floors should have drainage holes. Young birds will suffocate if the box is too hot, and drown or die of hypothermia if they are wet. Native cavity-nesting birds do not need perches to enter nestboxes.

Check Dimensions

Entry-hole dimensions must be appropriate. Make sure the hole is large enough to admit the bird you are trying to attract, and small enough to exclude undesirable species such as the House Sparrow and starling. House Sparrows are attracted to boxes with perches. If you are familiar with the birds that frequent the area of the nestbox, then you will have a fair idea as to your possible tenants. Generally, however, what will finally succeed in occupying the box for nesting is a guessing game. Approximately one dozen cavity-nesting birds will use boxes with a 1½-inch (3.8 cm) entrance hole. Depending on your location, these might include the Tree Swallow, the Violet-green Swallow, bluebirds, chickadees, wrens, nuthatches, and possibly titmice. Wrens will use holes that are smaller than 1⅛ inches (2.9 cm) in diameter. Woodpeckers, on the other hand, prefer larger holes. The Northern Flicker, Northern Saw-whet Owl, and Red-bellied

Woodpecker, for example, fancy entry holes 2½ inches (6.4 cm) across. Kestrels, screech-owls, Hooded Mergansers, and Wood Ducks require a 3-inch (7.6 cm) hole, but the Wood Duck's should be elliptical in shape.

Selecting a Site

The location you select for your nestbox must match the needs of the bird. All locations should have an abundance of food, protective cover, and water; however, different birds find these requirements in different and varied habitats. Some birds live in fields, others in open woodlands, still others along waterways and forest edges. If your nestbox is to be functional, it and its location must meet the basic needs of the bird you are trying to attract. If you put your nestbox in a field, for example, you might be providing an opportunity for Tree Swallows and bluebirds to nest. If you put it in a wooded area, on the other hand, nuthatches might take up residence. And some species, such as the Purple Martin and Tree Swallow, require a clear flight path to and from the nestbox. The location and box design that best match the bird's natural environment will be most likely to attract tenants.

Practical Considerations. Don't limit yourself to the boundaries of your backyard. If there is an open field nearby, obtain permission from its owner to mount a few boxes along the fencerow. (Stress that the landowner will not be inconvenienced by the nestboxes; their maintenance and monitoring will be your responsibility.) Many businesses, churches, nursing homes, and hospitals have appropriately landscaped areas around their buildings that might make appropriate box sites. Keep in mind that even though golf courses, cultivated fields, gardens, and yards offer great habitats for nest-boxes, these areas might also be exposed to herbicides, pesticides, house cats, and other predators.

Safeguards. In urban environments, boxes should be placed in areas not frequented by cats. As a safeguard, install baffles. This will also protect the occupants from other predators, such as raccoons. (Baffles and their installation are discussed on pages 161–167.) Finally, know the proper height above the ground to mount your box. Kestrels will not nest in boxes 10 feet (3 m) or less above the ground, for instance. Suggested mounting heights are listed in the profiles chapter and with nestbox plans.

When to Place Your Box. A good time to install new boxes is midwinter in the southern portion of North America, and early spring in northern sections. Frozen ground may make installation of posts or pipes impossible until later in spring in some areas, though; consider doing this in fall. The boxes themselves, however, should be erected no later than midwinter in the South and early spring in the North. Boxes need to be erected prior to the arrival of the birds. Once breeding males arrive, territories are established that include one or more nest sites.

Birdbox Don'ts

• Never purchase a box with a perch.

• Never purchase a nestbox that is glued or stapled; it should be bailed or screwed.

• Never paint, stain, or use preservatives on the inside of the nestbox, and never use any type of insect spray. The fumes from these substances may kill the young birds as well as adults.

The Importance of Monitoring

If you have never had the experience of watching birds develop over a period of time, you are in for a treat. You will learn more about the birds nesting in your box during this time than you ever anticipated. Monitoring the box is also one of the most important things you can do to help a brood fledge successfully. By checking the boxes, for instance, you can deter House Sparrows from nesting, especially if you remove their nests repeatedly.

Many people are unaware that checking boxes can be accomplished without inflicting any harm on the birds. Most birds have a very poorly developed sense of smell (vultures are an exception). You can therefore open the box, peek into the nest, and handle the eggs or young safely; the adults will not abandon the nest because of human scent. But you do need to be careful not to make too many trips to the nestbox, lest a trail be developed that could lead predators to it.

Winter Checks

If you have left your nestbox up over winter, you need to inspect it sometime before the breeding season starts. Midwinter through early spring is usually a good time for this, depending on your geographic location. If you find that over winter the box has been claimed by small mammals such as mice, don a rubber glove, stand upwind, and remove the contents. Be careful not to inhale the dust that might be present during this cleaning: Hantavirus, a respiratory infection carried by mice, might be present. This is also a good time to make repairs to the box if any are necessary.

Breeding Season Checks

During the breeding season, check the nestboxes frequently. Generally, checking the box once a week will be tolerated by the birds and will not harm them. When you are at the box, work quickly, efficiently, and quietly. Your visit should be approximately 30 seconds long. Walk slowly up to the box. Some people prefer to gently tap on the side of the box to make the bird aware of their presence. Open the top of the box (if possible), slowly and gently: If the box is not occupied by birds, it might have a mouse, wasps, or even a snake in residence.

Contrary to popular belief, careful handling of eggs and nestlings does not harm birds.

When Not to Monitor

There are times when boxes should not be checked. If you notice that the first egg has been laid, check the profiles in the following pages to get an approximate idea of the species' average clutch size. Allow enough time to elapse for all the eggs to be laid, then revisit the box, noting the number of eggs. Usually, one egg is laid a day. It is not a bad idea to add three to four days as a safety buffer. Check the box in the afternoon; most eggs are laid in the morning, and the female is more likely to leave the nest later in the day to feed.

Nestbox visitation should also be curtailed during the early stages of incubation. Most birds are very sensitive to disturbances during this time. If you keep track of the activity levels of the adult birds, especially the female, you should notice that eventually she begins leaving the nest for extended times. When this occurs, the incubation is well on its way, and you may check the nestbox.

Another time to refrain from checking on the young is when they are close to fledging. The approximate incubation durations and fledging ages are listed in the species accounts, but a good general rule is to limit your visits to the nestbox to the first 10 or 12 days after hatching. Bluebirds and Tree Swallows, for example, should be left alone after 12 days. If the young are disturbed after this time, they may leave the nest prematurely, lessening their chances for survival.

If the weather is cold, damp, or rainy, postpone checking the nestbox until another day. The adult birds need to be able to brood their eggs or young during these times. Checking the box might disturb the parents and keep them away for longer periods of time. This could be stressful to parents and to the developing young.

Note Taking and Record Keeping

Careful note taking is helpful. This becomes increasingly important with species whose breeding behavior and biology are not well documented. In such cases, your notes can make significant contributions to our understanding of these species. You can start taking notes as early as when you notice interested birds attending to your box. At this time, you might be privy to courtship behavior. Later, you can record notes on nest building.

Each time you inspect the nestbox, make careful observations. We find a pocket notebook helpful for this record-keeping task. Your observations should include the day, month, year, and time of day you visited the nestbox. Drawings can be a great aid to recording this data; photographs are wonderful, as well. It is extremely important, especially if you are monitoring more than one box, to record which box you are observing. Identify it by its location; some people number their boxes. The initial visit should include a written description of where the box is situated. The more detail you can include, the better. For example, it is better to note that box #1 is located in an unmowed field that has abundant Queen-Anne's-lace and buttercups blooming with occasional honeysuckle bushes, and that it is about 30 feet (9.2 m) from the forest's edge, than it is to just write that box #1 is in a field. Also include weather conditions such as air temperature, wind speed, and cloud cover.

Record what you see in the nestbox. For example, identify the bird species, the eggs' or nestlings' age (if known), their sex, and what is happening in the nest. Here, too, you need to be very specific. Record the number of eggs or young. Once the young are present, keep very accurate descriptions of the individuals. When necessary, do not be afraid

Contribute Your Data

If you are interested in formalizing your records and sharing your data, contact the Cornell Laboratory of Ornithology (see p. 191) and request North American nest-record cards. Submitting your data will help researchers compile information on nesting birds nationwide.

front

NORTH AMERICAN NEST-RECORD CARD PROGRAM			

Species: *TREE SWALLOW*

YEAR 1 1 9 **9 7** 5 ☐ 9 ☐ 14

Observer (two initials, last name) In squares in space opposite ➤ 15 **R** 17 **L A U B A C H**

Locality (in relation to nearest town) *PLEASANT VALLEY W.S., 2 MI. N., 2 MI. W. LENOX*

County *BERKSHIRE*

State or Province *MA* 34 ☐ 36 **1 3 4 0** 41

Elevation (in feet above sea level)

Latitude 29 **4 2** 31 **2 3** 33
Longitude 41 **7 3** 44 **1 8**

HABITAT (circle where appropriate)
1. Woods 2. Swamp 3. Marsh (4) Field 5. Grassland 6. Desert 7. Tundra 8. Suburban 9. Urban
0. Other (specify)
01. Coniferous 02. Deciduous 03. Mixed 04. Orchard 05. Cultivated 06. Fallow 07. No Veget. 08. Hedgerow
09. Shrub 10. Salt 11. Brackish 12. Fresh 13. Sandy Beach 14. Gravel Beach 15. Other (specify) 46
DOMINANT PLANT(S) IN HABITAT (list one or two)

goldenrod   cherry saplings 49 ☐ 55 ☐ 47

NEST SITE (circle where appropriate)
01 Bare ground 02 On ground in vegetation 03 Floating 04 Low vegetation 05 Shrub 06 Palm 07 Deciduous tree branch
08 Deciduous tree cavity 09 Conifer branch 10 Conifer cavity (11) Nest box 12 Other structure 13 Cliff or bank
14 Other (specify) 61
PRINCIPAL PLANT OR STRUCTURE SUPPORTING NEST *Metal pipe* 63 ☐

Height of Eggs Above Ground or Water in Feet (feet and tenths if under five feet) Feet **4** 72 Tenths **2** 76

If parasited by Cowbird check here and see instructions. ☐ If same pair had other nestings this year, indicate which this is (1, 2, 3) (use separate card for each nesting) 77

rev. 5-4-71 PLEASE COMPLETE BOTH SIDES OF THE CARD 78 79 80 1

back

No. Col. 1-12 (Col. 2-14, side 1) 13 If used for colonial nesting check here ☐ and see instructions

DATE Month	Day	Eggs	Young	Edit	Build-ing	Adult On	COMMENTS Stage of building, if eggs warm, age of young, if banded, etc.
6	6	0	0				*nest seemingly complete*
6	12	0	0				*same as above; saw adult swallow poking out of entrance hole 20 mins. earlier.* ✓
6	20	4	0				*eggs warm.*
7	1	4	0				*eggs warm.*
7	11	0	3				*9 day old? young; banded; adults flying overhead.*
7	16	0	3				*young well-feathered.*
7	22	–	1				*full-grown nestling at entrance; presumably ready to fledge.*
7	23	0	1				*1 dead nestling in box; other 2 presumed successfully fledged.*

01 Unknown because not revisited
02 Young seen leaving nest
03 Parent(s) excited near nest
04 Parent(s) with young near nest
(05) Nest empty, intact
06 Nest empty, damaged

OUTCOME INCLUDING CASES WHERE OUTCOME UNKNOWN (circle where appropriate)
07 Nest deserted
08 Failure due to weather
09 Failure due to predation
10 Failure due to invertebrate parasites
11 Failure due to cowbirds

12 Failure due to competition with other species
13 Failure due to human activities
14 Failure due to pesticides (give details separately)
15 Other (describe above) 76 77

Please complete both sides and return at end of season to your Regional Center or to Laboratory of Ornithology, Cornell University, Ithaca, New York 14850. We thank you for contributing your time and efforts to this program. 78 79 80 2

to carefully pick the young up. Remember, birds have a very poor sense of smell. Inspect the young. This is especially important for those species prone to blowfly infestations. Common sites of attachment for the blowfly are the fleshy parts of the chicks, such as the legs, underwing, and head. Do not hesitate to pull the blowfly larvae off the young. Make note of the number and places of attachment for the blowflies, and of how many young were affected. You might even need to gently lift the entire nest off the floor of the nestbox to check for blowflies. A spatula care-

The band on this 10-day-old Eastern Bluebird could yield valuable information in the future.

fully inserted under the nest and raised a few inches (centimeters) will allow the blowfly larvae and pupae, if any, to fall to the bottom of the nestbox; you can then use an old toothbrush to easily sweep them out. Diatomaceous earth (see the appendix for a list of suppliers) can be placed in the nestbox to discourage insects after the birds have hatched. When handling the young, you will occasionally be presented with fecal sacs. Discard these some distance from the nest, because they, too, could be subtle clues to predators that a potential meal awaits.

Note, too, whether you see both parents or just one. As you leave the nestbox, stand about 100 feet (30.5 m) from it and observe how long it takes before the parent(s) returns to the box. This is also a great time to note the adults' behavior. Behavioral notes will help you understand the relationship between the bird and its environment.

For biologists, accurate field notes are as important as detailed descriptions of bird sightings. Never change your notes. Before you visit a box, review your notes of that particular nest site. This will refresh your memory and help you anticipate the activity within the box. Reviewing the species profiles in this book will also tell you what you can expect before you open the nestbox.

The Unfortunate Few

Occasionally, nestlings will die, as will adults. Do not be alarmed at this, but do be aware that these dead individuals should be removed from the nest. This can be done easily by wearing gloves or by inverting a plastic bag over your hand and simply removing the dead individuals. Remember to dispose of the deceased away from the nest site, since they too might attract predators.

To Clean or Not to Clean?

Most people will instinctively clean the nestbox of its contents once the young birds have fledged. Indeed, it was once thought that after the old nest was discarded, gone also were a host of probable parasites; birds would therefore be attracted to this newly cleaned box. Recently, however, studies have indicated the opposite preference among some birds: A study in Kentucky on Eastern Bluebirds reported that of the 41 pairs studied, 38 preferred boxes with old nests. Still, Tree Swallows in British Columbia preferred cleaned boxes over those filled with old nesting material, and Purple Martins not only preferred compartments with old nesting material but also experienced a higher reproductive rate in them. Finally, House Wrens in Wyoming, given the choice of clean nestboxes or boxes that held old nests, showed no preference. Clearly, more research and data are needed. Results appear to vary not only by species but also geographically.

An Old Nest May Be a Good Nest

What could be the benefits of retaining old nests? For one, old nests may actually provide a more parasite-free environment than clean, empty nestboxes. In a number of cases, old nests have been found to harbor the larvae of a small wasp, the jewel wasp (*Nasonia* spp.). The adults of this wasp species parasitize the larvae of the blowfly, *Protocalliphora*. Perhaps this could explain why the Kentucky bluebirds preferred uncleaned nestboxes: The jewel wasp, found in old nests, could be a limiting factor for blowflies, reducing their nest infestations.

Infestations and Parasites

Why the concern with blowflies? They are ectoparasites (i.e., parasites that live on the exterior of their hosts) and feed on the blood of nestlings. Heavy nest infestations can seriously impact the survival rate of young birds. There are at least 26 different known species of blowflies in North America. If your nestbox is infested with blowflies, there is a very good possibility that more than one species is present. Adult blowflies overwinter in leaf litter. In spring, females deposit their eggs either directly onto the young nestlings or in the nest. Blowfly eggs hatch within 24 to 48 hours. This corresponds to the fledge stage of the birds: If the eggs took longer to hatch, the larvae would not have sufficient time to develop and feed on the nestlings. Blowflies remain in the larval stage for 7 to 15 days. During this time, they must feed on blood in order to develop. Larvae will therefore attach themselves to the fleshy parts of the young birds during the night; daytime

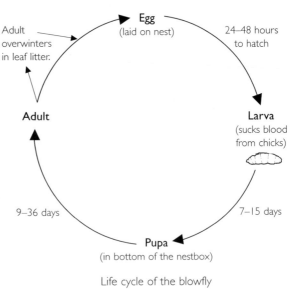

Life cycle of the blowfly

hours are spent in the nesting material. After a sufficient number of blood meals, the larvae pupate. The pupal stage may last from 9 to more than 36 days. When the adults emerge and young birds are still in the nest, mating will occur. Females subsequently lay eggs, and the cycle repeats. If no nestlings are available, though, the adult blowflies will become residents of the leaf litter until the following spring. Installing a hardware cloth platform ¾ inch (1.9 cm) above the bottom of the nestbox will reduce blowfly parasitism.

Jewel wasps are about ⅛ inch (.3 cm) in length, and can be easily recognized by their bright metallic colors. These wasps overwinter inside the case of the blowfly pupae. Their life cycle is interesting. In spring the wasp emerges and the female locates a nestbox that contains pupating blowflies. With the tip of her abdomen, she drills a small hole into the blowfly pupal case and deposits an egg. The wasp larva then consumes the pupating blowfly, and the now-vacant pupal case of the blowfly is used as a home by the pupating wasp! From egg to adult takes approximately 10 days. This is one serious argument for not cleaning out your nestboxes. However, this tiny wasp may not be present throughout all of North America; it is notably missing from the Midwest. More data are also needed to fully understand the relationship between blowflies and jewel wasps.

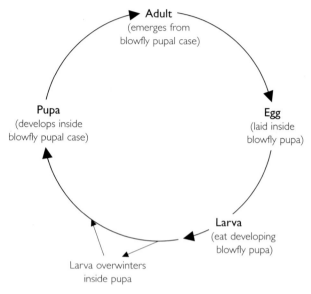

Adult
(emerges from blowfly pupal case)

Egg
(laid inside blowfly pupa)

Larva
(eat developing blowfly pupa)

Pupa
(develops inside blowfly pupal case)

Larva overwinters inside pupa

Life cycle of the jewel wasp

Some data from Ontario, Canada, have revealed changes in blowfly population numbers during the breeding season. The first bluebird nesting studied suffered from an intense population of blowfly larvae. Jewel wasp numbers were low; in fact, only 2 percent of blowfly pupae were parasitized. By midsummer, however, all nests contained not only blowflies but also jewel wasps. An amazing 60 percent of the blowfly pupae had been killed by the wasps!

Cleaning Options

Nestbox landlords have three options:

1. Remove the contents of the nestbox immediately after the young have fledged. If you discard the contents nearby onto the field or forest floor, any jewel wasp larvae present will become susceptible to predators. In turn, this will lead to a drop in the number of jewel wasps around to combat the blowfly pupae.

2. Leave the nesting material in the box until the beginning of the next breeding season. It is not yet known whether this is enough time for the jewel wasp to emerge from its hibernation-like state or whether, like the scenario above, this will hurt the wasp population.

3. Leave the nest in the box. If birds then build a new nest on top of the old one, however, the raised level of the new nest may make the young more vulnerable to predators. Still, this scenario may help the jewel wasps with their role in blowfly control. The Cornell Laboratory of Ornithology is conducting research on this topic. (For more information or to participate in the project, contact the Bird Population Studies Program at the Cornell Laboratory; see page 191 for the address.)

You may choose to seal nestboxes to prevent the overwintering of mice and to prevent House Sparrows from entering; you can also leave open the side panel of a cleaned nestbox. It is important to remember that boxes left out during winter can be and are used by other birds as roost sites. Although you need not check nestboxes during winter, such visits can provide interesting insights into "accidental" residents of your nestboxes. Chickadees have been documented to exhibit such behavior.

Cleaning Safely

It is advisable to wear gloves and perhaps a protective facial covering when you clean a nestbox. The fine dust resulting from both the nesting material and the fledglings may give you an allergic reaction; worse, hantavirus might be present. And raptors such as kestrels and owls could potentially harbor bacteria from decomposing carcasses. Nestboxes can be washed out with a 10 percent bleach solution (1 part bleach to 9 parts water). This is probably not necessary, though.

Profiles of Cavity Nesters

The profiles of birds most likely to use nestboxes featured in this chapter will give you insight into the complex and interesting lives they lead. These thumbnail sketches emphasize important aspects of breeding biology and are a distillation of currently known facts.

Each profile provides basic statistics about the particular species' breeding biology; relates information about its conservation status; outlines crucial habitat and housing needs; discusses its competitors, predators, and parasites; and suggests strategies for combating them. The bird's life cycle, including the development of its young and the role each parent plays in rearing, is the featured portion of each profile. We've also included references that you may want to consult in order to learn more. Range maps introduce each profile, to illustrate where the species resides during breeding and nonbreeding seasons. Portraits of each species will help you identify birds visiting your property or, even better, residing in your nestboxes. Each profile opens with the male ($\circlearrowleft$) of the species. When the sexes are identical, no sex is designated. In addition to the 25 featured species, we have included information about two exotic pest species — the European Starling and House Sparrow.

Key for Range Maps	
	summer range
	year-round range
	winter range

Armed with the information contained in these pages, you will be better able to gauge the likelihood of your success in attracting your chosen birds and to meet their needs. The profiles also will help you understand what is happening inside and outside your nestbox, once it is occupied. Observing birds is much more enjoyable when you're able to put a particular bird's behavior into context.

Monitoring your nestbox residents may reveal fertile ground for further research. It is surprising how little is known about the breeding biology of some of our more common birds. By careful observation and record keeping, you could add significantly to our knowledge.

Probably more than any other field of biology, ornithology has been greatly enriched by the diligent and dedicated work of amateurs. Think of these species profiles as a starting point, and consider this your formal invitation to add to our understanding of these marvelous creatures.

◄ Juvenile Northern Saw-whet Owls depend on their male parent for food for at least 1 month after leaving the nestbox.

Eastern Bluebird
(Sialia sialis)

See box plan on pages 131–137.

Length: 7 inches (17.8 cm)

Nest construction: Female

Eggs per clutch: 3 to 6, usually 4 to 5

Incubation: Female

Length of incubation: 14 days

Age at fledging: 15 to 20 days

Broods per season: 1 at northern limits of range, 2 in most of range, 3 in southern portions of range

Food: Predominantly insects and spiders in summer; fruit, berries, and seeds in winter

Description

This is one of our most beloved species. The Eastern Bluebird is a member of the thrush subfamily, of which there are 12 regularly nesting species in North America. Bluebirds are secondary cavity nesters that use the abandoned nests of woodpeckers, natural cavities in trees and fence posts, and nestboxes. Their beautiful plumage (the Algonquin once said that they carried the Earth on their breasts and the sky on their backs), winsome songs, habit of consuming insect pests, faithful family ways (as perceived by humans), and apparent propensity for nesting near human habitations endear them to nearly everyone.

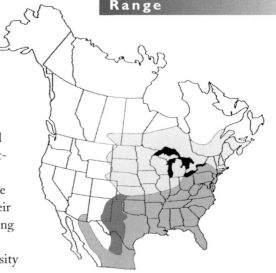

Range

Once greatly imperiled by loss of open breeding habitat, suitable nesting cavities, contamination of their insect food with DDT, and competition with exotic species (especially the European Starling and House Sparrow), Eastern Bluebirds have made a splendid comeback. Their populations are increasing at perhaps 6 percent a year, and once again these birds are gracing many a rural and semirural backyard. This is in large part due to the thousands of people who have erected and monitored nestboxes for these beguiling birds.

Habitat Needs

Eastern Bluebirds require semi-open land that provides largely treeless areas with short grass and gardens for feeding, surrounded by woodlands. Generally, they need at least 2 acres (.8 ha) of old field, hayfield, meadow, or lawn, with some of it mowed. Old (unsprayed) apple orchards once provided fine habitat. Bluebirds are ground feeders. From perches they scan the ground in search of prey. Males also require song posts for proclaiming their territorial rights.

Though more studies have attempted to determine the best box design for this species than for any other by far, the debate rages on. A large number of designs have been championed by various authors over the years, but none seems to have gained total acceptance by bluebirders continentwide.

Problems

Bluebirds often compete with Tree Swallows for nest sites, especially near water. One strategy to deal with this is to erect nestboxes in pairs 15 to 25 feet (4.6–7.6 m) apart. Tree Swallows will occupy one box, but will not tolerate the close presence of another pair of their own species. This leaves the other box available for bluebirds. Some studies indicate that Eastern Bluebirds are attracted to such two-box sites. Boxes should also be placed at least 120 feet (36.6 m) away from brush and trees, to discourage competition from House Wrens.

Predators, Parasites, and Diseases. Raccoons, house cats, squirrels, and snakes prey upon eggs, nestlings, fledglings, and adult bluebirds inside nestboxes. House Wrens will often pierce the eggs of bluebirds without consuming them; House Sparrows will

Housing Needs for Eastern Bluebirds

Box material: Wood

Floor dimensions: 4-inch (10.2 cm) or 5-inch (12.7 cm) square floor

Diameter of entrance hole: Must not exceed 1 ½ inches (3.8 cm), to exclude starlings

Box depth below hole: At least 6 inches (15.2 cm)

Mount: From 4 ½ to 5 ½ feet (1.4–1.7 m) above the ground, to facilitate monitoring without use of a stepladder

Suggestions: Place boxes at least 120 feet (36.6 m) from trees and shrubs, and orient so the box faces away from prevailing weather (generally east and south).

Spacing: As a rule, space 300 feet (91.5 m) or more apart.

Protection: A metal baffle or PVC pipe affixed to the pole, below the nestbox, can discourage predation by raccoons, squirrels, and house cats (see pages 164–167 for more information on predator guards).

kill both adult and nestling bluebirds. Mounting the nestbox at least 4½ feet (1.4 m) above the ground and installing predator guards in the form of metal cones or PVC pipe baffles below the box (see pages 164–167) will make it difficult, if not impossible, for climbing predators to reach the young. The application of axle grease to the supporting post may be necessary to deter climbing snakes.

Blowflies (*Protocalliphora* spp.) are common flies that as larvae suck blood from cavity-nesting birds such as bluebirds. Adults lay their eggs inside bluebird nests. The eggs hatch into larvae that attach themselves to the exposed skin of nestlings, especially their legs, feet, and wings. The larvae suck the nestlings' blood by night and usually retreat to the dark safety of the bottom of the nestbox by day. A heavy infestation can debilitate young bluebirds; in combination with insufficient feeding (often due to cold, wet weather), it can lead to their death. The larvae eventually change into dark pupae, and the adult flies emerge from the box days later, intent on finding a mate and starting the cycle all over again. Interestingly, nests that contain large quantities of pine needles are less apt to contain blowflies. Perhaps their acidity acts as a repellent.

What You Can Do. Monitoring enables you to regularly examine nests and young for blowflies. Do not be afraid to pick up the nestlings. You can remove the attached larvae and discard them from the nest. Also be sure to check under the nest for larvae and pupae. You can use a spatula to carefully lift up the nest (complete with young) within the box. This exposes the parasites and makes it possible for you to sweep them out.

The nests of House Sparrows should be removed at once. Trapping and elimination of House Sparrows may be necessary in some situations.

Life Cycle

In the North, male bluebirds return from their southern wintering areas as early as late winter. They return to the same territory they held previously; if breeding for the first time, they tend to choose a territory near where they were hatched. They are joined by the females about two weeks later. Females tend to disperse farther from their birth sites with regard to nesting location. After courtship that may last a few weeks, females select the nest site. Mating takes place over a period of days or even weeks. The female does most of the nest construction, but may be aided by the male. The circular cup is woven of dry grass and other plant fibers over the course of 4 to 5 days. After a few days, egg laying commences.

The average clutch size for the Eastern Bluebird is usually between four and five eggs.

The female, like most songbirds, lays one egg per day, usually during the early-morning hours. Once the clutch is complete, she begins incubation using her brood patch, a naked area on her belly. Incubation (all done by the female) lasts approximately 2 weeks. The clutch often hatches over the course of 24 hours. The young are naked and blind at birth. The female broods them continuously during their first few days of life, when they are incapable of producing their own body heat. The male brings food to the female during this time. At about 4 days of age, the young birds' eyes open; by this time they are also covered with soft down feathers. They grow very rapidly over the next 10 to 14 days, consuming huge quantities of insects which are brought to them by both parents.

Should one of the adults be killed at this stage, the other will strive to supply the necessary nourishment for the young by itself. Nestling bluebirds can usually be sexed by 10 days of age: The males show bright blue flight feathers (wings and tail), the females grayish blue feathers. The adults first eat and later remove the fecal sacs (fecal material covered in a gelatinous coating) with their bills, carrying them far from the nest so as not to attract the notice of predators.

Male Eastern Bluebirds share the responsibility of feeding their hungry nestlings.

Depending on the weather and the amount of food they have received, bluebirds fledge at between 15 and 20 days of age. Their first flight is usually to a nearby tree or shrub, although they are capable of flying some 300 feet (91.5 m). The male now assumes care of his fledglings, feeding them in the vicinity of the nest for another several weeks. The female may meanwhile begin a second or third clutch of eggs in the same or a different nestbox or natural cavity, usually with the same mate. The second clutch generally contains one egg fewer than the first. The young of the first brood have been known to bring food to the young of the second.

By early fall, feather molt has replaced the spotted breasts of the young with the species' characteristic brick orange coloring. They now closely resemble their parents. Young females will be ready to breed themselves the following spring when they are 10 months old. Bluebirds seldom live more than 3 years, although the current longevity record is 8 years. During our years of color banding studies, we never saw an individual more than 3 years old. Northern bluebirds usually migrate to the southeastern states in fall, while southern birds generally remain near their breeding territories year-round. Bluebirds tend to flock during winter.

Useful References
Grooms, S., and D. Peterson. *Bluebirds.* Minocqua, WI: NorthWord Press, Inc., 1991.
Zeleny, L. *Bluebird.* Bloomington, IN: Indiana University Press, 1978.

Western Bluebird
(*Sialia mexicana*)

See box plan on pages 131–137.

Length: 6½ to 7 inches (16.5–17.8 cm)
Nest construction: Female
Eggs per clutch: 3 to 8, usually 4 to 6
Incubation: Female
Length of incubation: 13 to 14 days
Age at fledging: Approximately 20 days
Broods per season: 2
Food: Predominantly animal matter (82 percent): insects (mainly grasshoppers, caterpillars, and beetles), as well as spiders; also wild fruits and a few weed seeds

Description

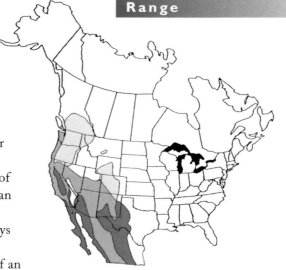

Range

The Western Bluebird, probably the least numerous of the three bluebirds, is very much the western counterpart of the eastern species, sharing many similarities of habit and lifestyle with its eastern brethren. The male is a darker, deeper blue; that beautiful color extends through the throat region to the top of the bird's breast. Observing these avian gems as they perch on fence posts or utility lines near ranch homes is always a treat for us.

The species has experienced less of an overall decline than its eastern cousin, but Western Bluebirds have suffered from a shortage of suitable nest sites. Population declines have been due in part to a decrease in suitable old cavity trees, and to competition with those two imported pests, the House Sparrow and European Starling.

This bird is as easily attracted to nestboxes as the Eastern Bluebird. Such boxes can make a substantial difference where natural and old woodpecker cavities are in short supply.

Habitat Needs

Western Bluebirds require open woodlands and pasturelands with old trees for nesting sites. They breed from oak woodlands above the elevation of deserts, in sycamores along stream corridors, in open coniferous forests such as ponderosa pine stands, logged-off or burned sections with scattered trees, and grassy clearings where there are a few tall dead trees, up to rather high elevations: 9,000 feet (2,745 m) in New Mexico. They are also found in farmland, nesting in roadside fence posts. Like other bluebirds, this species will frequently set up residence near houses. Western Bluebirds do not occur in closed boreal forest or open arid uplands.

Problems

Western Bluebirds compete keenly for nesting cavities with Violet-green Swallows (especially near water), House Wrens, and Eastern Bluebirds in areas where their ranges overlap, and House Sparrows and European Starlings.

Predators, Parasites, and Diseases. House Wrens are known to pierce the eggs and kill the young of this species. Deer mice eat the eggs and young of Western Bluebirds, and fire ants attack and kill the nestlings.

What You Can Do. Placing boxes well away from home, farm, and ranch buildings will limit their use by House Sparrows. Locating boxes away from shrubbery will reduce conflicts with wrens. Boxes can be erected in pairs 15 to 25 feet (4.6–7.6 m) apart where competition with Violet-green Swallows is fierce. Swallows may occupy

Housing Needs for Western Bluebirds

Box material: Wood
Floor dimensions: 5-inch (12.7 cm) square floor
Diameter of entrance hole: 1⁹⁄₁₆ inches (3.9 cm)
Box depth below hole: At least 6 inches (15.2 cm)
Mount: About 5 feet (1.5 m) above the ground
Suggestions: Locate boxes away from shrubbery, and orient so the box faces away from prevailing weather (generally east and south).
Spacing: As a rule, space 300 feet (91.5 m) or more apart.
Protection: Hanging boxes, which discourage climbing predators, have worked well in California and Oregon. Suspend boxes from small branches with hanging wire by means of a hook attached to the back of the box. A pole with an attached basket can be used to raise the boxes into place, and to lower them for monitoring (see page 164).

one box, but will not allow another pair of swallows to nest in a second box so close to them, thus leaving the other box available for bluebirds. Western Bluebirds have been known to drive out swallows, however. Hanging boxes from slender branches with wire can virtually eliminate attacks by climbing predators. Knotting an oil-soaked rag around the supporting wire will stop ants from reaching the box. Regular monitoring can help you deal with problems as they arise.

Life Cycle

Western Bluebirds are partially migratory; that is, they are migratory in parts of their range and year-round residents in others. In the latter case, they often move to lower elevations in winters. Most winter within the United States. Their breeding range overlaps that of their cousin the Mountain Bluebird. Males attempt to return for breeding to the place where they were hatched; if that is not possible, first-breeding-year birds tend to return to the same area that they frequented and got to know well as juveniles.

Once the male has appropriated a nesting cavity, he attempts to entice the female by singing (the song is less complicated than that of the Eastern Bluebird, but louder than that of the Mountain Bluebird) as well as with a colorful display: He half opens his wings and fans his tail, while at the same time dissuading rivals by flashing his brickred breast. He then perches beside the female, preens her, and may offer her food. Once the female has chosen her nest cavity and territory, which her male zealously protects from rivals, she begins nest construction. She uses dry grasses, forb stems, and pine needles, and occasionally adds hair or a few feathers. The inner cup is lined with fine grasses. The male accompanies her during nest building and may feed her, but does not take part in nest construction. The pair bond between them is thought to be monogamous.

The approach of this female Western Bluebird stimulates the feeding response in her nestlings.

Females usually lay four to six eggs, darker than those of the Mountain Bluebird, over a period of 4 to 6 days; then they begin incubation. After approximately 2 weeks, the young emerge from their entrapping shells. Only the female is capable of brooding the young using her highly vascularized brood patch. When the male arrives during brooding, the female leaves the nest in order to feed herself. Both parents feed their nestlings, primarily insects. Western Bluebirds do catch insects on the wing but they most often feed off the ground, spotting prey from perches. The young experience a rather long nestling phase of about 3 weeks, after which they leave the box on their first brief flights.

A few days after the first brood fledges, the female begins laying a new clutch of eggs. While she is thus occupied, the male takes over total care of the fledglings, which remain together as a group. The young become independent about 2 weeks after fledging but continue to beg for food from their parents if the adults do not begin a second brood. After the second brood leaves the nestbox, both sets of young and parents join in a family flock and remain in the neighborhood. By the time of the juvenile molt in late summer, the young birds greatly resemble their parents. Banding records indicate a maximum longevity to date of 5 years and 1 month.

Useful References

Thrushes, Kinglets, and Their Allies. In Bent, A. C. *Life Histories of North American Birds.* Washington, D.C.: United States National Museum, 1949.

Mountain Bluebird
(*Sialia currucoides*)

See box plan on pages 131–137.

Length: 7 inches (17.8 cm)
Nest construction: Female
Eggs per clutch: 4 to 8, usually 5 to 6
Incubation: Female
Length of incubation: 13 to 14 days
Age at fledging: 18 to 23 days
Broods per season: 1 at high elevations, 2 at lower altitudes
Food: Predominantly insects and spiders; also fruit, berries, and seeds

Description

The Mountain Bluebird is certainly one of our most beautiful species. Its exquisite all-blue plumage can take your breath away. Sighting these gorgeous birds is always a highlight of our midspring trips to the piñon-juniper lands of the American Southwest, where wintering flocks feed upon the abundant juniper berries. Like its two cousins, the Mountain Bluebird is a secondary cavity nester that utilizes natural tree cavities, abandoned woodpecker nest sites in trees, fence posts and utility poles, and nestboxes. The great majority of these birds now probably use nestboxes. In fact, most of what is known about the Mountain Bluebird has been gleaned from studies on birds using nestboxes.

In general, the Mountain Bluebird suffered from a less severe population decline than its eastern cousin in the first half of the twentieth century, but gradually it, too, has come to face some of the same negative factors that so affected Eastern Bluebirds; especially competition for nest cavities from European Starlings and House Sparrows. Also, fire suppression practices and the decline of the logging and livestock industries actually caused population reductions of Mountain Bluebirds, which require more open habitats than other bluebirds.

Range

The placement of nestboxes and bluebird "trails" (series of boxes) has had a major positive impact upon the size of Mountain Bluebird populations in many western states and provinces. One trail in Saskatchewan stretches for an incredible 2,500 miles (4,033 km)! Generally speaking, populations now seem to be holding their own in most areas.

Habitat Needs

Mountain Bluebirds require predominantly open country with scattered trees. They have a wide habitat tolerance: They can nest from plains to timberline. Despite its name, the species breeds in grasslands, sagebrush flats, along forest edges, in open woodlands of piñon pine and juniper, in aspen or cottonwood groves in open country, in burned or cutover areas (with sufficient nest sites), near human habitations, as well as in ponderosa pine parklands and along the edges of alpine tundra (up to 12,350 feet, or 3,767 m). Nestboxes should not be located near cropland, however. Mountain Bluebirds need short grasses or bare ground for hunting, and they require perches from which to locate insect prey.

Problems

Mountain Bluebirds compete fiercely for the limited supply of suitable nest sites with other secondary cavity nesters, including other species of bluebirds where their ranges overlap. Among these are the Tree Swallow, Northern Flicker, European Starling, House Sparrow, House Wren, and chickadees.

Placing boxes away from croplands reduces competition with swallows, while placement away from shrubbery discourages their occupation by wrens. By situating nestboxes away from forest, chickadees are less apt to use them. An entrance hole 1½ inches

Housing Needs for Mountain Bluebirds

Box material: Wood

Floor dimensions: 5-inch (12.7 cm) square floor

Diameter of entrance hole: 1⁹/₁₆ inches (3.9 cm), unless starlings are a problem; then 1½ inches (3.8 cm)

Box depth below hole: 6 to 7¾ inches (15.2–19.7 cm)

Mount: From 4½ to 6 feet (1.4–1.8 m) above the ground

Suggestions: Open grassland is often a good location. Orient so the box faces away from prevailing weather (generally east and south), as well as roads and utility lines.

Spacing: As a rule, space 300 feet (91.5 m) or more apart.

Protection: Mount boxes on metal pipes fitted with aluminum collars or predator guards. Position boxes away from trees, and from 1,200 feet (366 m) to ½ mile (807 m) from barns and homes. Monitor for blowfly larvae regularly.

The female Mountain Bluebird lacks the cerulean blue hue of her mate and the rusty breast of her female Eastern and Western Bluebird relatives.

(3.8 cm) in diameter excludes starlings. At least in some areas, however, Mountain Bluebirds may require a slightly larger hole size.

Predators, Parasites, and Diseases. Cooper's and sharp-shinned hawks, northern harriers, American Kestrels, House Sparrows, and American crows, as well as weasels, squirrels, eastern chipmunks, and mice are known to prey upon Mountain Bluebirds, their nestlings, and/or their eggs.

As with other bluebird species, blowfly larvae suck blood from nestlings (refer to page 13). Blackflies have been known to kill young nestlings.

What You Can Do. Poles or pipes supporting nestboxes can be fitted with aluminum collars or predator guards (see pages 164–167) to keep climbing predators out. Mounting boxes on metal pipes will keep mice from gaining entry. Boxes should be positioned away from trees to discourage squirrels. They should be placed from at least 1,200 feet (366 m) and as much as a ½ mile (807 m) from barns and homes where House Sparrows are a problem. Regular monitoring will enable you to remove blowfly larvae from the nest (see pages 12–15).

Life Cycle

Mountain Bluebirds return to their breeding areas in late winter and early spring, with the males arriving from a few days to a few weeks ahead of the females. Adults show a strong attachment to territories and boxes where they bred successfully in previous years. One banded female is known to have used the same nestbox for 4 consecutive years. Birds returning for their first breeding season radiate out to new areas away from where they were fledged. Although Mountain Bluebirds are able to withstand below-zero temperatures, late storms can delay their nesting. Males begin singing with the establishment of a territory as soon as they arrive back on the breeding grounds. Some people feel that their song is weak in comparison to that of the Eastern Bluebird.

The female selects a nest site from among those that male bluebirds show her, and thus she chooses the male defending it only indirectly. Territories can be more than 12.4 acres (5 ha) in size. There may be fierce competition for nesting cavities among this species and Eastern and Western Bluebirds where their ranges overlap, and between Mountain Bluebirds and Tree Swallows, especially near cultivated fields. Mountain Bluebirds seem to dominate in competitions with their bluebird relatives, although they have been known to hybridize with both species. The male guards the female closely to protect his paternity interests from other males.

The female constructs the nest, usually over a period of 4 to 6 days, from dry grasses and forb stems; sometimes she lines it with a few feathers. Quite a long time may elapse between nest building and egg laying. Female Mountain Bluebirds lay one very pale blue or bluish white egg per day, and begin incubation with the laying of the last or next-to-last egg. The male brings food to the nest for his mate. Clutches of this species are on average larger than those of other bluebirds. The young hatch following approximately 2 weeks of incubation. Cold, wet weather can result in heavy mortality of young early in the season. Females often change territories and mates if the first nesting attempt fails.

Clutches of the Mountain Bluebird are generally larger than those of Eastern Bluebirds and thus require larger nestboxes.

Females brood their young for 6 or 7 days, at which time the young are well covered with down and capable of maintaining their own high body temperatures. During this time the female spends the night in the nest cavity, while the male roosts nearby. Both parents feed the young about evenly, although the male does nearly all of it during their first few days of life. Caterpillars are the preferred food, although grasshoppers also make up a major percentage of the young birds' diets. For the first few days they are fed by regurgitation, then a mixture of regurgitated and fresh foods; later on they are fed only fresh food. The young grow very rapidly, doubling their weight every day for the first week or so. By 12 days they are well feathered.

Nestlings become fledglings after about 20 days in the nest cavity. They are dependent upon their parents for food and protection from predators for up to several additional weeks. Quite commonly, the female will begin a second clutch shortly after the first brood fledges. Second clutches usually contain fewer eggs than the first. The male continues to care for the fledglings, although the duration of that care depends to a great extent upon the weather. Later the young, with mottled breasts, follow their parents about as they forage. By September the young closely resemble their parents.

Adult Mountain Bluebirds hunt insects from perches, by fly catching, and by hovering. This species, in fact, uses hover-hunting much more than its two bluebird relatives. Most hunting is done early morning and in early evening.

Mountain Bluebirds gather into family groups in late summer, and then into larger congregations in preparation for migration. They are the most migratory of the three bluebird species. Birds in northern breeding areas tend to leave before those breeding in more southerly areas. Migration can continue well into late fall. Individuals that bred at high elevations move to lower levels. Some birds winter as far south as central Mexico, while others winter in the breeding range, but at lower elevations. This species is known to have lived at least 5 years and 11 months in the wild.

Useful References

Power, H. W., and M. P. Lombardo. "Mountain Bluebird *(Sialia currucoides)*." In *The Birds of North America*, No. 222 (A. Poole and F. Gill, eds.). Philadelphia and Washington, D.C.: The Academy of Natural Sciences and The American Ornithologists' Union, 1996.

Tree Swallow
(*Tachycineta bicolor*)

See box plan on page 131.

Length: 5 to 6 inches (12.7–15.2 cm)

Nest construction: Female

Eggs per clutch: 2 to 8, usually 4 to 7

Incubation: Female

Length of incubation: 11 to 19 days, usually 14 to 15

Age at fledging: 15 to 25 days, with an average of 18 to 22

Broods per season: 1

Food: Insects and (when available) berries, primarily bayberries

Description

The Tree Swallow, one of eight swallows found in Canada, the United States, and Mexico, returns early from its wintering grounds. Frequently, cold temperatures and lack of insect prey present hazards to these swallows. These birds, unlike other swallows, can survive for long periods of time on bayberries. Tree Swallows can be best identified by the beautiful iridescent, greenish blue plumage on their heads and backs, and white underparts. First-year females, however, have a mixture of brown and greenish brown feathers; they resemble juvenile birds. Females attain adult plumage in two years. Juvenile Tree Swallows can be recognized in summer by the brown feathers on their heads and backs, and the white undersides that carry a dusky brown wash across their chests.

Range

Tree Swallows are birds of open country and can be easily spotted flying over open fields, meadows, marshes, or lakeshores. Under the current forestry practice of removing standing dead trees, their available nesting sites have been greatly reduced. This species will readily accept and use nestboxes. In southern California, Tree Swallows were once eliminated because of agricultural practices. With the introduction of nestboxes, however, the Tree Swallow population there has returned and increased.

Tree Swallows are currently considered indicators of pollutants and potential health hazards. PCBs and high levels of DDE have been found in adults, eggs, and nestlings in the western part of their range. Indications suggest that these residues may be harmful to this species. Mortality rates for older egg-laying females have increased. Birds residing in more acidic wetlands tend to have smaller young and to fledge fewer individuals overall, implying that acid precipitation may affect reproductive success.

Habitat destruction and water pollution in wintering areas may also have serious effects on Tree Swallow numbers. Loss of marshes can result in greater concentrations of birds into smaller areas for roosting. Consequently, local food supplies will be depleted more rapidly. Roosting birds may also become more vulnerable to adverse local weather conditions. Pollution of rivers and marshes could lead to food scarcity or food contamination by toxins.

Habitat Needs

Tree Swallows forage over both land and water, catching insects while they fly. Open areas, preferably near water, are favored by this species. These include fields, marshes, wooded swamps, open water, and shrubby areas.

Housing Needs for Tree Swallows

Box material: Wood

Floor dimensions: 5-inch (12.7 cm) square floor

Diameter of entrance hole: 1½ inches (3.8 cm)

Box depth below hole: 6 to 7 inches (15.2–17.8 cm)

Mount: 4½ to 5½ feet (1.4–1.7 m) above the ground; such a mount also provides a convenient perch for the male during the nesting period

Suggestions: Placement should be based on local weather conditions, such as prevailing winds. In general, though, boxes should face open fields and away from roads. If nestboxes are paired, Tree Swallows seem to prefer the one that faces south.

Spacing: At least 50 to 70 feet (15.3–21.4 m) apart

Protection: Construct the box with an extended roof overhang (up to 7 inches, or 17.8 cm), and add a ¾-inch (1.9 cm) block of wood over the entrance hole, to deter raccoons; baffles may also help. To avoid competition with other birds, place nestboxes in pairs about 15 to 25 feet (4.6–7.6 m) apart, and/or locate them in open areas away from forest areas and buildings. To deter snakes, grease the nestbox's mounting pole, or affix a ¼-inch (.635 cm) mesh hardware cloth guard.

Problems

Tree Swallows receive intense competition for cavities from several species. House Wrens will add sticks and twigs to the Tree Swallow's nest, causing the nest to be deserted. Occasionally eggs and nestlings are destroyed. Tree Swallows will often avoid nesting too close to wooded areas, in part to avoid the wrens. House Sparrows and Northern Flickers will destroy all nest contents. House Sparrows have been known to kill adult Tree Swallows in their efforts to gain nest sites. Eastern and Mountain Bluebirds will often successfully defend their cavities against Tree Swallows, although Tree Swallows can kill nestling bluebirds if they gain access to the nest.

Predators, Parasites, and Diseases. Raccoons are the most frequent predators of Tree Swallow nests. Other predators include the black rat snake, black bear, common grackle, American crow, Northern Flicker, chipmunks, weasels, deer mice, and feral cats. Flying or perching swallows are prone to predation by the sharp-shinned hawk, American Kestrel, merlin, peregrine falcon, great horned owl, and black-billed magpie.

Blowflies (*Protocalliphora* spp.) can affect the nestlings' rate of growth, which in turn affects the length of time that the young remain in the nest. Other Tree Swallow parasites are mites, jumping spiders, book lice, bark beetles, ants, ichneumon wasps, chalcid wasps, and bird lice.

What You Can Do. Being a vigilant monitor of the Tree Swallow's nesting activities and checking the box on a regular basis are the most beneficial contributions you can make. An extended roof overhang (up to 7 inches, or 17.8 cm), coupled with the addition of a ¾-inch (1.9 cm) block of wood over the entrance hole, serves as some protection against raccoons. Other baffles have also proven to be an effective deterrent for raccoons. (See pages 164–167 for baffle design and construction.)

To avoid competition with bluebirds, nestboxes can be placed in pairs about 15 to 25 feet (4.6–7.6 m) apart. Tree Swallows will occupy one box, leaving the other to be occupied by bluebirds. Placing the nestbox in open areas and away from forest edges will prevent aggressive competition from the House Wren. Mounting nestboxes away from buildings such as barns may also decrease competition from such birds as House Sparrows.

Many female Tree Swallows will sit tight on their nests. Do not be afraid to gently pick the female off the nest and examine the nest, eggs, or newly hatched young. Do not handle birds that are older than 12 days; this might cause premature fledging. If blowflies are found in the nest or attached to young, do not hesitate to remove them; discard them away from the nest. (See pages 13–15 for more about blowflies.) In areas where snakes present a problem, several solutions can be tried. If the nestbox is mounted on a pole, you might apply grease to the pole. Or you can affix a ¼-inch (.635 cm) mesh hardware cloth guard to the pole. (See page 166 for design and installation procedures.)

Life Cycle

Older Tree Swallows arrive at the breeding grounds before first-year birds, and males arrive before females. Females generally arrive up to a week later, forming pair bonds shortly thereafter. Breeding territory is defended immediately after pairs have been formed. Pair bonds last for the duration of the breeding season. Often, the same pair will mate in consecutive breeding seasons. This is perhaps a result of both individuals returning to the same nest site year after year rather than lifelong pair bonding.

Nests, built almost exclusively by the female, consist of an accumulation (up to 2¾ inches, or 7 cm) of dry grass and straw. This material may be collected near water on the ground, usually within 100 feet (30.5 m) of the nesting site, and transported in the beak to the nesting site. The nest is hollowed out by the female pushing with her breast into the plant material to form the cuplike structure; 10 to 50 feathers are added to line the nest. Some nests have been found containing more than 100 feathers. Males deliver the feathers when the grass nest construction is complete and egg laying has begun. It is the female, however, that arranges the feathers to form a canopylike structure over the eggs. The feather lining is important in that it increases the insulation within the nest.

A first-breeding-year female, identified by her drab plumage, feeds a well-developed nestling.

The shafts of feathers are pointed down, and the broad vanes point up and over the brood. This reduces heat loss, thereby encouraging the brood to develop faster. By the time the eggs hatch, enough feathers have worked themselves into the nest to provide the young chicks with a soft cushion. Most of the nest building is accomplished during the morning; it may take anywhere from a few days to 2 weeks to complete. A week or more may pass before eggs are laid.

This feather-lined Tree Swallow nest also contains two Black-capped Chickadee eggs (speckled eggs at top).

Like other songbirds, the female Tree Swallow lays one egg per day, but gaps may develop between the laying of consecutive eggs, especially during cold and wet weather. Incubation may be delayed by up to 2 weeks. Eggs do not lose their viability. Eggs are usually laid within 2 hours of sunrise, in early morning. Incubation starts on the day that the next-to-last one is laid. Males guard the nestbox when the female leaves on her feeding forays.

During the last few days of incubation, the male gives "contact calls" to the eggs. It is thought that this might act as a stimulant for the eggs to start pipping. Most clutches hatch over a 2-day period. The female removes eggshells from the nest, along with the fecal sacs that are usually deposited in the nest at the time of a feeding. The fecal sacs are carried away, often being deposited over water (in our own case, over our neighbor's garden). The young are brooded for the first 3 days. At 15 days of age, the nestlings will come to the entrance of the box to be fed, often with their heads sticking out of the hole and looking like miniature killer whales. Nestlings fledge at between 15 and 25 days of age. The parents continue to feed the young for at least 3 days after they depart the nest.

Cold, wet weather tends to account for greatest fledgling mortality in the nest. Tree Swallows live an average of about 2.7 years. Longevity records list 11 years as the maximum life span. A banded Tree Swallow female in Ontario, Canada, has been reported to be 10 years old. Another banded female produced 54 eggs and 47 fledglings in her 8-year life span. One female, sitting tight on eggs, was banded at the Pleasant Valley Wildlife Sanctuary in Lenox, Massachusetts, in 1992. From her plumage, it was known that she was not a first year bird. She returned to the sanctuary and brooded eggs in 1993, 1995, and 1997, making her at least 6 years old. At Broadmoor Sanctuary in Natick, Massachusetts, a Tree Swallow has been recorded to be 7 years old.

Useful References
Robertson, R. J., B. J. Stutchbury, and R. R. Cohen. "Tree Swallow." In *The Birds of North America,* No. 11 (A. Poole, P. Stettenheim, and F. Gill, eds.). Philadelphia and Washington, D.C.: The Academy of Natural Sciences and The American Ornithologists' Union, 1992.

♂

Violet-green Swallow
(*Tachycineta thalassina*)

See box plan on page 131.

Length: 5 to 5½ inches (12.7–14 cm)

Nest construction: Both male and female

Eggs per clutch: 4 to 6

Incubation: Female

Length of incubation: 14 to15 days

Age at fledging: 23 to 24 days

Broods per season: 1

Food: Almost exclusively insects

Winter range: From Mexico south to Guatemala, El Salvador, and Honduras

Description

In his 1923 publication, *Birds of California,* ornithologist William Leon Dawson referred to Violet-green Swallows as "children of heaven." An apt description for this western counterpart of the Tree Swallow, especially when it is skimming close to the ground or water, or circling at great heights in pursuit of its prey. This swallow tends to fly higher than any other.

The Violet-green Swallow can be distinguished from the Tree Swallow by the white on the cheek, which then extends above the eye. White flank patches also extend onto the sides of the rump (the area

Range

above the tail on the lower back). The back and top of the head are a soft velvety green or greenish bronze, with faint shades of purplish violet concentrated on the nape (the back of the neck). The female is duller than the male and can be distinguished by the browner color of the sides of her face. Her throat has a slight ashy brown wash. Likewise, her head is browner with a bronze-green shade, but it is never as bright as that of the male. Juveniles show more gray-brown feathers on the back. White areas, other than the rump, are mottled or grayish in appearance. Frequently, juveniles will show a dingy throat and chest that blends gradually with darker areas on the head.

Juveniles acquire adult plumage by molts in early to midfall. Interestingly, Violet-green Swallows might be more closely related to Central and South American species than to the Tree Swallow.

Despite the Violet-green's extensive distribution, less is known of it than nearly any other North American swallow. All current knowledge is based on reports from the 1940s and 1950s involving observations of a few pairs.

Habitat Needs

The Violet-green Swallow prefers nesting sites to be located in open deciduous, coniferous, and mixed woodlands. Parts of its breeding range are shared with the Tree Swallow. Violet-green Swallows, however, are found in more open habitats and will nest in rock crevices, holes in dirt banks, or columnar cacti. These birds prefer trees in open areas, such as open groves or woodland edges. Some records dating back to 1908 indicate that Violet-green Swallows will also nest in sand banks, streamside cut banks, and old nests of cliff and bank swallows. They will occupy nestboxes when natural cavities or old woodpecker holes are not available. They have been known to nest in boxes under the eaves of buildings or in trees.

Problems

The most intense competitors for nest sites tend to be the House Wren, mountain chickadee, and House Sparrow.

Housing Needs for Violet-green Swallows

Box material: Wood
Floor dimensions: 5-inch (12.7 cm) square floor
Diameter of entrance hole: 1½ inches (3.8 cm)
Box depth below hole: 6 to 7 inches (15.2–17.8 cm)
Mount: On trees or posts 4 to 10 feet (1.2–3.1 m) above the ground
Suggestions: Take prevailing weather conditions into consideration when you place boxes; in general, though, they should face toward open fields and away from prevailing winds.
Protection: Place nestboxes away from human habitation to avoid competition with House Sparrows and European Starlings.

Female Violet-green Swallows are duller above than their mates and have a brownish wash on the sides of their heads.

Predators, Parasites, and Diseases. Among adults, several blood parasites (the protozoans *Haemoproteus, Leucocytozoon,* and *Trypanosoma* spp.) and two nematodes (*Acuaria coloradensis* and *Angularella* spp.) have been reported. Botflies (*Cuterebridae* spp.) have been noted infecting nestlings. After larvae (maggots) were removed, no resultant fatalities were reported. Bird lice infested one nest so heavily that the adults abandoned it just as the nestlings were beginning to get their feathers. Finally, fleas (*Ceratophyllus idius* and *C. celsus*) were collected from nests in Alaska.

What You Can Do. Monitoring the nestboxes, especially in early spring, is the best safeguard against nestbox occupation by House Sparrows. Boxes mounted away from human habitation generally encounter fewer problems from either House Sparrows or European Starlings. House Sparrows tend to start nesting earlier than Violet-green Swallows. If you detect a House Sparrow, remove its nesting material immediately. This process might require several repetitions, because House Sparrows will start to renest immediately if their nest is destroyed. Another method is to remove and destroy the eggs of the House Sparrow. This, too, might require several repetitions. Once the swallows become established, however, they are not easily driven out. Please note that House Wrens and mountain chickadees are federally protected birds: Do not remove their nests. House Sparrows and European Starlings are nestbox birds whose nests may be destroyed.

Monitoring nestboxes also provides the opportunity to check each nest for blowflies and their larvae. (See pages 13–15 for more about blowflies.)

Life Cycle

Violet-green Swallows return from their wintering grounds in Mexico and Central America in early to midspring. By early to mid-April, these swallows have become fairly well established in their chosen breeding localities. Pairs form by mid-April. Courtship and copulation generally take place in early morning, frequently before sunrise.

Nest building generally occurs from mid-April to mid-May. Both male and female participate in gathering material for the nest. The female, however, visits the nest twice as often as the male. Nest materials consist of grass or weed stems, twigs, fur, and hair. The male brings feathers to the nest after the female has started laying eggs. Feathers, almost exclusively chicken feathers, are placed by the female with their shafts down, creating a domelike structure over the eggs. They are thought to act as an insulator and help conserve heat, thus hastening the development of the young. Nest construction spans a period of from 6 days to 3 weeks; it generally takes place in the morning and early afternoon. Eggs are laid one per day until the clutch is complete. Although little information is available on the dates that first eggs are laid, it appears to be in mid-May. Eggs may be laid before the nest is completely built, or one to two days after its completion.

Eggs, which are indistinguishable from those of Tree Swallows, hatch within 14 or 15 days after incubation has started. It may take 5 days before all eggs are hatched. Eggshells are removed soon after hatching. Information is scarce on brooding, but one published account reported a female brooding her young for 10 days after hatching. Additional brooding may protect the young from mosquitoes. Although no research has been conducted on the diet of the nestlings, it is presumed that the young are fed insect matter such as gnats and flies. The young nestlings increase their weight steadily until by day 10, the weight of the young equals that of their parents (.6 ounce, or 16 g). Eyes open when the nestlings are 1 to 2 days old. Much like Tree Swallows, Violet-green Swallow adults remove fecal sacs early in the nestlings' life. This practice diminishes as the adults encourage the young to leave the nest. By day 16, young can be seen looking out of the box when the parents are absent. The young fledge after 23 to 24 days. This can occur during any part of the day, and sometimes over several days. The adults continue to feed the young for a short time after fledging, although most of the feeding is done by the female. It is not known when the young become totally independent of the parents. Fledged birds may or may not return to the nestbox.

Violet-green Swallows are very sensitive to weather conditions. Those returning in early spring are frequently confronted with cold weather, and many retreat to slightly warmer surrounding areas. Under such conditions, insect food becomes scarce and many swallows have a difficult time finding sufficient food. Deaths are common in these circumstances. The longest living Violet-green Swallow was recorded to be 6 years and 10 months.

Useful References

Brown, C. R., A. M. Knott, and E. J. Damrose. "Violet-green Swallow." In *The Birds of North America,* No. 14 (A. Poole, P. Stettenheim, and F. Gill, eds.). Philadelphia and Washington, D.C.: The Academy of Natural Sciences and The American Ornithologist's Union, 1992.

Purple Martin
(Progne subis)

See box plan on page 138.

Length: 7 ¼ to 8 ½ inches (18.4–21.6 cm)

Nest construction: Female

Eggs per clutch: 3 to 6, usually 4 to 5

Incubation: Both sexes (male insulates, but does not incubate)

Length of incubation: 12 to 20 days, usually 15 to 18

Age at fledging: 24 to 31 days, usually 28

Broods per season: 1, rarely 2

Food: Flying insects: dragonflies, wasps, flies, beetles, true bugs, and ants

Winter range: South America, especially eastern Bolivia and Brazil

♂

Description

Considered by many who live in its wide range as the true harbinger of spring, the elegant Purple Martin is North America's largest swallow. Martins have a large and exceedingly loyal following that is second in size, but hardly commitment, only to the many people who erect nesting boxes for bluebirds. So dedicated are Purple Martin aficionados that at least $30 million is spent on their behalf annually. The fact that they consume large quantities of insects (mosquitoes represent only a minuscule percentage of their diet, quite at odds with what was once heralded), coupled with their gregarious nature, has made these big swallows a much-sought-after species for centuries.

Human efforts to attract Purple Martins go back to well before colonial settlement of the continent, when Native Americans of the southeastern United States hung gourds for the glossy purplish blue swallows around their gardens. Originally, martins nested singly or in small colonies within large trees riddled with abandoned woodpecker

Range

cavities. Today, populations of Purple Martins east of the Great Plains nest virtually nowhere but in the houses or gourds put up specifically for them. They are thus completely dependent upon humanity for housing. Western martins, on the other hand, are much less likely to occupy artificial nesting sites.

Populations seem to be diminishing over much of northern North America. However, recent increases have occurred along the Atlantic Coast, from Georgia to Virginia, and in portions of Tennessee and Kentucky west to Kansas and Oklahoma. The birds are common in the Deep South, where milder climatic conditions prevail. Martins are very susceptible to cold, wet weather that lasts for more than 3 or 4 days and the resulting scarcity of insect food; entire regional populations have been wiped out due to such weather conditions. Perhaps the major reason for their steady decline in the North has been competition for nest sites with those introduced exotics, the European Starling and House Sparrow.

Do not become involved with Purple Martins unless you are prepared to invest a significant amount of time, money, and energy on their behalf. Providing housing for this species can be far more complex than for any other cavity-nesting bird.

Habitat Needs

Purple Martins originally occupied open woodlands interspersed with fields, woodland edges, lumbered forests, burned areas with snags, and agricultural land. In the East, they now nest almost exclusively in towns and rural areas around human settlements, including golf courses, and sometimes even in large cities in the South. In the West, martins

Housing Needs for Purple Martins

Box material: Aluminum, wood, or gourd

Floor dimensions: 6-inch (15.2 cm) square floor

Diameter of entrance hole: 2 inches (5.1 cm)

Box depth below hole: 2 inches (5.1 cm)

Mount: Erect houses on poles, or hang gourds from wires, 12 to 20 feet (3.7–6.1 m) above the ground. Martins generally will not nest in houses less than 8 or 9 feet (2.4–2.7 m) above the ground.

Suggestions: Install houses or gourds a minimum of 40 feet (12.2 m) from limbs or buildings.

Protection: To thwart predators, attach a predator guard to the supporting pole, keep the entrance hole small, and/or (for great horned owls) wrap wire mesh around your martin house. To avoid competition with House Sparrows and European Starlings, do not erect nestboxes or hang gourds until Purple Martins have reappeared in spring; also, larger martin colonies seem better able to resist intrusion.

prefer woodpecker cavities in trees; in the Southwest, saguaro cacti. Colonies are generally located near water, and breeding areas must contain adequate perches.

Purple Martins usually nest in colonies of from a few to very rarely hundreds of pairs. Multi-unit apartment houses, groupings of single nestboxes, as well as gourds hung in clusters have all been used successfully by martins, although there is little agreement over which arrangement is more attractive to the species; it seems to vary geographically. Only 10 percent of all martin houses contain Purple Martins, however; most of the others actually work to their detriment by providing nest sites for competing starlings and House Sparrows.

Most commercially available houses have 6-inch (15.2 cm) square compartments. Larger apartment sizes are recommended, though. A 2-inch (5.1 cm) distance from the entrance hole to the bottom will reduce loss of eggs due to accidental brushing or lifting out of the nest by the martins. Single boxes should be outfitted with slide-out trays to facilitate monitoring. Ideally, houses should have a fully controlled ventilation system (to be opened only when outside air temperature reaches 90°F, or 32.2°C, insulated compartment ceilings, removable compartment fronts for monitoring, and porches with a ⅝-inch (1.6 cm) vertical lip. They must be predator-proof and able to be raised and lowered by means of a winch (telescoping pole) system.

Whether aluminum or wooden houses are preferable is also a matter of some debate, but aluminum houses have the advantages of being lighter and easier to raise and lower during monitoring and cleaning; they also last longer. On the other hand, wooden houses often have larger compartments, may be less expensive to construct from a materials-only standpoint, and they tend to remain cooler during high temperatures. Houses with 24 to 36 compartments are better than smaller models, but most commercially available houses have only 12. Houses and gourds should be painted white in order to create cooler temperatures within. Even white plastic gourds with screw-off access ports and molded-in rain canopies are available.

Open space around nest sites is important. Established houses should not be moved. Playing a tape recording (see the appendix) of the martin's dawn song sometimes succeeds in attracting the species to a new nest site.

Problems

European Starlings (especially in lowland areas) and House Sparrows are major nestbox competitors. To a lesser extent, the Tree and Violet-green Swallows, house finch, Northern Flicker, Great Crested Flycatcher, and Eastern Bluebird also compete. House Wrens will pierce martin eggs.

Predators, Parasites, and Diseases. Raccoons, house cats, black rat snakes, and owls (especially screech and great horned) prey on martin adults and young; the blue jay, black-billed magpie, and fish crow do so to a lesser extent. Starlings have been known to kill adult martins, and House Sparrows destroy their eggs.

Nest parasites include blowflies (*Protocalliphora* spp.), lice, a flea *(Ceratophyllus idius)*, bedbugs, ticks, and the martin mite *(Dermanyssus prognephilus)*. These mites can have major detrimental effects upon colonies.

The female of North America's largest swallow, the Purple Martin, has a pale gray chest and lacks the male's iridescent plumage.

What You Can Do. Raccoons, house cats, black rat snakes, and other climbing predators can be excluded by attaching a predator guard to the supporting pole (see pages 164–167). Keeping the entrance hole diameter to 2 inches (5.1 cm) will exclude most screech-owls and the American Kestrel. You can thwart great horned owls by wrapping hardware cloth (galvanized wire mesh) around your martin house once this large raptor has been identified as the nocturnal predator; cut 2½- to 3-inch (6.4–7.6 cm) openings in front of the entrance holes. Monitoring is recommended at 5-day intervals until the nestlings are 22 days of age; after that, extra care should be taken to avoid premature fledging.

Because House Sparrows and European Starlings begin nesting earlier in the season than martins, do not erect nestboxes or hang gourds until resident martins have arrived back on the scene. Bigger apartment houses and larger colonies seem better able to resist intrusion by House Sparrows. If all fails and you are unable to dissuade or control sparrows or starlings, it is better to remove the martin house altogether than to increase pest numbers.

James R. Hill III, the founder of the Purple Martin Conservation Association, has excellent advice for increasing the likelihood of establishing a new colony. If competition with native species is a problem, plug the entry holes with paper cups, and erect alternate housing for the competing species. For example, after tree swallows have established themselves in the newly placed single nestboxes, remove the cups. If you are setting up a martin house in an area where no colony currently exists, be sure not to make housing available too early. The first migrant martins, sometimes erroneously called scouts, pass through an area 4 to 5 weeks prior to the actual return of first-year breeders, looking for a site to colonize. At unestablished sites, it is vitally important that you leave open a few of the entrance holes as an invitation to potential colonizers.

Life Cycle

Purple Martins return very early from their South American wintering grounds; as early as mid-winter in the Deep South. Males usually arrive a few days before the females and establish territories. Fully adult males (which don't attain their shiny dark plumage until their second return from migration) generally return to where they formerly bred, and mate with the females shortly after the latter's return. First-year breeders mate later and mostly in areas up to 50 miles (80.7 km) or so from where they hatched. Females actually choose a mate and nest site combination.

Both sexes contribute fresh green leaves to the nest cup, which may help to discourage parasites.

The female constructs the nest using dry grasses, leaves, stalks, feathers, and even mud, amid much vocal chatter. Nest construction begins 1 to 4 weeks prior to egg laying. Mud walls are commonly built near compartment entrances. The nest is characteristically lined with fresh green leaves, collected by both sexes, which may aid in discouraging parasites (not yet proved). Martins lay an average of four to five pure white eggs at intervals of one per day. After 15 to 18 days of incubation by the females (males sometimes insulate the eggs, but do not have a brood patch), the eggs hatch. Both parents feed and care for the nestlings. Feedings increase in frequency until the nestlings attain maximum weight, and then decline. Martins consume an average of 1.25 ounces (35.4 gm) of insects per day, caught on the wing. Adult dragonflies are the major food given to older nestlings. Young martins are brooded by their mother until 10 days old. Their eyes are almost totally open by 11 days of age. By 12 days of age, they weigh as much as their parents. At 17 to 18 days, they begin poking their heads out of the entrance hole; they also begin defecating out of the entrance at this age.

When 4 weeks old, the nestlings are ready to leave the house. They may spend several days on the martin house's porch before finally fledging. The young may return to the nestbox for a week or so 1 to 12 days after fledging, especially during inclement weather. These returnees often receive food from later-nesting adults, which may not be able to distinguish their own young from the interlopers.

Purple Martins gather into huge premigratory flocks at summer's end that have numbered up to 700,000 individuals! Flocks roost in trees or under cement bridges. Martins are early migrants and make the longest migratory flight of any North American swallow. The average life span is 7 to 8 years; the record is 13 years, 9 months.

Useful References

Brown, C. R. "Purple Martin *(Progne subis)*." In *The Birds of North America*, No. 287 (A. Poole and F. Gill, eds.). Philadelphia and Washington, D.C.: The Academy of Natural Sciences and The American Ornithologists' Union, 1997.

Hill, James R., III. "Attracting Purple Martins." *Bird Watcher's Digest.* 1993;4:32–37.

Slabaugh, Chris J. *Purple Martins: 400 Questions and Answers.* Published by the author, 1994.

Bridled Titmouse
(Baeolophus wollweberi; formerly *Parus wollweberi)*

See box plan on page 144.

Length: 5 ¼ inches (13.3 cm)
Nest construction: Unknown
Eggs per clutch: 5 to 7 (white)
Incubation: Poorly known; probably female
Length of incubation: Unknown
Age at fledging: Unknown
Broods per season: Poorly known; probably 1
Food: Poorly known; mostly insects, probably feeding on adults, larvae, and eggs

Description

The Bridled Titmouse, in our estimation, is the most attractive of all the crested tits with its distinctive black and white facial pattern. Among the titmice, this is the only one with a black bib. The rest of the bird is gray with whitish underparts. Its pert, pointed crest adds an air of distinction. These titmice are highly curious, frequently emitting squeaking noises as they glean foliage or investigate some irregularity in their area. This is coupled with an amazing display of acrobatic abilities that might rival those of the chickadee. To see the Bridled Titmouse, you must travel to southern Arizona and New Mexico, as well as to the highlands of Mexico. Its calls or songs are similar to those made by chickadees and other titmice but more rapid and somewhat higher in pitch. The song is a two-syllable phrase resembling that of the Plain Titmouse (now Juniper and Oak Titmouse), repeated several times. One of its common calls is a variation of *chick-a-dee.*

Range

Habitat Needs

Bridled Titmice are permanent residents of the oak and pine-oak woodlands of mountainous areas in their range. Occasionally they can be found in cottonwood-willow-mesquite areas. They are less common and more localized in the riparian woodlands at lower elevations.

Problems

No known competitors have been reported in the literature.

Predators, Parasites, and Diseases. The literature discusses neither predators nor parasites of this bird.

What You Can Do. Even though the literature does not mention any predators of this species, it would still be a good idea to equip this box with predator guards. See pages 164–167 for designs and installation procedures.

Life Cycle

The breeding biology of the Bridled Titmouse is virtually unknown. Nests are generally lined on the bottom and up the sides with a mat composed of cottonwood down, shreds of decayed grasses, and some rabbit fur. In some cases, needles of the Apache Pine make up the nesting material on the bottom of the box. One nest, reported by Herbert Brandt, "was made entirely of silvery, curly leaves, an inch or two in length, fashioned into a shallow basket form, held loosely together." During the nonbreeding season, Bridled Titmice usually form flocks of 25 or more individuals, sometimes mixed with species of insectivorous birds. Longevity record for the Bridled Titmouse is 6 years and 7 months.

Useful References
Jays, Crows and Titmice. In A. C. Bent. *Life Histories of North American Birds.* Washington, D.C.: United States National Museum, 1964.

Housing Needs for Bridled Titmice

Box material: Wood
Floor dimensions: 4-inch (10.2 cm) square floor
Diameter of entrance hole: 1 ¼ inches (3.2 cm)
Box depth below hole: 6 to 8 inches (15.2–20.3 cm)
Mount: 6 to 15 feet (1.8–4.6 m) above the ground
Suggestions: Bridled Titmice will use nestboxes of the same design as those for bluebirds.
Protection: Equip boxes with predator guards.

Plain Titmouse

(Baeolophus inornatus and *B. ridwayi;* formerly *Parus inornatus)**

See box plan on page 144.

Length: 5¾ inches (14.6 cm)
Nest construction: Female
Eggs per clutch: 3 to 9, usually 7
Incubation: Female
Length of incubation: 14 to 16 days
Age at fledging: 15 to 18 days
Broods per season: Unknown
Food: Insects, spiders, caterpillars, leaf galls, seeds of poison oak, acorns, juniper berries, and elderberries

Description

Both the common name, Plain Titmouse, and the scientific one, *Parus inornatus,* are apt for this plain-looking bird. It is, however, a charming fellow with its jaunty crest (like a miniature jay), its sprightly movements, and its melodious voice. The gray-brown plumage provides excellent camouflage against the trunks of the oaks Plain Titmice like to forage in for insects, frequently emitting *tee-le-doo.* During one of our excursions to Arizona, our attention was drawn to a little gray bird that was continuously erecting his crest and intensively and furiously pecking at the bark of an oak. Occasionally he would produce a single sharp note, along with one that seemed to have a more definite air of authority. At other times he appeared to be angry. Then his notes seemed to come faster and harsher: *see-dee-dee* or *chica-dee-dee.* Shortly thereafter he extracted a nice fat, juicy grub. His song became sweeter and his crest was lowered. He flew to another tree and we lost sight of him. Plain Titmice can be found from southern Oregon, east to Nevada and Utah, southeast to Oklahoma and south to Baja California, Arizona, southern New Mexico, and western Texas.

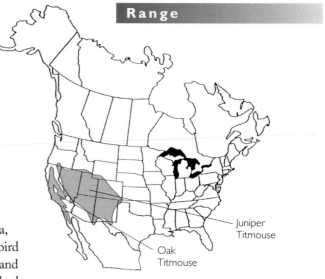

Range

Juniper Titmouse

Oak Titmouse

Habitat Needs

Plain Titmice favor live oaks and deciduous growth of all kinds, as well as oak wood-lands, cottonwoods along streams, forest edges, and mixed oak-piñon-juniper wood-lands. They also occur in river bottom groves, towns, parks, and suburban gardens.

Problems

There is one unusual case of a Plain Titmouse reusing a nest of an Ash-throated Flycatcher. Apparently this flycatcher had nested successfully the previous year in that particular nestbox. Upon returning, she found her nestbox occupied by a Plain Titmouse. The titmouse had relined the nest and then laid six white eggs. When the box was checked, the Ash-throated Flycatcher was incubating both her eggs and those of the titmouse. The titmouse eggs did not hatch. Most likely the flycatcher had driven off the titmouse after she laid her own eggs.

Predators, Parasites, and Diseases. Plain Titmice, like all other small birds, have to be constantly on the alert to avoid becoming prey of predatory birds and mammals. Jays appear to have an affinity for this species: They have often been seen near nestboxes containing young titmice, and sometimes even perched on the box peering in. Scrub jays have been known to dive at fledglings as they leave the nestbox.

Housing Needs for Plain Titmice

Box material: Wood
Floor dimensions: 4-inch (10.2 cm) square floor
Diameter of entrance hole: 1 ¼ inches (3.2 cm)
Box depth below hole: 6 to 7 inches (15.2–17.8 cm)
Mount: On a tree or post 5 to 10 feet (1.5–3.1 m) above the ground
Suggestions: Locate boxes in areas that have a variety of trees present, in addi-tion to some surrounding areas that are open. To encourage nesting, place hair, fur, feathers, or thread near the box.
Protection: Equip boxes with baffles and predator guards.

* The Plain Titmouse has been recently split into the Oak Titmouse (see photo, p. 46) and the Juniper Titmouse, based on electrophorensic analysis of proteins. The two former subspecies of Plain Titmouse are almost as different from each other as both are from the other two species of titmouse. The Oak Titmouse, *Baeolophus inornatus*, occurs in open oak-pine or oak-juniper forests along the Pacific slopes of California; the Juniper Titmouse, *Baeolophus ridwayi*, can be found inland in the Joshua Tree–juniper woodlands of the Little San Bernardino Mountains. The best traits for distinguishing between them are vocalizations and bill sizes. The Pacific slope birds sing by repeating phrases that consist of a high-pitched syllable followed by a lower-pitched syllable. The interior birds either sing a single repeated note or, when notes alternate, emphasize one syllable. The Juniper Titmouse also has a longer bill.

What You Can Do. Equipping the nestbox with baffles and predator guards is the only preventive measure that can be taken.

Life Cycle

It appears that Plain Titmice frequenting the interior of the United States have a tendency to form flocks in winter. Those found along the West Coast, however, tend to remain in their breeding territories. Pairs are formed while these birds are in flocks and before territories are established. Courtship or pair formation is initiated by the males, when they begin to sing *witt-y, witt-y, witt-y* or *ti-wee, ti-wee, ti-wee*. This is followed by "approach threats" toward the females, and chases that simulate mating flights. The female "accepts" the male by being submissive, and with gestures such as wing quivering and soft calls. The male responds by feeding the female, and the pair bond is established.

Oak Titmice often line their nests with feathers and fur.

The female Plain Titmouse searches for a nest site alone and also gathers the materials to fill the chosen cavity. The male feeds the female from the time she commences to build the nest through the time the young are no longer brooded. After this, both parents feed the young equally. The young titmice are fed by regurgitation during the first 4 days after hatching. After the fourth day, worms and insects are stuffed into the mouths of the nestlings. The young will forage close to the nest site after they have fledged. By the time they are 5 weeks old, they are foraging for themselves and gradually are driven from the area by the parents. Juveniles in some cases establish temporary territories on their own, but most are nearly a year old before they can successfully defend and maintain their own breeding territories. The Oak Titmouse has been known to live as long as 8 years.

Useful References
Jays, Crows and Titmice. In A. C. Bent. *Life Histories of North American Birds.* Washington, D.C.: United States National Museum, 1964.

Tufted Titmouse
(*Baeolophus bicolor;*
formerly *Parus bicolor*)

See box plan on page 144.

Length: 6½ inches (16.5 cm)
Nest construction: Female
Eggs per clutch: 3 to 9, usually 5 to 6
Incubation: Female
Length of incubation: 12 to 14 days
Age at fledging: 15 to 18 days
Broods per season: 1, occasionally 2 in the South
Food: Insects, seeds, and fruit

Description

Along with its family members the chickadees, the Tufted Titmouse ranks among the most curious of species found in the eastern deciduous forest. A common visitor to feeders during fall and winter, the Tufted Titmouse can be recognized by the gray feathers on its back, which give way to the white plumage of the breast and belly. A rusty to pinkish wash graces its sides. The most diagnostic feature is the gray crest, which can be either erected or laid flat, especially when the bird's curiosity is aroused. The large black eyes are also striking. A small black patch can be detected at the base of the beak. A year-round resident, this bird has during the past 50 years expanded its range northward, probably because of climatic warming and increased bird feeding. Generally it can be found in nearly the entire eastern half of the United States, excluding only the northern parts of Maine, New Hampshire, Vermont, and New York, and the southernmost tip of Florida. In 1983 the black-crested titmouse of Texas was merged with the Tufted Titmouse into one species.

Watching these inquisitive fellows at our feeder, we came to the conclusion that titmice will always choose the largest sunflower seed available to them. This, we later

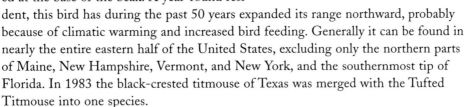

found, is substantiated in published accounts. Titmice will cache food during fall and winter. Watch your feeder during this time and you will soon come to the conclusion that titmice take only one seed at each excursion to the feeder. The seed is then shelled and stored. Seeds are generally stored on small to medium-size branches and twigs, in trees with medium and large trunks. The seed itself is placed on the top surface of these branches. Seeds are also stored under loose pieces of bark, in cracks and rotted areas of trees, and on the ground between two branches. With the increased use of the forests and their related products, titmice could see a decline in numbers. This is already happening in Ohio, in fact; there, this species has become uncommon in farmlands and fragmented forests.

Habitat Needs

Tufted Titmice prefer areas that have tall vegetation and a forest with a dense canopy that contains a large variety of trees. These birds are mostly limited to deciduous forests but can be found in mixed deciduous-coniferous forests, swamps, orchards, parks, and suburban areas. In eastern and southern Texas, titmice are found in riparian and mesquite habitats.

Tufted Titmice prefer to nest in natural cavities. With the decline in the availability of these cavities, nestboxes could become increasingly important to this species.

Problems

No known competitors for Tufted Titmouse nest sites have been reported in the literature. House Wrens can be assumed to be threats to titmice if the nestbox is placed relatively low, along a shrubby area, or along the forest edge. House Wrens habitually

Housing Needs for Tufted Titmice

Box material: Wood
Floor dimensions: 4-inch (10.2 cm) square floor
Diameter of entrance hole: 1 ¼ inches (3.2 cm)
Box depth below hole: 6 to 7 inches (15.2–17.8 cm)
Mount: On a tree or fence post in semishade 5 to 15 feet (1.5–4.6 m) above the ground
Suggestions: Locate boxes in areas that have a mixture of trees and open space. To attract this species, place nesting materials such as hair (human, cat, or dog), fur, feathers, and even thread no more than 3 or 4 inches (7.6–10.2 cm) long near the box.
Protection: Equip boxes with predator guards.

take over and build nests in many cavities in their territories, and puncture the eggs of competing species.

Predators, Parasites, and Diseases. Not known in detail. The most typical predators of adults are apparently house cats, hawks, owls, and snakes, especially black rat snakes. Cowbirds have been reported to have laid eggs in the nests of the Tufted Titmouse, but rates of parasitism were low. Several external parasites have been reported, including two lice (*Myrsidea incerta* and *Phillopterus* spp.), a mite *(Trombicula irritans)*, and a tick *(Hoemaphysalis leporis-palustris)*.

What You Can Do. Since no specific predators or parasites appear to plague the Tufted Titmouse, the best that we can contribute to the breeding success of this species is continued awareness of potential predators. Know if your area has wandering cats that could disturb the nesting of the titmice. Also be aware of other mammalian and reptilian predators; taking proper measures, such as installing predator guards, will decrease the chances of titmice falling prey to them. Constructing the box according to the measurements given on page 144 and mounting it properly will increase the chances of a successful fledging.

Life Cycle

A sure sign that winter is drawing to a close and spring is in the air is the *peter-peter-peter* call of the titmouse. When that call is heard, winter flocks disperse as young birds form monogamous pairs that last several years. The male starts to feed his mate from the time the pair begins prospecting for a nest site until the end of incubation. Usually, this mate feeding is accompanied by wing quivering by one or both of the birds.

This clutch of seven Tufted Titmouse eggs is only slightly larger than the average five to six.

The nest itself is completed exclusively by the female. The foundation of the nest is composed of damp leaves, green moss, dried grass, hair, strips of bark, and occasionally feathers. The nest cup is then lined with hair, fibers, fur, wool, cotton, and various related materials. Over the 6- to 11-day period needed to complete a nest, titmice may actually gather hair or fur from live mammals. Eggs are laid first thing in the morning, just prior to the female leaving the nestbox each day. During the egg-laying period, titmice partially cover the eggs with nesting material.

Only the female incubates the eggs. During this time, she is fed by the male both on and off the nest. After an incubation period of about 2 weeks, the clutch may take from 10 to 24 hours to hatch. The young, born naked and blind, are brooded for the first few days after hatching. Their eyes open by day 8 and, by day 10, the young are completely feathered. The female stops brooding by day 12 and helps the male with the feeding of the nestlings. Titmice have an interesting behavior: It is thought that the young from the previous brood will assist in the feeding of the current young. Fledging occurs at 15 to 18 days after hatching. Generally, birds leave the nest at any time during the day. For the first 4 days after they leave the nest, the fledglings are relatively inactive, seemingly more content to sit and be fed in heavy shrub cover. On day 5, the fledglings start feeding themselves, and they forage independently by 6 weeks of age. The longevity record for a Tufted Titmouse is 13 years, 3 months.

Useful References

Grubb, T. C., Jr., and V. V. Pravosudiv. "Tufted Titmouse *(Parus bicolor)*." In *The Birds of North America,* No. 86 (A. Poole and F. Gill, eds.). Philadelphia and Washington, D.C.: The Academy of Natural Sciences and The American Ornithologists' Union, 1994.

White-breasted Nuthatch
(Sitta carolinensis)

See box plan on page 144.

Length: 5¾ inches (14.6 cm)
Nest construction: Female
Eggs per clutch: 5 to 8, occasionally 3 to 10
Incubation: Female
Length of incubation: 13 to 14 days
Age at fledging: 26 days
Broods per season: 1
Food: Insects, nuts, and seeds

Description

One year in late June, we were entertained at home by a female nuthatch that had discovered a novel way to break open the sunflower seeds she had just acquired from our feeder. Midmorning she would stick a seed between the shingles of our roof, hammer away at it, then fly away with her newly excavated treasure. This continued for several weeks. In midsummer she returned, this time with three fledglings and her mate. They, too, would stick a seed between the shingles, hammer away, then fly off and alight on a nearby tree trunk. Nuthatches in general appear to have personalities. This might be attributed to their long, slightly upturned bills, and their habit of descending a tree headfirst. Adding to their character is their slow, nasal *ank-ank-ank* call. Sexes can be distinguished. The males have a black crown; the female's crown is gray. Both have bluish gray plumage, white breasts, and a beautiful rusty accent under the tail that extends somewhat to the sides. Females in the southeastern United States have crowns that are so dark as to appear black in most conditions.

Despite its wide distribution, very little is known about the White-breasted Nuthatch. This is partly due to the fact that nuthatches prefer to nest in cavities found in large, old trees, making it difficult for researchers to examine the nests. Forestry

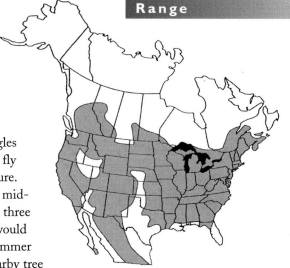

Range

practices that involved the removal of old, dead trees might have affected the populations of these birds. When old trees with natural cavities and woodpecker holes become less available, nestboxes are a good alternative. Other than several reports that these birds have used boxes, very little further information is available.

Habitat Needs

White-breasted Nuthatches prefer to inhabit mature deciduous and mixed deciduous-coniferous forests. They tend to nest near open areas and along forest edges. The nest is often located near water, fields, and orchards. These birds are not common users of nestboxes but will use them if placed in a mature forest near a cleared area.

Problems

There are no reported competitors for the nuthatch. One bird that could potentially inflict harm is the House Sparrow. R. W. Williams in 1918 described an incident of two red-headed woodpeckers attacking a nuthatch's nest and young.

Predators, Parasites, and Diseases. There have been rare reports of brown-headed cowbirds victimizing the nuthatch. Two flies have been noted on the plumage of these birds, *Ornithonica confluenta* and *Ornithomyia anchineuria*. Overall, however, flies do not seem to pose a major threat to nuthatches. Small hawks and owls probably prey on this species.

What You Can Do. Because the nuthatch nestbox must be mounted so high off the ground, monitoring might be a problem. However, you should be aware of the potential predators present. Affix the correct guard (see pages 164–167 for predator guard designs and installation procedures) to the box prior to mounting. Placing the nestboxes inside a

Housing Needs for White-breasted Nuthatches

Box material: Wood
Floor dimensions: 4-inch (10.2 cm) or 5-inch (12.7 cm) square floor
Diameter of entrance hole: 1¼ inches (3.2 cm)
Box depth below hole: 7 inches (17.8 cm)
Mount: 12 to 20 feet (3.7–6.1 m) above the ground
Suggestions: These birds will use the same box design as the titmice. Locate the box in a mature forest near a cleared area.
Protection: Equip the box with predator guards. Place it inside a mature forest and away from buildings to protect against House Sparrows.

Female White-breasted Nuthatches are distinguished from males by their grayish crowns.

mature forest and away from buildings is the best protection against House Sparrows. Interestingly, nuthatches have been observed "bill sweeping" their nest site with crushed insects. Most of the insects used by these birds tend to exude a strong-smelling substance. It is thought that the nuthatches perform this behavior to deter against mammalian predators such as squirrels and raccoons.

Life Cycle

White-breasted Nuthatches are monogamous, remaining together for many years. The pair maintain their bond and defend their breeding territory year-round, which is more convenient for this species than others, because nuthatches are generally nonmigratory (in some years there is some irruptive movement). Birds that relocate are most likely young birds that have left because of low food supplies.

Courtship starts with the breeding song sung by the male, frequently during the first half hour of a wintry morning. As the female approaches, the male will continue to sing, displaying his plumage to her. Frequently *hit-tuck* notes are exchanged between the two partners. *Phee-oo* notes reflect a high level of interest. The male will feed the female prior to copulation, and during egg laying and incubation.

Exclusively the female builds the nest starting as early as April. Little is known about the nest construction or structure, although nuthatches have been observed carrying hairs and pieces of bark to the nest cavity. One nest in Oregon was lined with wadding from an old mattress lying beside the trail, while another description notes that the nest cavity was "floored with bark flakes and strips and lumps of earth; with a cup of finer bark shreds, grasses and rootlets, but mainly with fur, wool, hair and feathers." Eggs are thought to be laid one per day until the clutch is complete. Incubation starts with the laying of the final egg.

Rather little is known about the construction or composition of the White-breasted Nuthatch's nest.

The female broods the young birds for at least the first 3 days after hatching. During this time, the male feeds both the female and the young. As the young become older, the female broods less and begins to assist the male in feeding the young and removing the fecal sacs. The young remain in the nest for as long as 26 days. The young stay with parents for several weeks, then disperse. After dispersal, most young nuthatches establish their own territories, usually in pairs. They breed in these territories the following year.

Data is sparse on the life span of White-breasted Nuthatches. Of 21 banded individuals, 10 disappeared in less than 2 years. The longest reported living nuthatch was 9 years, 10 months old.

Useful References

Pravosudov, V. V., and T. C. Grubbo Jr. "White-breasted Nuthatches *(Sitta carolinensis).*" In *The Birds of North America,* No. 54 (A. Poole and F. Gill, eds.). Philadelphia and Washington, D.C.: The Academy of Natural Sciences and The American Ornithologists' Union, 1993.

Bewick's Wren
(*Thryomanes bewickii*)

See box plan on page 143.

Length: 5½ inches (14 cm)
Nest construction: Both sexes may work on the nest, but the female does most of the building
Eggs per clutch: 4 to 11, usually 5 to 7
Incubation: Female
Length of incubation: 10 to 14 days
Age at fledging: 14 days
Broods per season: Probably 2
Food: Insects, small vertebrates, and carrion

Description

The Bewick's Wren has been described as a "gentle and confiding creature" in its range from British Columbia east to the Appalachians and south to southern Mexico. Slightly larger than the House Wren, the Bewick's Wren is rather plain in appearance. Eastern birds are reddish brown above (see photo), while western birds are grayish brown. This wren also has a long white eyebrow strip, but lacks the white throat of the Carolina Wren. When the Bewick's Wren fans its tail, the white outer tips of the feathers are very conspicuous, as is its unique slow, sideways flicking of the tail.

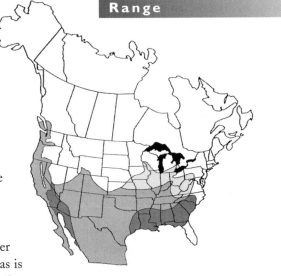

Range

Like other wrens, the Bewick's is a nervous, restless, and inquisitive bird, examining a woodpile one moment and investigating a knothole in a shed the next. Its behavior is almost reminiscent of a mouse. The wren is most likely using its long, narrow, slightly downcurved bill to scavenge for insects and spiders. The Bewick's Wren's loud and cheerful song has been described as sweet and tender. It usually begins with a soft buzz, as if the bird was inhaling, followed by a trill and a series of slurred notes. The wren can frequently be seen singing, perched high in its foraging areas. Many consider the Bewick's Wren among the finest singers of all birds. If an intruder enters that territory, the wren scolds with a harsh *vit–vit–vit* along with a harsh, drawn-out buzzing note. The Bewick's Wren was Blue Listed from 1972 to 1986. Its populations have been declining everywhere east of the Mississippi for inexplicable reasons.

Habitat Needs

Bewick's Wrens can be found on or near the ground in brush-covered, partly open areas, including the edges of deciduous forests, coniferous woods with underbrush, chaparral, and piñon-juniper woodlands. This wren avoids swampy woodlands. With the encroachment of housing developments, the Bewick's Wren can also be found in suburbs within its range.

Almost any suitable cavity will attract this bird to nest. Like other members of its family, it will nest in such unusual places as empty barrels, deserted automobile oil wells, and the slightly more conventional crevices in stone, brick, or tile walls. Bewick's Wrens will readily accept a nestbox if one is available.

Problems

The Bewick's Wren will occasionally attack the nests of its own species as well as those of other birds nesting nearby, such as the dusky-capped flycatcher, cassin's kingbird, and bushtit. No other information on competitors is available for this wren.

Predators, Parasites, and Diseases. The Bewick's Wren is most likely preyed upon by predatory birds, mammals, and reptiles such as snakes. Two interesting reports can be found in the literature of this wren serving as prey for a roadrunner and a rattlesnake. No parasites are known for this wren.

Housing Needs for Bewick's Wrens

Box material: Wood
Floor dimensions: 4-inch (10.2 cm) or 5-inch (12.7 cm) square floor
Diameter of entrance hole: 1 inch (2.5 cm)
Box depth below hole: 6 inches (15.2 cm)
Mount: 4½ to 10 feet (1.4–3.1 m) above the ground
Suggestions: These birds will use the same box design as the House Wren. Some designs feature a slot instead of a round hole; it looks like a letter drop in a mailbox and gives the wrens more room to maneuver the long twigs they use as a foundation for their nests. It should be cut 1 to 1¼ inches (2.5–3.2 cm) high, 3 inches (7.6 cm) long, and 4 to 6 inches (10.2–15.2 cm) above the floor.
Protection: Equip boxes with predator guards.

What You Can Do. As with any other species, this wren's nestboxes should be equipped with predator guards (see pages 164–167 for guard designs and installation directions). Because the range of the Bewick's Wren covers vicinities that shelter larger populations of snakes, predator guards would protect the nestbox not only against mammalian hunters but against these predators as well.

Life Cycle

The Bewick's Wren is less migratory than the House Wren, and will often remain in an area year-round. Only severe cold and/or the lack of food will cause these birds to migrate. It is not uncommon for Bewick's Wrens to take over the area occupied by House Wrens after they leave in fall, only to be forced out in spring. In some parts of its range, the Bewick's Wren breeds earlier and in thicker habitats than the

Like other wrens, Bewick's Wrens often build nests in unusual places, like this wooden canoe hull.

House Wren in order to avoid competition. In late spring, males establish their breeding territories, which encompass several potential nest sites. Some males appear to be bigamous or even polygynous. Advertisement for a mate commences when the male starts singing on his territory. It is of interest that the male's song shows marked geographic variations. For example, males in Arizona sing a short, simple song but have repertoires of 15 or more songs. Males in Colorado, on the other hand, sing long, complex melodies but have only about 10 to choose from. Population density, habitat, and possibly the songs of other bird species in the area may influence the nature of geographic song variations. Pairing occurs quite rapidly once a territory has been established.

Generally, nests are not built until the female is present. (Males build crude dummy nests at times.) Although both sexes may work on construction, the female does most of the work. In some instances, females have been known to fabricate the nest alone. The nest is built in about 10 days. The base is usually composed of a number of short sticks generally placed in the nestbox by the male. The female will frequently rearrange these sticks until they eventually cradle the nest cup in one corner. The nest cup is lined with fine fur, cottony plant material, occasional feathers, and snake or lizard skins. Eggs are white with irregular brown, purple, gray spots and dots. Once the clutch is complete, the female does all the incubation. The male feeds the female during this time. Both parents feed the fledgings during the 14-day nestling period and will continue to feed the young for another 2 weeks after they have fledged. This wren has a longevity record of 8 years.

Useful References
Bent, A. C. *Life Histories of North American Nuthatches, Wrens, Thrashers and Their Allies.* New York: Dover Publications, Inc., 1964.

Carolina Wren
(*Thryothorus ludovi-cianus*)

See box design on page 143.

Length: 5 ½ inches (14 cm)

Nest construction: Both sexes, but the female does most of the lining

Eggs per clutch: 4 to 8, usually 5 to 6

Incubation: Female

Length of incubation: 14 days

Age at fledging: 12 to 14 days

Broods per season: Probably 2

Food: Insects, small vertebrates, and occasionally seeds

Description

The folklore and tradition of the Old World mark the wren as a tiny bird, and this has carried over into American literature. Darius Green characterized this family as "the little chatterin' sassy wren, no bigger'n my thumb." The Carolina Wren is certainly not a tiny bird among the wrens, however. In fact, it is so large that early American ornithologists referred to it as the Great Carolina Wren, with the accent on the Great. Notwithstanding its size, it possesses the temperament of most wrens, with continuous nervous, excited, eloquent, and curious activity. Its abundant energy is expressed both by voice and up-and-down tail movements.

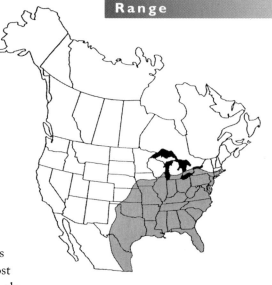

Range

Carolina Wrens have been described as being much more handsome than the mouse brown House Wren. Carolina Wrens have a richer rusty brown above and a warm buff below. A bold white eye stripe as well as a white throat also help you distinguish this wren from the others. We associate Carolina Wrens with the warm weather of the sunny South, but they can be found north to the central parts of Wisconsin, Michigan, New York, and southern New England.

These birds rank among our own favorites, because their song is loud, cheery, and easy to learn: a series of triplet whistles, *TEA-kettle, TEA-kettle, TEA-kettle,* that is unmistakable and can be heard nearly year-round. It has been called the Mocking Wren, because some of its notes resemble those of other birds, particularly the whistle call of the Tufted Titmouse and a song of the cardinal. Carolina Wrens, however, have experienced population declines in the Northeast and parts of the Midwest. They were Blue Listed in 1980 and 1981, and a species of Special Concern from 1982 to 1986.

Habitat Needs

Carolina Wrens favor thick, thorny shrubbery along waterways and in swamps, as well as woodland thickets, hammocks, and isolated clumps of trees and bushes on the prairies and in the pine barrens. Brushy forests, forest margins, cut-over forests, and cultivated fields with brush heaps or old buildings can also provide suitable habitat for the Carolina Wrens, as can suburban parks and gardens. Carolina Wrens tend to associate less with humans than House Wrens.

Natural nests are extremely difficult to find, however. Much like the House Wren, the Carolina Wren will use a wide variety of receptacles to house its nest. These include tin cans, coffeepots, pails, hats, caps, and pockets of old clothes left hanging in sheds or on porches. Other nests have been constructed on artificial structures such as shelves, doorjambs, and other flat surfaces protruding in sheds, barns, and abandoned buildings. It is no surprise, then, that this species will readily adopt and use nestboxes.

Problems

The Carolina Wren overlaps to some extent with the House Wren in its breeding range. Apparently, this does not represent a significant conflict between these two species. The Bewick's Wren, on the other hand, is dominated by the slightly larger Carolina Wren during disputes in areas where both individuals occur.

Housing Needs for Carolina Wrens

Box material: Wood
Floor dimensions: 4-inch (10.2 cm) square floor
Diameter of entrance hole: 1⅛ inches (2.9 cm)
Box depth below hole: At least 4¼ inches (10.8 cm)
Mount: 4½ to 10 feet (1.4–3.1 m) above the ground
Suggestions: Orient the box to face away from prevailing weather. An alternative entrance hole is a slot 1½ inches (3.8 cm) high and 3 inches (7.6 cm) wide placed 1 to 6 inches (2.5–15.2 cm) above the box floor; this provides wrens more room to maneuver their sticks into the box during nest construction.
Protection: Equip with predator guards.

Predators, Parasites, and Diseases. The literature does not cite specific predation by animals on this species. However, if nestboxes are near human habitations, domestic cats can be a problem. Raccoons can also be attracted to humans, and they, too, can prey on the wrens and their young. Three types of external parasites have been identified for the Carolina Wren. These include four species of ticks, two of mites, and one louse.

What You Can Do. Since cats inflict the greatest mortality of any predator on wildlife, it is a good idea to keep all pet cats at home and not let them stray in the outdoors. Keeping your refuse securely stored will also decrease the incidence of wren death due to raccoon predation. Some deaths of both young and adult Carolina Wrens have been attributed to pesticide use. It is generally a good idea to use pesticides only if all else fails. Their effects on all organisms, including ourselves, tend to be negative.

Life Cycle

Carolina Wrens are resident birds in their range. Males start declaring their territory in late winter by their songs. Some males may sing throughout the year. Males do not begin to build their nests until they first become mated. When mating has occurred, the pair begins to seek out suitable sites. Both sexes contribute to building the nest; it can be completed within two days. Almost any soft and pliable material is used to construct it, including bulky masses of leaves, twigs, rootlets, weed stalks, strips of inner bark, and any other handy debris. The interior structure is surprisingly domed, with a side entrance. It is lined with feathers, hair, moss, wool, and fine grasses. Most, if not all, of the nest lining is accomplished by the female. Also incorporated into the nest might be

In characteristic wren fashion, these Carolina Wrens have constructed their nest atop a plastic bucket.

sections of snakeskin. No practical explanation has been given for the use of this material other than that it is fairly easily manipulated, making it suitable for building a nest. One nest in Texas was found to contain small twigs, corn husks, pieces of paper, string, thread, wool rags and leaf skeletons!

Usually, the first egg is laid 5 days after the nest building has started. Each of the subsequent eggs is laid daily until the clutch is finished. Eggs of the Carolina Wren are usually pure white, but often pinkish, or creamy white. Generally they are more heavily marked, with large reddish brown spots, than other wrens' eggs. The spots are irregularly scattered and often concentrated into a ring at the large end. The male feeds the female to some extent during nest building, incubation, and brooding. These wrens will also spend an unusually long period of time on the nest when incubating. Carolina Wrens will leave the nest cavity only six to seven times a day, compared to the House Wren, which leaves an estimated 27 to 43 times daily. Eggs generally hatch after 14 days of incubation. The young fledge at 12 to14 days of age. The extent of double-brooding and polygyny between broods is not known. The male will, however, sometimes take care of the newly fledged brood so that the female can begin a second clutch in a new nest that the male prepared during the time the female was incubating the eggs. Longevity records indicate a life span of 6 years and 2 months.

Useful References

Bent, A. C. *Life Histories of North American Nuthatches, Wrens, Thrashers and Their Allies.* New York: Dover Publications, Inc., 1964.

House Wren
(Troglodytes aedon)

See box plan on page 143.

Length: 4½ to 5¼ inches (11.4–13.3 cm)
Nest construction: Male and female
Eggs per clutch: 5 to 8, usually 6 to 7
Incubation: Female
Length of incubation: 12 to 15 days
Age at fledging: 12 to 18 days
Broods per season: 2, occasionally 3
Food: Insects and small invertebrates, such as spiders, snails, and millipedes

Description

No one can deny the boundless energy of House Wrens, especially when the males first return in spring to their breeding grounds and start singing. They continue their beautiful, bubbling song through summer. Watching such a performance, you cannot miss the wren's quivering throat and the flicking of his upcocked tail. And of all the birds, the wrens are probably the most eccentric in their choice of nest sites. This tiny brown bird with buff underparts and faint eyebrows will come and go all day long carrying small twigs into several prospective nest sites, only to be interrupted briefly to scold intruders.

Range

The House Wren, however, has been involved in some controversy. Problems started for this species in 1925. Althea Sherman, who for a number of years had made careful observations of the wrens nesting in her backyard, wrote a spirited article in which she reviewed at great length the destructive tendencies of House Wrens toward species that come into direct competition with it by nesting in the same area. Over the years, humans may in fact have contributed to this problem. House Wrens originally nested in cavities; with the introduction of nestboxes, we contributed to the species' population increase. This was, in fact, the case in Ms. Sherman's backyard. The wren, to heighten its own brood's chances for survival, eliminates competitors; Ms. Sherman failed to note this motive, however.

Habitat Needs

House Wrens will nest practically anywhere. They have been found nesting along forest edges, in shrubby areas, swamps, fields, farmlands, and suburban parks. Characteristics of a preferred nesting site for a wren include being enveloped in vegetation and facing somewhat downhill. Small openings within the vegetation will allow the wren to move freely about its domain. These areas need also to have high perches from which the male may sing to proclaim his territory and attract a mate.

This species has been known to nest in rather unique sites, such as the radiator of a dismantled car, an empty cow skull, the leg of a pair of pants on a clothesline, the pocket of a scarecrow, and shoes. However, more conventionally the House Wren will occupy a nestbox of the same design as the Black-capped Chickadee.

Problems

House Wrens receive fierce competition from bluebirds and Tree Swallows, primarily because they coexist in the same type of habitat. There is also intense competition among wrens themselves for nest sites. Using boxes with 1½-inch (3.8 cm) diameter entrance holes will encourage swallows and bluebirds, while a 1-inch (2.5 cm) diameter hole will encourage the nesting of wrens and chickadees. Placing boxes along forested edges will also encourage wren usage.

Housing Needs for House Wrens

Box material: Wood
Floor dimensions: 4-inch (10.2 cm) square floor
Diameter of entrance hole: 1 inch (2.5 cm)
Box depth below hole: 6 inches (15.2 cm)
Mount: 4½ to 10 feet (1.4–3.1 m) above the ground
Suggestions: Locate the box close to a shrubby area, in a large tree, under the eaves of a building, or along a fencerow. Unlike all other nestboxes, this one need not be securely anchored; it can be left free hanging.
Protection: Install baffles or apply heavy coats of grease or carnauba wax to discourage climbing animals. To avoid competition with Tree Swallows and other wrens, do not pair boxes.

Predators, Parasites, and Diseases. Domestic cats are the wren's number one enemy, especially because the bird often nests near humans and cats are common pets. Cats appear to be especially destructive when House Wren young are disturbed and fledge prematurely. In such incidents, the young birds are easy pickings for the cat. Other predators of the House Wren are red and gray foxes, and the great horned and screech-owls. Wasps, bumblebees, field mice, red squirrels, and chipmunks have been noted to be somewhat troublesome at times.

Two lice and three species of mite have been found to be external parasites on House Wrens. The presence of these parasites in the nest is not usually fatal, but heavy infestations may affect nestlings. Nests have been found to be infested with the larvae of the blood-sucking blowfly *Protocalliphora splendida sialia*. These have not traditionally been as major a problem for House Wrens as for bluebirds and swallows. They have, however, been proved to be contributors to the mortality of nestlings, especially when coupled with bad weather and the lack of food.

What You Can Do. Owners of domestic cats should not let their pets stray outdoors. Cats have been known to have a great impact on wildlife. Even a slight disturbance will cause premature fledging, which can have fatal results for the young birds. After birds have left the nestbox once, they will not stay in it again even if you return them. Be aware, too, of the consequences of using herbicides or pesticides. Many sprays will affect the insects that the wren eats and may have detrimental effects on both young and adults. Domestic pets may also be affected by these sprays.

Careful monitoring of the nestbox can avoid serious problems with external parasites and other unwelcome guests in the box. (Refer to pages 12–15 for information about dealing with blood-sucking blowfly larvae.) If wasps or bumblebees are found in residence in the nestbox, careful removal will avoid any problems later. Generally, if mammals are found inside the nestbox, removing the nesting material will discourage them from using the box. You might have to repeat this several times. Avoid visiting the nestboxes too frequently to discourage predation by foxes. Frequent visits will leave not only worn paths but also scent trails to the box. Installation of baffles or the application of heavy coats of grease or carnauba wax might also discourage climbing animals. House Wrens often have a negative impact on the nests of Tree Swallows and other wrens when occupying adjacent, paired boxes; not pairing boxes could alleviate some of this problem.

Life Cycle

Males arrive from their wintering grounds in the southern United States and Mexico sometime in April. Most males will return to the same breeding territory year after year. Females arrive an average of nine days after the males. Once the male establishes or reestablishes his territory, mainly by singing from perches within the selected area, he starts to build several nests. The male wren strives to fill each nest cavity with sticks, leaving only a narrow passageway to a comparatively small nesting cavity that will eventually house the female and eggs or young. After one nesting season, we cleaned out a wren box and counted all the twigs that filled it: 387 twigs. This means that a wren had made 387 separate flights to deposit the sticks in this one box alone! One male reportedly built an amazing seven "dummy" nests. All nest sites are vigorously defended throughout the breeding season.

A male may pair with one female for part of the season to raise a brood, then mate with a different female to raise a second or third brood. Some males have been known to have two mates simultaneously. Once a female enters a male's territory, his singing changes, becoming more high pitched and squeaky. He accompanies his singing with wing quivering and will lead the female around his territory, displaying the various different sites at which he has started to build nests. She accepts a site by constructing a nest cup from various materials such as moss, grass, plant fibers, rootlets, feathers, spider cocoons, hair, and anything else she may come across, including strips of plastic or string. The nest cup is actually built behind the pile of sticks the males has accumulated in the nesting cavity. This ritual is repeated every time a new mating takes place.

The female lays one egg per day until the clutch is complete. She begins to incubate the eggs when the next-to-last egg is laid. The male occasionally will feed the female while she is incubating; otherwise, she must leave the nest and forage for herself. Eggs generally hatch all on the same day. Nestlings are brooded for their first 3 days of life. Both parents care for the young; the male does not enter the nest but passes the food to the female, who feeds the young. Interestingly, however, when the young are older, the male will enter the nest and feed them, but only when the female is not in the box. Both parents remove fecal sacs from the nest. Young will fledge at between 12 and 18 days of age, and are capable of flight. They continue to be fed by both parents for approximately another 2 weeks. The female may begin to renest while the young are still being fed. In such cases, the male becomes the primary caregiver.

Close to fledging, these House Wren nestlings peer out of their natural nesting cavity.

House Wrens lay as many as eight eggs, often in a corner of the nestbox.

Wrens have a comparatively high metabolic rate: Food can pass through their bodies in approximately an hour and a half. Food therefore must be constantly replenished. In order to withstand long periods without food at night, adult birds can lower their body temperatures. However, a body temperature of 71°F (21.7°C) is lethal. To maintain their regular body temperatures (males: 104.4°F, or 40.2°C; females: 105°F, or 40.6°C), wrens feed mostly on insects. This insect prey includes grasshoppers, beetles, caterpillars, stink bugs, leafhoppers, cabbage worms, and gypsy moths. When these birds first return in early spring, they almost exclusively feed on ants. Spiders appear to be a favorite, perhaps because they are easily found in the wren's haunts: woodpiles, brush, stone walls, hollow logs, and sheds. No fruit or vegetative matter has been reported to be consumed by this species. House Wrens have been reported to have a life span of as long as 9 years.

Useful References

Bent, A. C. *Life Histories of North American Nuthatches, Wrens, Thrashers and Their Allies.* New York: Dover Publications, Inc., 1964.

Black-capped Chickadee

(Poecile atricapillus; formerly *Parus atricapillus)*

See box design on page 143.

Length: 4¾ to 5¾ inches (12.1–14.6 cm)
Nest construction: Female
Eggs per clutch: 5 to 10, usually 6 to 8
Incubation: Female
Length of incubation: 11 to 13 days
Age at fledging: 14 to 18 days
Broods per season: 1
Food: Insects, large caterpillars, spiders, snails, slugs, centipedes, seeds, berries, and fat from dead vertebrates such as deer and skunks

Description

At one time or another, all of us have taken a gentle stroll in the out-of-doors only to encounter an inquisitive chickadee or two. When this happens, chickadees energetically hop from one branch to another, vocalizing an array of *chick-a-dee* calls. Usually the leader of the flock emits the loudest calls, only to be echoed by other members of the group. The amount of energy expended and the commotion produced would lead you to believe that these little birds are much larger than their actual size. If fact, the average chickadee weighs the equivalent of a quarter, nickel, and dime put together, or about .4 ounce (11 g).

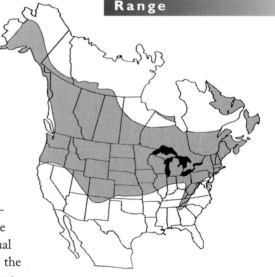

Range

We have spent hours being entertained by these birds as they glean the surfaces of leaves or hang from a twig, upside down, to pick off food. Indeed, chickadees have specialized leg muscles that help them hang upside down. We have also seen them hover at the feeder anxiously waiting for a free perch, or fly off their perch in pursuit of insects in midair, much the way a hawk pursues its prey. Backyard feeding stations can be excellent spots to determine the pecking order of a flock. Chickadees have a linear hierarchy in that a main pair will dominate all other individuals of their respective sexes. Over the many years of banding that we have done, chickadees are our most frequently banded bird. When held in the hand, their assertive personalities are easily seen: They will attempt to peck their way out, raising and lowering their crown feathers.

The Black-capped Chickadee has a wide range that includes much of Canada and about the northern two-thirds of the United States, coast to coast. Being so widespread, it is a familiar bird to many and can be easily recognized by its black cap and throat, white cheeks, gray back, and dull white to buff underparts. Most are year-round residents in their range and able to withstand short days and very cold temperatures, especially in northern areas. Chickadees have the amazing capacity to enter a state of "regulated hypothermia" on cold nights: The bird can drop its body temperature 18 to 22°F (10–12°C) below its daytime norm, thus conserving energy overnight. Banding records seem to indicate that some chickadees migrate, because local populations experience an influx of new individuals in fall and a departure in spring. We see these trends at our banding station in western Massachusetts.

Forests are being cleared and destroyed daily, affecting many bird species. The Black-capped Chickadee, however, has benefited from this clearing, especially when woods are transformed into agricultural fields. Chickadees prefer to nest along forest edges. With the forest cleared or fragmented, more edge habitat is available, thereby providing potentially more nesting sites. It must be kept in mind that overzealous forest management can reduce or eliminate natural nest sites. Where natural sites are rare, nestboxes may be accepted and provide excellent alternative nesting sites. Feeders have also enhanced chickadees' survival, especially in the northern parts of their range.

 ## Housing Needs for Black-capped Chickadees

Box material: Wood

Floor dimensions: 4-inch (10.2 cm) square floor

Diameter of entrance hole: 1⅛ inches (2.9 cm)

Box depth below hole: 6 inches (15.2 cm)

Mount: 4½ to 15 feet (1.4–4.6 m) above the ground

Suggestions: A Black-capped Chickadee will occupy a nestbox of the same design as used for the House Wren. Orient the box to receive sunshine 40 to 60 percent of the day. Locate it in clearings or edges of mature hardwood forests or, in agricultural areas, woodlots along the perimeter of farmlands. Place about 1 inch (2.5 cm) of wood chips or shavings in the bottom of the box.

Protection: Keep the box away from shrubby areas, and keep the entrance hole small. Install baffles to deter mammalian predators.

Habitat Needs

The Black-capped Chickadee prefers deciduous and mixed deciduous-coniferous woodlands, open woods and parks, willow thickets, and cottonwood groves. It can also be found in disturbed areas such as old fields or suburban areas, as long as suitable nest sites and adequate food for the dependent young are available. Usually chickadees are more common near the edges of wooded areas, but they can also be found in the middle of a large forested tract of land.

Problems

The only competitor that the chickadee has to contend with is the House Wren, because both will use a nestbox design that has a small-diameter entrance hole. House Wrens will destroy the egg clutches and young of competitors.

Predators, Parasites, and Diseases. Chickadees are preyed upon by the small, fast-flying sharp-shinned hawk, northern shrike, Eastern Screech-Owl, and Northern Saw-whet Owl. Mammalian predators include raccoons, squirrels, opossums, and possibly weasels. Chickadees also fall prey to certain snakes.

No major outbreaks of any disease have been reported for this species. A few blood parasites have been reported, but at extremely low levels. This is also true for ectoparasites. Low to no infestation by ectoparasites is partly due to this species' habits of digging new cavities each time it nests, and occupying cleaned nestboxes.

What You Can Do. To discourage competition from the House Wren, proper placement of the nestbox is necessary. Keep the box away from shrubby areas favored by the House Wren. The diameter of the entrance hole (1⅛ inches, or 2.9 cm) excludes the House Sparrow and European Starling from entering and nesting. This also excludes entrance by the brown-headed cowbird and thereby prevents brood parasitism.

Constructing baffles is the only tested method to deter mammalian predators and snakes. (See pages 164–167 for designs and installation procedures.) To encourage the reuse of nestboxes in succeeding breeding seasons, clean them immediately after the young have fledged. This will also provide cavities for chickadees to roost in during extremely cold winter nights. Nestboxes need to be checked again and cleaned, if necessary, in spring.

Life Cycle

Our faith that winter will not last forever is renewed whenever we hear the chickadee's *fee-bee* call in late winter. As the sun climbs higher and the days become longer, this call is given more and more frequently by the males. The small winter flocks begin to break up, and the males start to define their territories. The *fee-bee* call then becomes the predominant sound of the outdoors. At times, males appear to be answering one another.

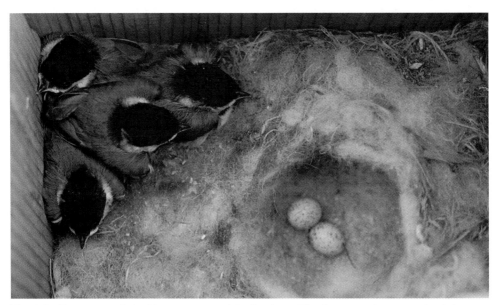

Two infertile eggs remain in this moss-covered, fur-lined nest. The fur acts as important insulation.

Most pairs are formed in fall; some pairs form during winter and spring. Pairs formed in winter and spring are generally new birds that have joined the flock. Most likely, these are first-year birds that have dispersed from their hatching area. Needless to say, some birds die during winter, and the survivors must find new mates in spring.

Black-capped Chickadees are monogamous and their pair bonds last for several years, if not for life. Both pair members excavate a nesting cavity by using their beaks to remove rotten wood. Chickadees meticulously carry away the wood chips produced during the excavation. Each bird will alternately take a chip of wood into its beak, fly to a nearby perch, and drop the wood chip. Excavation of a cavity takes from 7 to 10 days. The nest itself is built exclusively by the female in 3 to 5 days. She uses coarse materials such as moss, then lines the nest with finer materials such as rabbit fur or wool from the cinnamon fern. In early May we once observed several chickadees plucking fur from our sleeping dog, Taos. Her malamute coat would certainly provide a warm, soft lining for eggs and young.

Eggs are laid within a day or two of nest completion. Typically, one egg is laid early in the morning. Interestingly, the female may add some nesting material during the egg-laying period. Incubation is done exclusively by the female and starts when the next-to-last egg is laid. She will develop a brood patch by the time the last egg is deposited, which helps the eggs stay warmer and develop faster. Some males develop brood patches, but there is no evidence that they assist in incubation. When the female is absent from the nest, the eggs are covered with nesting material.

The incubation period is 11 to 13 days. The male regularly brings food to the female. At other times, both male and female leave the nest site and forage together. Typically, eggs will hatch within 12 to 30 hours of each other, and in the order they were laid. Eggshells are removed from the nest, taken some distance, and either dropped or eaten.

Nestlings are brooded by the female for a few days after hatching. As they mature, less and less time is spent brooding, until at about 12 days, all brooding ceases. The male does most of the feeding at this point, assisted by the female. Young generally leave the nest at 16 days of age. If the nest is disturbed, however, fledging might occur as early as 12 days. Most young fledge in the morning, and the nest is completely abandoned within 2 hours of the first fledgee. Young are fed by parents for the next 2 to 4 weeks. These fledglings emit frequent *dees* in efforts to solicit food. The yellow corners of the young bird's mouth are soon lost after leaving the nest, and their wings and tail grow rapidly; 7 to 10 days after leaving the nest, they are indistinguishable from the adults.

Juvenile birds disperse suddenly in random directions. This may occur because of aggression from adults or decreased feeding by the parents. These young birds will soon form winter flocks composed of local breeding birds and unrelated hatching-year individuals. Most young chickadees will remain with one flock; a few may become winter floaters; and in years with poor food supplies, some move south in search of more productive feeding areas. Chickadees may also join birds such as warblers, titmice, kinglets, and others to form a more cosmopolitan "mixed flock." The average life span of a Black-capped Chickadee is 2½ years. Many young do not survive their first summer. The currently published longevity record for a chickadee is 12 years, 5 months. Our oldest banded Black-capped Chickadee in western Massachusetts was an individual at least 8 years old.

Useful References

Smith, S. M. "Black-capped Chickadee." In *The Birds of North America*, No. 39 (A. Poole, P. and F. Gill, eds.). Philadelphia and Washington, D.C.: The Academy of Natural Sciences and The American Ornithologists' Union, 1993.

Carolina Chickadee

(Poecile carolinensis; formerly *Parus carolinensis)*

See box design on page 143.

Length: 4¾ to 5 inches (12.1–12.7 cm)
Nest construction: Female
Eggs per clutch: 5 to 8, usually 6
Incubation: Female
Length of incubation: 11 to 12 days
Age at fledging: 13 to 17 days
Broods per season: Probably 1
Food: Insects: moths and caterpillars; spiders, berries, and seeds, including those of poison ivy

Description

The Carolina Chickadee was one of the four birds discovered by John J. Audubon in the coastal areas of South Carolina. This chickadee is by no means confined to the Atlantic and Gulf coastal plains, however: It is resident from central New Jersey, Ohio, Missouri, and Oklahoma south to Florida and Texas. These birds are so similar in appearance to the Black-capped Chickadee that Audubon did not realize that they were separate species until 1834, over a century after "the" chickadee had been discovered by the Europeans. The Carolina and Black-capped Chickadees are also alike enough in their

needs that they do compete, especially during the breeding season. Carolina Chickadees prefer valleys and foothills, whereas the Black-capped Chickadee generally can be found at higher elevations.

Any chickadee is easily recognized by its black cap and bib, and white cheeks. The Carolina Chickadee can be carefully differentiated by its wings, which lack the white edgings present in the Black-capped, and by an examination of its bib, which appears to have a more definite edge, especially along the bottom. The best method of distinguishing these birds is their voices. The Carolina's call is characteristically higher and renders a faster version of *chick-a-dee-dee-dee* than the Black-capped. Another familiar song of the Carolina Chickadee is *fee-bee, fee-bay*. Based largely on their vocalizations, it has been proposed that the Black-capped Chickadee and the Carolina Chickadee are the same species, but recent biochemical analysis seems to indicate that they are separate species. Hybrids of the Carolina and Black-capped Chickadees are common, although restricted to a narrow area from Kansas east to Illinois.

Habitat Needs

Any wooded area will attract the Carolina Chickadee, whose habitat requirements are nearly identical to those of the Black-capped. Carolina Chickadees are associated with open deciduous, mixed deciduous, and coniferous forests, especially those in riparian areas and swamps as well as in thickets, cultivated areas with scattered trees, and suburban parks. They are frequent backyard residents.

Problems

Like the Black-capped Chickadee, the Carolina Chickadee's competitor is the House Wren, because both will nest in boxes of the same design and use the same size of entry hole. House Wrens will destroy not only the eggs of their competitors but also their young. European Starlings and House Sparrows will also attempt to use the box, if given the opportunity.

Housing Needs for Carolina Chickadees

Box material: Wood
Floor dimensions: 4-inch (10.2 cm) square floor
Diameter of entrance hole: 1 ⅛ inches (2.9 cm)
Box depth below hole: 6 inches (15.2 cm)
Mount: 4½ to 15 feet (1.4–4.6 m) above the ground
Suggestions: A Carolina Chickadee will occupy a nestbox of the same design as used for the House Wren and Black-capped Chickadee. Locate it in sunny areas along forest edges or agricultural fields. Place about 1 inch (2.5 cm) of wood chips or shavings in the bottom of the box.
Protection: Keep the box away from woody and shrubby areas, and keep the entrance hole small. Install baffles to deter mammalian predators.

Predators, Parasites, and Diseases. Like all small birds, the Carolina Chickadee must be continually on the watch for small accipitrine hawks, cats, snakes, and small mammals. Screech-owls apparently do not prey upon this bird.

Carolina Chickadees host numerous external parasites, including lice and mites.

What You Can Do. The best way to discourage the House Wren from occupying a nestbox is to locate that box in the proper habitat for the bird you wish to attract. Placing it away from shrubby areas should dissuade wren occupancy. Entrance holes measuring 1⅛ inches (2.9 cm) across will prevent starlings and House Sparrows from using the box. If for some reason these birds do succeed in entering a nestbox, remove the nesting material and/or eggs immediately. Several repetitions of this might be necessary in order to keep these species away.

Native predators can be excluded from the boxes by equipping them with baffles. (See pages 164–167 for designs and installation directions.) Cats should be kept indoors. They have a tremendous impact on wildlife. Keeping them inside is the only way to keep them from being predators on birds and other animals.

Life Cycle

Carolina Chickadees start their pair bonding when a female persistently pursues a male. The male will react by attacking the female. If the female is able to endure his attacks and remains persistent, eventually a pair bond will form. This can occur at any time during the year. Territories are established by singing, chasing other birds from the area, and restricting the pair's activity to the selected area. Both sexes will spend up to a month looking for a suitable nest site. It is the female, however, that makes the final choice. Nests are built by females. The nest itself is constructed on a moss base with a delicately woven cup of grass, plant down, and feathers. The nest is lined with finer materials such as fine grass, fur, and hair.

Carolina Chickadee eggs are indistinguishable from those of its black-capped relative.

Eggs are laid one a day. During this egg-laying period, the female covers the incomplete clutch with nesting material whenever she leaves the nest. Incubation starts with the laying of the next-to-last egg and is done exclusively by the female. The male will bring food for the female while she is incubating and brooding. Females are reluctant to leave the nest; when one is flushed, she will generally make a hissing sound as she leaves the nest.

The young are brooded for a few days after hatching. Once the young have more control over their metabolisms, they are attended by both parents. Nestlings fledge when they are 13 to 17 days old but remain dependent on the adults for food and protection for the next two to four weeks. Parents may abortively attack the young, causing them to

Nestlings this well developed should probably not be handled, lest they fledge prematurely.

disperse and start their independent living. Although it is not known how many broods are raised a season, it is commonly thought to be only one. Carolina Chickadees will renest, if necessary, when a brood is lost. These chickadees are winter residents in their areas. Pairs will stay together on their territories throughout the year. In winter, they will forage in small mixed-species flocks that include titmice, warblers, nuthatches, woodpeckers, and kinglets. Little is known about the dispersal of juveniles. Carolina Chickadee longevity records report a maximum life span of 10 years and 11 months.

Useful References
Bent, A. C. *Life Histories of North American Jays, Crows and Titmice.* New York: Dover Publications, Inc., 1964.

Northern Flicker
(Colaptes auratus)

See box design on page 145.

Length: 12 to 14 inches (30.5–35.6 cm)

Nest construction: Both sexes excavate cavities in trees; no nest construction is required in an artificial nestbox.

Eggs per clutch: 3 to 12, usually 5 to 8

Incubation: Both sexes

Length of incubation: 11 to 14 days, usually 11

Age at fledging: 25 to 28 days

Broods per season: 1; 2 in southern United States

Food: 75 percent animal matter: ants (45 percent of all food) and other ground-dwelling insects, including beetle larvae; 25 percent plant material: seeds, nuts, acorns, and grain from late fall to early spring

Description

The brightly colored and vocal Northern Flicker is a large, very widespread, and interesting woodpecker. It is a primary cavity nester that excavates many of the natural cavities subsequently used by numerous secondary cavity-nesting species of bird. For this reason, it is an important component of woodland ecosystems.

Unlike its relatives, the flicker spends much of its time on the ground, searching for and feeding upon ants. These birds use their remarkably long and sticky tongues, which can be extended up to 1½ inches (3.8 cm) beyond the bill, for this purpose. Ants, in fact, make up a larger proportion of the flicker's diet than that of any other North American bird.

Although still an abundant species, the yellow-shafted subspecies of the East dwindled by 52 percent between 1966 and 1991. Populations of the western red-shafted subspecies decreased by 19 percent between 1968 and 1991. Loss of habitat and competition with European Starlings for nesting cavities have been blamed for these declines. The two subspecies hybridize in their narrow zone of overlap in the Great Plains. The Gilded

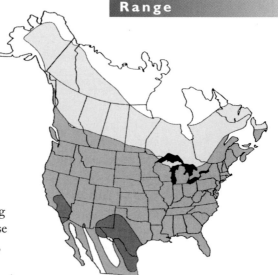

Range

Flicker of the desert Southwest was recently separated out as a full species. Flickers, unlike most woodpeckers, use nestboxes regularly and have adapted well to human habitats, although they much prefer to excavate their own nest cavities.

Habitat Needs

Northern Flickers require semi-open country. They nest in open woodlands (deciduous, coniferous, or mixed), woodlots, groves, farms, orchards, shelterbelts, roadsides, parks, suburban areas, cities, and edge or replacement growth in northern coniferous forests. Tall trees along watercourses are an especially important habitat in the Great Plains. Flickers will also nest in swamps with numerous snags, beaver ponds, burned forests with standing stubs, and clearcuts with scattered snags. They also require open ground for feeding.

Problems

European Starlings, squirrels, screech-owls, House Sparrows, and American Kestrels compete with flickers for nest cavities. Starlings are especially fierce competitors.

Predators, Parasites, and Diseases. Peregrine falcons and other hawks kill and eat adults, while the eggs and young of flickers are taken by squirrels, weasels, mice, crows, jays, red-headed woodpeckers, black rat snakes, and bull snakes; they are also preyed upon by house cats and raccoons.

What You Can Do. Competition with starlings for nesting cavities is a common problem facing flickers both in natural and artificial cavity situations, especially early in the breeding season. Starlings usually win out in a direct contest with flickers for a nest site, despite the woodpecker's larger size. Regular monitoring and willingness to control

Housing Needs for Northern Flickers

Box material: Wood
Floor dimensions: 7½-inch (18.4 cm) square floor
Diameter of entrance hole: 2¼ inches (6.4 cm)
Box depth below hole: 16 to 18 inches (40.6–45.7 cm)
Mount: 6 to 20 feet (1.8–6.1 m) above the ground
Suggestions: Locate the box in a generally sunny location and orient it to face away from prevailing weather (usually south or east). Fill it with wood shavings to allow the flickers to simulate excavation.
Protection: To deter raccoons and other climbing predators, mount the box on a metal pole at least 6 feet (1.8 m) high and install a predator guard on the pole.

starlings are essential. Flickers that have lost their cavity to starlings usually renest later in the season.

An experiment that involved placing nestboxes within 3 to 5 feet (.9–1.5 m) of active flicker nests in Ohio did not enable the flickers to compete successfully against starlings. Both flickers and starlings vastly preferred the flicker-excavated cavities over the nestboxes, perhaps because the boxes were mounted too close to the cavities that had been usurped by starlings.

Screech-owls are unable to enter a box that has a 2½-inch (6.4 cm) diameter opening. To keep raccoons and other climbing predators from reaching the nestbox, mount it on a metal pole at least 6 feet (1.8 m) high, and place a predator guard on the pole (see pages 164–167).

Life Cycle

Males tend to arrive on the breeding grounds in early spring a few days before females, and soon begin drumming and giving location calls to advertise their ownership. Both sexes seek out their former territories and nest sites, often using the same nest cavities year after year. Winter home ranges varied in size from 119 to 250 acres (48.2–101.3 ha) in a Colorado study. Flicker breeding territory ranges are not well understood. Courtship is quite elaborate and involves much touching of bills, bobbing, and spreading of wings

Eggs of primary cavity nesters, like the Northern Flicker, are usually white and unmarked.

to expose the brightly colored underside. The "mustache" mark distinguishes male and female adult Northern Flickers. Both sexes drum and call and defend their nesting territory tenaciously. Flickers usually begin breeding at one year of age, but young birds are more likely than older birds to disperse from their hatching sites for nesting.

Males usually select the nest site. Copulation occurs just before the nest is completed, at least in natural situations. Females lay one pure white, glossy egg per day, usually around dawn, and incubation begins one or two days before the last egg is laid. Both sexes incubate, with the female doing most of it during daylight hours; her mate takes his turn at night. If a predator destroys the eggs, the pair will quickly renest, but in a different cavity.

The young hatch after about 11 days. Both parents feed them regurgitated ants and other insects initially. Both also brood their nestlings for up to 2 weeks. The nestlings consume roughly their own weight in food each day. After 4 days, the young are able to create their own body heat. After 9 days or so, the adults begin carrying away their nestlings' fecal sacs (prior to this, they eat the sacs). By 10 days of age, the nestlings' eyes are partially open, and they fully open by 12 to 15 days. Nestling flickers make a buzzing sound that some believe is an attempt to make predators think twice before entering a hive of bees. After 15 days, the adults visit the nest site much less often than before. At between 2 and 3 weeks of age, the young climb to the entrance hole, where they are fed by their parents.

Top. Both sexes of the "yellow-shafted" form exhibit a red nape patch; the male has a black "mustache." *Bottom.* In contrast, the "red-shafted" form lacks the nape patch; the male's "mustache" is red. (♀ = female)

After 26 days or so of confinement in the cavity, the young leave on their first flights, generally in the order that they hatched. This first flight averages 163 feet (50 m). At this stage, both male and female fledglings sport mustache marks. The adults continue to feed the young birds after they leave the nest, but their dependence upon their parents does not last long, only about 2 weeks. In the southern portion of their wide range, the female sometimes begins laying a second clutch of eggs. The pair bond continues through the breeding season.

Prior to southward migration, Northern Flickers gather in family groups. Birds from the northern parts of their range are strongly migratory, while those breeding in southern areas tend to remain year-round. Flickers in northern areas move southward in late autumn, mostly at night. The maximum recorded life span for the species is 9 years, 2 months for the yellow-shafted subspecies, and 7 years, 7 months for the red-shafted.

Useful References

Moore, W. S. "Northern Flicker *(Colaptes auratus)."* In *The Birds of North America,* No. 166 (A. Poole and F. Gill, eds.). Philadelphia and Washington, D.C.: The Academy of Natural Sciences and the American Ornithologists' Union, 1995.

♂

Red-bellied Woodpecker
(Melanerpes carolinus)

See box design on page 145.

Length: 9 to 10½ inches (22.9–26.7 cm)

Nest construction: As with most other wood-peckers, both sexes excavate cavities in trees; no nesting material is added to excavated cavities or nestboxes.

Eggs per clutch: 3 to 8, usually 4 or 5

Incubation: Both sexes; the male incubates at night

Length of incubation: 12 to 14 days

Age at fledging: 20 to 27 days

Broods per season: 1 in northern portions of range; 2 and occasionally 3 in southern areas

Food: 50 percent animal: wood-boring beetles, grasshoppers, ants, bugs, and crickets; some spiders are also taken. 50 percent vegetable: acorns, beech-nuts, wild fruits, corn, and oranges; sap is also con-sumed. Young are fed insects and berries.

Description

The Red-bellied Woodpecker is conspicuous for both its bright and contrasting plumage as well as its loud calls. Some calls may be mistaken for those of the gray tree frog. The "zebra-back" is an attractive and vocal bird that resembles no other species across its rather wide range in eastern North America.

Common in the southeastern United States, it may be abundant in open swamps and bottomland woods. In the Great Plains, at the western edge of its range, the Red-bellied is still spreading westward along wooded river valleys. This species has also shown a steady expansion of its range northward and is now found regularly in southern New England. We were pleased and surprised to find one of these "southern" woodpeckers one January

Range

in our yard at 1,525 feet (465 m) in elevation in the heavily wooded hills of western Massachusetts. Like the Tufted Titmouse and Northern Cardinal, which have extended their breeding ranges northward since the 1940s, Red-bellieds also patronize bird feeders during winter, which is one plausible explanation for the advance.

In Texas where their ranges overlap, this bird has been known to hybridize with the similar-appearing and closely related golden-fronted woodpecker.

Habitat Needs

Red-bellied Woodpeckers favor open woodlands, the edges of forest openings, suburban backyards, groves, orchards, swampy woodlands, and wooded river corridors. Deciduous forest is preferred in the North, whereas pine woodland is sometimes the chosen breeding habitat in the South.

Like most woodpeckers, these birds prefer to nest in cavities that they excavate in trees. Cavity excavation is an important part of courtship in this family of birds. Red-bellieds do, however, use artificial nestboxes regularly. Log nestboxes built with slab lumber that retains the bark may be more successful at attracting this species and its relatives.

Problems

Starlings are probably the major competitor for nest cavities, especially early in the season. These introduced birds sometimes force the woodpeckers to abandon their excavated cavities immediately after completion. Red-bellieds have also been known to compete with the red-headed woodpecker and Great Crested Flycatcher for nest sites.

Predators, Parasites, and Diseases. Little is known about specific predators but presumably climbing snakes, raccoons, and squirrels prey upon Red-bellied Woodpecker eggs and nestlings. Sharp-shinned and Cooper's hawks probably kill adults and fledglings,

Housing Needs for Red-bellied Woodpeckers

Box material: Wood
Floor dimensions: At least a 6-inch (15.2 cm) square floor
Diameter of entrance hole: 2 inches (5.1 cm)
Box depth below hole: 15 inches (38.1 cm)
Mount: 8 to 20 feet (2.4–6.1 m) above the ground
Suggestions: Pack the entire nestbox tightly with wood chips or shavings so that the pair can "excavate" the cavity. Mount it on a tree, or hang it by a flexible wire or chain.
Protection: Install metal flashing and/or baffles to deter climbing predators such as raccoons. (See page 166.)

as do owls. A starling is presumed to have killed an adult Red-bellied Woodpecker in Mississippi at a tree cavity excavated by the woodpecker.

What You Can Do. Foiling European Starlings, as we have stated numerous times elsewhere in this book, is a major challenge that may require drastic action: starling capture and elimination. Packing the nestbox tightly with sawdust and wood chips may perform a twofold function: enable the woodpeckers to simulate cavity excavation, and make the box less desirable to starlings.

Install metal flashing and/or baffles to create barriers for climbing predators such as raccoons (see pages 164–167). As an alternative to mounting the box on a tree, you may wish to hang it from a 3¼-foot (1 m) long flexible wire or chain at least 8 feet (2.4 m) above the ground.

A female Red-bellied Woodpecker, distinguished from the male by a gray crown, brings food to her nestlings.

Life Cycle

Northern birds that migrate southward in fall arrive on the breeding grounds early in spring and begin preparations for nesting almost immediately. In southern portions of their range, Red-bellied Woodpeckers remain on their territories year-round, but without defending those territories as they would during the breeding season. For birds nesting in tree cavities that they create, courtship begins with excavation, done by both sexes. The simulated excavation of sawdust and wood chips packed into nestboxes may enable Red-bellied Woodpeckers to satisfy this important component of their courtship. In addition, woodpeckers often enlarge the entrance hole of a nestbox even when it is already large enough to admit them, perhaps also an innate effort to satisfy the need to excavate a nest cavity with a mate.

Red-bellied Woodpecker eggs are rather dull when laid but become somewhat glossy with incubation.

Where both species exist, starlings often force Red-bellieds to abandon their completed nesting cavities so that they can use them. During one study in Mississippi, researchers found that Red-bellied Woodpeckers harassed by starlings tended to lay their eggs later and have smaller clutches than Red-bellieds without these problems.

Females lay one pure white egg each day until the clutch, usually four or five, is complete. Incubation begins with the laying of the final egg. Both birds incubate, but the

These birds' nestling phase is nearing completion, as evidenced by their advanced development and the quantity of fecal matter in the nestbox.

male does most of his at night, as in some other species of woodpecker. There is some speculation that the more aggressive male may be better suited to drive off nocturnal predators than his mate. If the eggs are lost to a predator, the female will lay a second clutch. After 12 to 14 days of incubation the eggs hatch, often over a span of 2 days.

Parent birds share about evenly the duties of feeding their nestlings a diet of insects and berries. The adults occasionally procure food on the ground. Red-bellied Woodpeckers habitually store acorns, nuts, fruit, and insects for later consumption. The male also broods the nestlings at night, while his mate does so during daylight hours. Nestlings develop their juvenile plumage prior to leaving the nest at about 3 weeks of age.

In situations where their parents begin a second nesting, fledglings remain with the adults for only a few weeks, rather than until fall as they would otherwise. In autumn these family groups dissolve, and the young birds are totally on their own.

Red-bellied Woodpeckers withdraw from higher elevations and the northern edges of their range in winter, with a general southward movement from northern and north-eastern breeding grounds. These migratory wanderings may be predicated on the food supply. In the South some Red-bellieds flock, often in association with yellow-bellied sapsuckers, with which they also share the habit of drinking sap. The longevity record for this species, based on banding results, is 12 years and 1 month.

Useful References

Bent, A. C. *Life Histories of North American Woodpeckers.* Smithsonian Institution United States National Museum Bulletin 174, 1939.

Ingold, D. J. "Woodpecker and European Starling Competition for Nest Sites." *Sialia* 11:3–6, 1989.

Wood Duck
(Aix sponsa)

See box design on page 149.

Length: Male: 18¾ to 21 inches (47.6–53.3 cm); female: 18½ to 19⅞ inches (47–50.5 cm)

Nest construction: Female

Eggs per clutch: 6 to 15, usually 10 to 12; clutches of 16 or more indicate laying by more than one female

Incubation: Female

Length of incubation: 25 to 37 days, usually 30

Age at fledging: 60 to 70 days

Broods per season: 1 or 2

Food: Seeds, fruits (especially acorns), and aquatic and terrestrial vertebrates; young are fed insects

Description

Populations of this exquisitely plumaged duck, found only in North America, dropped to levels so low in the 1930s that it was considered on the verge of extinction. Historic factors leading to this state of affairs included overhunting, logging of mature timber, and the loss and degradation of forested wetland habitats. Populations were also decimated in Massachusetts via the destruction wrought by the hurricane of 1938.

Range

yr = year-round
s = summer

Today, in marked contrast, the Wood Duck is the most common breeding waterfowl species in the eastern United States. What brought about this amazing turnaround? The maturation of eastern forests has played an important role, as have hunting regulations, a significant increase in beaver-created wetlands, and the addition of artificial nest sites. Wood Duck populations grew steadily over a 70-year period until about 1985, but have since leveled off, due perhaps to an absence of nest cavities in suitable breeding habitat. Nestbox programs can have at the least a very positive effect on local populations of this elegant duck.

Habitat Needs

Wood Ducks prefer wetlands that combine flooded shrubs, water-tolerant trees, and small areas of open water resulting in 50 to 70 percent cover. A mixture of shallow freshwater wetland types is best. Beaver ponds; shrub swamps with buttonbush, willow, and alder; and marshes with dense stands of emergent plants such as bur reed, arrow arum, duck potato, smartweeds, and American lotus are favored. In the West, narrow timbered corridors along rivers serve as important Wood Duck habitats. The ideal habitat contains mast (acorn, nut, and berry) producing hardwoods that border streams and permanent freshwater lakes. Stable water levels are likewise very important to brood survival.

Wood Ducks are secondary cavity nesters that readily use nestboxes provided for them. They prefer to nest directly over or adjacent to water, and good visibility is important; the entrance should be conspicuous, and vegetation should not obstruct the front of the box. Boxes should generally be no more than ¼ mile (.4 km) from water, although ½ mile (.8 km) is acceptable. The box should be mounted high enough to avoid flooding, but in any event it should be at least 4 feet (1.2 m) above water and 5½ feet (1.7 m) or more above the ground. Higher boxes are obviously more difficult to monitor and maintain. The nestbox should be mounted in a level position, not with a backward tilt. Since Wood Ducks are not territorial, boxes can be mounted in pairs or clusters.

Initially, wooden boxes are more acceptable to the ducks than metal ones, but metal nestboxes have a higher nest success rate. Cylindrical galvanized sheet metal boxes lined with automobile undercoating have been highly successful. Metal boxes should be painted to keep them cooler. Wooden boxes should not be painted or stained, and they should be fitted with conical or other types of predator guards (see pages 164–167).

Housing Needs for Wood Ducks

Box material: Wood or metal

Floor dimensions: 10 inches (25.4 cm) by 10 inches

Diameter of entrance hole: 4 inches (10.2 cm); or use an elliptical hole 3 inches (7.6 cm) high by 4 inches (10.2 cm) wide

Box depth below hole: 17 inches (43.2 cm)

Mount: At least 4 feet (1.2 m) above the water and 5½ feet (1.7 m) above the ground

Suggestions: Fill the box 3 to 6 inches (7.6–15.2 cm) deep with wood chips or shavings. Metal and smooth-lumber boxes must be fitted with galvanized wire or plastic mesh ladders to enable ducklings to climb out.

Spacing: 50 feet (15.3 m) apart, or even in pairs or clusters

Protection: Fit wooden boxes with cone-shaped metal predator guards at least 18 inches (45.7 cm) in diameter below the box on support posts, and/or attach a 5¾- by 5½-inch (14.6 x 14 cm) square by 8-inch (20.3 cm) long wooden tunnel to the entrance to discourage mammalian predators. To discourage starlings, mount metal boxes horizontally.

Plastic boxes, especially in the southern part of the range, should be avoided due to high heat buildup inside them.

Problems

Hooded Mergansers and European Starlings nest in boxes intended for Wood Ducks, as do tree squirrels, white-footed mice, and opossums. Honeybee swarms sometimes take up residence in them as well.

Predators, Parasites, and Diseases. Raccoons, black rat snakes, foxes, mink, and fox squirrels consume the eggs, while the great horned owl, mink, snapping turtle, bullfrog, large fish, and American alligator prey on the young. Adults are killed by great horned owls, mink, raccoons, red and gray foxes, and alligators.

What You Can Do. Inspect boxes at least annually to make sure that they are in good repair. Deep boxes are less apt to be vulnerable to predators than shallow ones. Attach cone-shaped metal predator guards at least 18 inches (45.7 cm) in diameter below the box on support posts, and/or attach a 5¾- by 5½-inch (14.6 × 14 cm) square by 8-inch (20.3 cm) long wooden tunnel to the entrance to keep mammalian predators at bay (see pages 152, 166). Elliptical entrance holes tend to restrict entry by raccoons, except small individuals more common in the South. If starlings are a problem, mount metal boxes horizontally.

Monitoring should be done during the early evening, just after the incubating hens leave the nests to feed and exercise, in order to minimize disturbance. *Do not continually disturb incubating birds, as desertion may result.*

Within 24 hours of hatching, ducklings leave the nest, often taking tremendous leaps to the ground without injury.

Life Cycle

Much of the population forms pair bonds in fall or winter, prior to their arrival on the breeding grounds in early spring. The breeding season in this species is quite long, up to six months. The male helps the female seek out suitable nest sites, but the female chooses the nest cavity. Most females return to nest in the same cavity they used previously, or in close proximity to it. Many hens begin breeding as yearlings, although the majority of young adults do not return to their hatching sites to nest. Wood Ducks are not territorial and so the nest site is not defended.

No nest material is carried by the ducks. In natural situations, they rely on the wood chips found in the bottoms of old pileated woodpecker cavities. It is important to provide a bed of wood chips or shavings as a base in the nestbox. Females cover the eggs with this debris during the egg-laying phase. Hens lay one creamy white egg per day, usually in the early morning, but they may skip a day. Quite interestingly, Wood Duck eggshells are only half as thick as those of Hooded Mergansers. When about half the clutch has been laid, the female begins to add down feathers from her breast

As clutch size increases, the female plucks progressively more down from her breast until the eggs are well insulated.

to the depression where the eggs rest. She increases the amount of down as the clutch grows. Females spend 85 percent of their day on the eggs. Renesting is common if the clutch is destroyed.

Wood Ducks, like Hooded Mergansers, are brood parasites, laying eggs in the nests of other Wood Ducks or those of mergansers. Female Wood Ducks do accept eggs and nestlings that are not their own, although parastized nests have lower hatch rates than unparasitized ones.

After 1 month of incubation the eggs hatch, although cool temperatures, disturbance, and large clutches can lengthen incubation. The male deserts the female after incubation is completed and takes no part in the care of the young.

The downy young leave the nest cavity 24 hours after hatching by climbing to the entrance hole and leaping out, sometimes from incredible heights. Ducklings have been known to leap 289 feet (88 m) to the ground without injury! Females immediately lead their broods to rearing areas up to 1.2 miles (2 km) away. Stream channels provide valuable travel corridors during this vulnerable stage of the ducklings' lives. They are brooded by their mother for about 2 weeks after hatching, and they feed mainly upon invertebrates for 2 to 3 weeks. As they get older, their diets change gradually to plant

Wood Duck eggs, here partially covered by down and other nesting material, have shells that are only half the thickness of Hooded Merganser eggs.

foods. Adults feed largely on acorns, nuts, seeds, and berries. The hen stays with her young for 1 to 2 months, and sometimes begins a second nesting. This is more common in the southern portion of the range, where up to 18 percent initiate second clutches. By 60 to 70 days of age, the young are able to fly.

Wood Ducks often make dispersal flights in early fall after the breeding season. Many northern birds move southward, but some move in other directions. These dispersal flights can be quite long. Birds from Vermont have been found as far away as Texas and Newfoundland. This movement is independent of true southern migration. In true migration, which begins later, the ducks move southward, following their preferred habitat with the advancing season.

Nearly two-thirds of all Wood Ducks are killed during their first year of life; the oldest known bird lived to be 22 years and 6 months of age.

Useful References

Bellrose, F. C., and D. J. Holm. *Ecology and Management of the Wood Duck.* Harrisburg, Penn.: Stackpole Books, 1994.

Hepp, G. R., and F. C. Bellrose. "Wood Duck *(Aix sponsa)."* In *The Birds of North America,* No. 169 (A. Poole and F. Gill, eds.). Philadelphia and Washington, D.C.: The Academy of Natural Sciences and The American Ornithologists' Union, 1995.

♂

Hooded Merganser
(Lophodytes cucullatus)

See box design on page 149.

Length: Male: 16¾ to 19 inches (42.5–48.2 cm); female: 15⅝ to 18 inches (39.7–45.7 cm)

Nest construction: Female

Eggs per clutch: 6 to 13, usually 10 to 12 (larger clutches are considered the result of nest parasitism)

Incubation: Female

Length of incubation: 26 to 41 days, usually 30 to 33 days

Age at fledging: 70 days

Broods per season: 1

Food: A diverse diet of aquatic insects, small fish, and crustaceans, particularly crayfish; also some mollusks and amphibians

Description

This lovely duck of woodlands and associated freshwater wetlands is the smallest of our three merganser species. The male, with his regal white crest outlined in black, is virtually unmistakable. The Hooded is the only merganser restricted to North America. It is most common in the Great Lakes region, while its population in the southern United States is spotty.

Hooded Mergansers historically suffered from deforestation, hunting, and perhaps pesticides. The lack of suitable nest cavities due to logging probably limits their breeding in once suitable habitats. Logging may also decrease water clarity, making foraging more difficult. In general, however, populations now seem to be stable and are perhaps even increasing in some areas.

Range

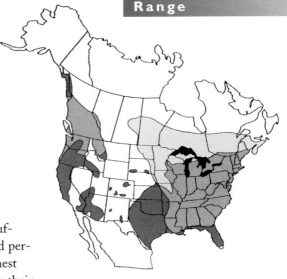

This female's bill is well adapted for grasping slippery aquatic food items.

A significant portion of the breeding population may be vulnerable to the effects of acid rain: Aquatic invertebrates, the merganser's food supply, are greatly reduced in waters with pH levels below 5.5 (7.0 being neutral). PCBs may cause eggshell thinning, while mercury contamination of water bodies can poison the birds. Lead poisoning is not thought to be a significant threat to this duck, due to its diet and feeding methods.

Hooded Mergansers readily use the nestboxes usually installed for Wood Ducks. Providing these attractive birds with artificial nesting sites in suitable habitat can have a positive effect on local populations.

Habitat Needs

Hooded Mergansers are closely tied to forested wetland systems, although they have nested in boxes located in grassland areas (in Minnesota, for instance). They breed in a wide range of forest types: from spruce-fir to mixed pine-hardwood, cottonwoods and oak-cypress-tupelo woodlands. They prefer to breed very near water but will nest as far as .3 mile (.5 km) from it. These mergansers favor bottomlands, woodland ponds, rivers, and sheltered backwaters that support large numbers of aquatic invertebrates and small fish. The wetland communities that they use include marshes, swamps, beaver ponds, small lakes, and forested creeks. They nest less often on large lakes. Clear, generally shallow (less than $4\frac{9}{10}$ feet, or 1.5 m, deep) water is required for locating prey. Hooded Mergansers must also have access to exposed areas such as rocks, logs, and bars that can serve as loafing sites.

Housing Needs for Hooded Mergansers

Box material: Wood or metal
Floor dimensions: 10 inches (25.4 cm) by 10 inches
Diameter of entrance hole: Use an elliptical hole of 4 inches (10.2 cm) by 5 inches (12.7 cm)
Box depth below hole: 16.5 inches (41.9 cm)
Mount: At least 3 1/4 feet (1 m) above the ground
Suggestions: Fill the box 3 inches (7.6 cm) to 6 inches (15.2 cm) with wood chips or shavings.
Spacing: As close as 50 feet (15.3 m) apart
Protection: Install predator guards on poles and trees that support boxes to discourage mammalian predators, and/or outfit entrance holes with tunnel guards. To dissuade rat snakes, place nestboxes on poles over water.

Nestboxes located over or near water are preferred and wood or metal boxes are selected by Hooded Mergansers over plastic ones. Boxes mounted on poles and trees are used equally. Orientation toward a given compass direction does not appear to be important in this species. Females prefer to nest in boxes containing wood shavings or sawdust, and to reuse boxes that they have utilized previously.

Problems

Wood Ducks, for which most nestboxes tend to be erected, compete with Hooded Mergansers, especially in the southern part of the merganser's range. The common goldeneye competes with the Hooded Merganser in the northern portion of the latter's range. Honeybee swarms sometimes take up residence in Wood Duck and Hooded Merganser nestboxes.

Predators, Parasites, and Diseases. Raccoons, mink, and black rat snakes prey on incubating females. Merganser eggs are eaten by these three species plus the black bear and pine marten. The European Starling, Northern Flicker, red-headed woodpecker, and Red-bellied Woodpecker are known to destroy this duck's eggs.

Internal parasites of this merganser include nematodes and flatworms.

What You Can Do. Install predator guards on poles and trees that support boxes (see pages 161–167) to keep raccoons, pine martens, and other climbing mammalian predators from reaching them. Outfit nestbox entrance holes with tunnel guards that make it impossible for these same predators to reach the female, eggs, or young (see page 152). Preventing rat snakes from reaching the nestbox is more of a challenge, but placing nestboxes on poles over water may work.

Life Cycle

Males and females initially form pair bonds during their second winter of life, with females first breeding at age two. Early-spring migrants tend to arrive within a few days of ice leaving waterways in the North. Older birds have a strong tendency to return from their wintering grounds to the same nesting sites that they used before, or to locations nearby. Courtship takes place in small groups consisting of at least one hen and several drakes. Copulation occurs on the water. The female selects the cavity, for which she may have begun prospecting the previous summer.

Experienced birds start nests earlier than first-time breeders, and egg laying begins with nest construction. The nest is essentially a depression

Clutches larger than 13 indicate the work of more than one female.

in wood shavings or chips placed in the bottom of the box by the monitor. The female may also add some sparse vegetation to the nest lining. She lays one white, almost spherical egg every other day. *She may abandon the nest if disturbed before the clutch is complete.* Following completion of the clutch, the female plucks down from her breast and uses it to line her nest. It is sometimes possible to replace the female on the eggs after a nest check once incubation has begun. The hen incubates throughout the night. She commonly defecates when disturbed during incubation. The pair bond is seasonal: The male leaves the female after she begins incubation.

Hooded Mergansers are known to lay eggs in the nests of their own species. Such nest parasitism is quite common, with one-third to nearly one-half of all clutches containing the eggs of more than one female. Clutches larger than 13 eggs are assumed to be the work of more than one hen. This species also parasitizes and is in turn parasitized by the common goldeneye, common merganser, and Wood Duck. Interestingly, the eggs of Hooded Mergansers possess shells that are twice as thick as those of Wood Ducks, which serves to distinguish these two species' eggs.

After approximately one month of incubation, all the eggs hatch over a span of only four hours. The female broods her hatchlings until it is time for them to leave the box. Within 24 hours of hatching, the young, after hearing their mother call to them from the water, use their sharp claws to climb to the entrance hole, then leave the nest by leaping to the ground. First, however, their mother inspects the vicinity to determine if it is safe. Females will often lead their young for distances of up to 1¼ miles (2 km) from inland nest sites to water or between water bodies.

The ducklings are able to feed themselves from day 1 and begin diving immediately. They feed mostly on aquatic insects, using their excellent underwater vision. Only the female cares for the young. By about 70 days of age, the ducklings are able to fly.

Hooded Mergansers are late migrants, leaving their northern breeding grounds just before ice closes the ponds. Most are short- or intermediate-distance migrants, and all winter north of the U.S.-Mexico border. They winter primarily in forested freshwater wetlands, brackish estuaries, and tidal creeks. The oldest known individual of this species lived to 11 years, 3 months, based upon banding returns.

Useful References
Dugger, B. D., K. M. Dugger, and L. H. Fredrickson. "Hooded Merganser *(Lophodytes cucullatus)."* In *The Birds of North America,* No. 98 (A. Poole and F. Gill, eds.). Philadelphia and Washington, D.C.: The Academy of Natural Sciences and The American Ornithologists' Union, 1994.

Eastern Screech-Owl
(Otus asio)

See box design on page 153.

Length: 6¼ inches (smallest males) to 10 inches (largest females) (15.9–25.4 cm)

Nest construction: None

Eggs per clutch: 2 to 7, usually 4 to 5

Incubation: Female

Length of incubation: 21 to 28 days, usually about 26

Age at fledging: 27 days

Broods per season: 1

Food: Insects, crayfish, songbirds, rodents, reptiles, amphibians, and fish

Description

All of us, at one time or another, have heard calls of the screech-owl, which rarely screeches. It is a favorite among filmmakers, used to add an ambient flavor to evening scenes. This owl also produces a curious variety of barks, hoots, rasps, chuckles, and screeches that can be heard throughout its wide range. The Eastern Screech-Owl can be found east of the Rocky Mountains, from southern Canada to near the Tropic of Cancer in Mexico. A permanent resident in its range, the screech-owl is often the most common predator in wooded suburban and urban areas.

Range

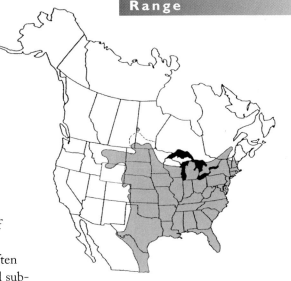

Screech-owls have two color phases, gray and red. Specifically, the red phase, more prevalent in the South, is more of a chestnut-red in appearance, while the gray phase, found in the North and in southernmost Texas, is brownish gray. As with all owls, the sexes look alike in this species. This owl has bright yellow eyes and usually a pale bill. Ear tufts are prominent if raised; when flattened, however, the screech owl has a round-headed appearance. The underparts are marked with bars and streaks, with especially heavy black streaks on the upper breast; this provides wonderfully cryptic camouflage, especially when individuals stretch and elongate themselves. We were birding along the Cape Ann coast of Massachusetts when we heard about a screech-owl in the cemetery. The bird was sunning himself in the knot of a huge maple tree on a bitter-cold mid-winter day. It seemed to take forever for us to eventually spot this individual: Its plumage and "stick" posture made it virtually invisible.

The Eastern Screech-Owl was once on the National Audubon Society's Blue List, reflecting a concern due to a decline in its numbers. Recently, however, this owl appears to have extended its range westward to the Great Plains, where forests are present in river valleys. The warming climate and an increase in urbanization have also promoted a northwestward range expansion. Trees planted in deforested or naturally grassy areas encourage population expansion. In reforested habitats, nestboxes are essential, especially where trees are young.

Habitat Needs

The Eastern Screech-Owl will inhabit most wooded landscapes below 4,875 feet (1,487 m) in elevation, including mixed forests, woodlots, swamps, farms, orchards, stream edges, and suburban parks. These owls prefer an open subcanopy with sparse shrub cover; this facilitates flying, foraging, and perhaps predator detection. Needless to say, these birds will occupy and adapt to a variety of environments. We rescued a young screech owl from a front lawn in the center of Des Moines, Iowa, and we were entertained by these owls at night in semirural Westport, Massachusetts.

Housing Needs for Eastern Screech-Owls

Box material: Any wood variety more than ¾ inch (1.9 cm) thick
Floor dimensions: 7¾ inches (19.7 cm) square
Diameter of entrance hole: 2¾ inches (7 cm)
Box depth below hole: 9 inches (22.9 cm)
Mount: 15 to 50 feet (4.6–15.3 m) above the ground; mount on a straight trunk that is wider in diameter than the box itself
Suggestions: Cut ⅝ inches (1.6 cm) off each of the floor's corners to create drainage holes. In addition, the front sloping lid should be 2 inches (5.1 cm) above the entrance hole, overhanging it by 2½ inches (6.4 cm). The box may be stained or painted dark brown on the outside only. Place about ¾ inch (1.9 cm) of dry deciduous leaf litter, or 2 to 3 inches (5.1–7.6 cm) of wood chips in the bottom. Locate the box in the shade where an unobstructed flying area is available.
Spacing: At least 100 feet (30.5 m) apart
Protection: Install predator guards on the pole or tree.

Screech-owls will use a number of artificial nest cavities, including Purple Martin and wren nestboxes, in addition to mailboxes, porch columns, and even boxes discarded on the ground.

Problems

Fox squirrels and occasionally the European Starling and Northern Flicker have been known to displace incubating or roosting Eastern Screech-Owls. Squirrels may eat the eggs, while the two birds will build over the nest or toss out the owl's eggs. Because the American Kestrel has similar nesting requirements as the Eastern Screech-Owl, these two species might compete for potential nest sites.

Eastern Screech-Owl, like this gray-phase bird with raised ear tufts, is the owl species most likely to accept nestboxes.

Predators, Parasites, and Diseases. Large owls, hawks, and screech-owls themselves will eat adults and fledgings. Black rat snakes, opossums, raccoons, and ringtail cats eat eggs and nestlings, but rarely adults. Hippoboscid flies are uncommon in their association with this owl. When present, however, they may be responsible for spreading mites. Heavy mite or fly egg infestations have been found on the wings of nestlings, but not adults. Only one death of a nestling has been attributed to heavy fly infestation. Two first-year females have been reported with only one functioning eye; they disappeared shortly after the breeding season. Several nestlings have been reported with a dysfunctional foot. The screech-owl that we "adopted" in Des Moines likewise had one foot that was dysfunctional. By the time "Dude" was 6 months old, both feet were crippled. He died at the age of 9 months.

What You Can Do. To prevent the nestbox from being used by squirrels, place it on a pole with a predator guard. This will also deter raccoons, black rat snakes, opossums, and ringtail cats. Starlings tend to select more open vegetation types than these owls do; keep this in mind when you are selecting a site. As with all other starling incidences, careful monitoring of the nestbox is your best ally. If starlings do succeed in their nesting efforts, you must evict their eggs and destroy the nest. This bird is not protected by federal law. Interestingly, in central Texas, live blind snakes have been found in screech-owl's nests. Rarely eaten, the sequestered snakes live in the owl nest debris, feeding on ants and fly larvae and pupae. In this way they reduce insect competition and contribute to faster growth of nestlings, which subsequently have a lower mortality rate than those in nests that do not host these snakes.

Life Cycle

Eastern Screech-Owls are primarily solitary, except when breeding and occasionally when mates share a winter roost cavity. Courtship usually starts in late January and continues through mid-March. Pair bonds generally form for life, although new mates may be sought after a death, or a "divorce" may result during or after an unsuccessful nesting. Courted females sometimes beg, crouching and, with partly extended wings, rasping at males arriving with food. After a series of vocalizations, copulation usually follows.

No nest is constructed. The female makes a depression with her body as she lays the eggs onto the nesting debris. She remains in the nest cavity for 6 days before the first egg is laid. The first three or four eggs are laid one day apart, with increasing intervals thereafter. The female stays in the cavity except for brief excursions at dusk, and sometimes near dawn. During this time she defecates, drinks, bathes, casts pellets, and is fed by her mate. Screech-owls produce one to two pellets daily.

Eggs peep for 1 or 2 days before hatching. Chicks emerge naked and with their eyes closed. The female may eat the eggshells, or may carry them out and away from the nest. The male catches all food throughout brooding, delivering single items to the female, who tears up large ones for the small nestlings. As time passes, the male may provision the older owlets.

The nestling period is approximately 28 days, with slight regional variations. Most fledging occurs within 1 hour of sunset: Parents stimulate it by withholding food. Hungry young will seek out parents who are outside the box; this causes the owlets to fledge. Food caches may also be left to accumulate in the nest in order to encourage the young birds to seek food on their own. The parents may encourage the young to leave by vocalizing. Chicks leave the nest in hatching order over a 1- to 2-day period, unless they are interrupted by intruders or bad weather. Fledglings generally cannot fly for the first

Incubating females, like this red-phase bird, have prey (note the blue jay feathers and mouse) delivered to them by their mates.

Chicks usually fledge in the order of their hatching. For their first 2 to 3 days, they are unable to fly, but instead climb and jump-flap to nearby limbs.

2 or 3 days but can climb into the nest tree, jump-flap to a nearby limb, and climb higher. The young remain dependent on their parents for 8 to 10 weeks. The female stays close to the young. In the second and third weeks after fledging, the young begin their predatory attempts, capturing mostly insects. By weeks 7 through 9, the young birds are becoming more adept predators, like their parents.

A maximum age of 13 years, 6 months has been recorded for the screech-owl. First-year survival in suburbs has been estimated at 36 percent; 30 percent in rural areas. Juveniles constitute the largest percentage of dead individuals. Most are killed by cars on roads, while others are shot, drowned, killed by cats and dogs, trapped, and poisoned.

Useful References

Gehlbach, F. R. "Eastern Screech-Owl *(Otus asio)*." In *The Birds of North America,* No. 165 (A. Poole and F. Gill, eds.). Philadelphia and Washington, D.C.: The Academy of Natural Sciences and The American Ornithologists' Union, 1995.

Gehlbach, F. R. *The Eastern Screech Owl: Life History, Ecology, and Behavior in the Suburbs and Countryside.* College Station: Texas A & M Press, 1994.

Western Screech-Owl
(*Otus kennicoottii*)

See box design on page 153.

Length: 8½ inches (21.6 cm)

Nest construction: None

Eggs per clutch: 2 to 5, occasionally 6

Incubation: Female

Length of incubation: 21 to 30 days

Age at fledging: 28 days

Broods per season: 1

Food: Small mammals, insects, small vertebrates, and birds

Description

Like its eastern counterpart, the Western Screech-Owl is a small bird with bright yellow eyes and usually a dark bill. Ear tufts are prominent if raised; when they are flattened, this owl appears to have a rounded head. Western Screech-Owls are generally gray, but some of the birds in the humid coastal Northwest are brown. The upper parts of this bird are marked with blackish streaks and thin bars. Nocturnal by nature, it is best located and identified by voice. Two common calls of the Western Screech-Owl are a series of short whistles that accelerate with tempo, and a short trill followed by a longer trill.

Western Screech-Owls tend to vocalize more in fall than Eastern Screech-Owls, which are more vocal in late winter and spring. In areas where the Western Screech-Owl's range overlaps with that of the whiskered screech-owl, the Western Screech-Owl is generally found at lower elevations.

Range

Habitat Needs

The most favored localities for this owl are open and in the immediate vicinity of water, either fresh or salt. Deciduous forests seem to be preferred over fir woods, although during the day birds tend to roost in the dark foliage of some young fir tees. Breeding territories usually include woodlands, especially oak and riparian, scrub, orchards, and woodlots.

Problems

Western Screech-Owls are challenged for their nest sites by squirrels, starlings, Northern Flickers, and possibly other Screech-Owls. If the nestbox is located in an open area, a potential competitor for the box could be the American Kestrel. Squirrels have been known to eat both eggs and young, and to nest over the owl's existing nest.

Predators, Parasites, and Diseases. Other raptors such as large owls and hawks will prey upon the Western Screech-Owl, as will members of its own species. Snakes, opossums, and raccoons have been known to eat the eggs and nestlings, but seldom the adults.

What You Can Do. Placing boxes in the proper areas and habitats will encourage Western Screech-Owls to use them. Because neither of the parents builds any type of nest, but relies on debris left in the cavity, placing wood chips in the bottom of the nestbox is a great asset to the hatching success of the eggs. Be aware of what types of predators are present in the areas where you erected boxes, and take appropriate safeguards. (See pages 164–167 for predator guard designs and installation procedures.) If snakes are a problem and the box is mounted on a pole, applying grease to the pole may be a deterrent.

Housing Needs for Western Screech-Owls

Box material: Wood
Floor dimensions: 7¾ inches (19.7 cm) square
Diameter of entrance hole: 2¾ inches (7 cm)
Box depth below hole: 9 to 10 inches (22.9–25.4 cm)
Mount: 5 to 30 feet (1.5–9.2 m) above the ground on a tree or pole
Suggestions: Western Screech-Owls will use a nestbox of the same design as for the American Kestrel. Place several inches (cm) of wood chips in the bottom of the box.
Protection: Install predator guards on the pole; to deter snakes, apply grease to the pole as well.

Life Cycle

According to A. C. Bent, nests of the species are rarely found, partially due to the birds' secretive behavior. One unusual nest was reported to have been located in a lone dead fir tree stub that stood in a vacant city lot. The nest cavity was apparently excavated only to a depth of about 6 inches (15.2 cm). Nest cavities of this species are generally 2 to 3 feet (.6–.9 m) deep and situated in well-wooded localities.

Early writings about Western Screech-Owls contain several interesting accounts of their predatory habits. Stomach contents of one bird examined on a cold January morning in 1917 contained cutworms, centipedes, mole crickets, goodsize beetles, and various other insect remains. Screech-Owls are incubating either eggs or young at this time of year; insect prey would most likely be fed to the young, along with small birds. Nest

Western Screech-Owl, like the Eastern Screech-Owl with which it was once considered to be a single species, is strictly a nocturnal hunter.

cavities have been found to be garnished with a sprinkling of feathers, presumably the discarded remnants of meals. Other writings from the turn of the century report Western Screech-Owls attempting to take domestic ducks for prey. Dr. G. D. Shaver's farm announced that during the winter of 1914 and 1915, two golden pheasants and five ring-necked pheasants had been killed by a pair of Western Screech-Owls in one morning. The following year, at the same farm site, a similar incident occurred in February, with four bantams and two cock golden pheasants dead. Although no one could be certain how the dead birds had met their demise, Dr. G. D. Shaver liberally laced one of the bantams with strychnine (not legal today) and replaced the body in the farmyard. The next morning, the body of a screech-owl with the claws of one foot firmly embedded in the dead chicken was found. Generally, these owls prey mostly on small rodents, insects, and other invertebrates.

The Western Screech-Owl generally incubates each of its two to five white, moderately glossy eggs as they are laid. This causes the eggs to be hatched in a sequence. The young within the brood vary widely in size and age. This adaptation permits the adults to raise all their young if food is plentiful, or only the first few if food is scarce. Population fluctuations are mostly controlled by increases and decreases in the populations of mice and meadow voles. The longevity record for this species of owl is 12 years, 11 months.

Useful References
Birds of Prey, Part 2. In A. C. Bent. *Life Histories of North American Birds*. Washington, D.C.: United States National Museum, 1961.

Northern Saw-whet Owl
(Aegolius acadicus)

See box design on page 153.

Length: Males: 7 to 8 inches (17.8–20.3 cm); females: 8 to 8½ inches (20.3–21.6 cm)
Nest construction: None
Eggs per clutch: Usually 5 to 6; occasionally 4 to 7
Incubation: Female
Length of incubation: 27 to 29 days, hatching asynchronous (eggs hatch at different times)
Age at fledging: 27 to 34 days
Broods per season: 1
Food: Small mammals, birds, insects, and other invertebrates

Description

The Northern Saw-whet Owl is one of the smallest and most common northern owls; it is found across southern Canada and the northern United States. Much remains to be learned about its populations, distribution, behavior, and breeding biology. Its diminutive size and tame behavior often lend this species to a particular fondness among humans. Frequently, individuals are found by chance encounters or by the excited activity and noisy protests from sparrows, warblers, chickadees, and kinglets. We will never forget the first saw-whet we saw. We came upon it in a dense grove of red cedars next to cornfields and water in central Iowa; it had just returned to its perch with a mouse between his talons. These owls can be easily approached to within a few feet. Often, a saw-whet can be carefully lifted off its perch by hand. This is not recommended, however, because it stresses the bird unduly.

This small owl can be identified by its petite size and rounded head with no ear tufts. Its reddish brown plumage above and white feathers below, streaked with a reddish brown, are other diagnostic features. The facial disk is also reddish and does not have a

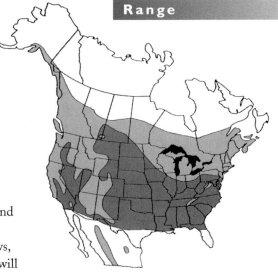

Range

dark border. (Dark-bordered facial disks can be observed on screech-owls.) The bright yellow irides draw your attention immediately to its face.

Although this bird is common in its range, its nocturnal and retiring habits contribute to its being seldom seen. Saw-whets fly low to the ground with rapid wing beats, often suggesting a woodpecker. Generally, they swoop up to a perch. This bird is also seldom heard at night except for a few weeks during the mating period.

Even when hunting habitat and prey are available, a lack of nest sites can result in non-reproducing saw-whet owls. Accelerated logging in southern Canada and the northern United States has reduced suitable breeding habitat, particularly through the loss of nesting snags. Old, dead trees, which provide the best natural sites for cavity nesters, are the first to be felled by landowners. The recent increase in popularity of wood-burning stoves could lead to a loss of nest sites for all cavity nesters, not just the saw-whet owl. Whenever possible, these nest sites should be preserved. Where sites do not presently exist, furnishing artificial nestboxes is one way to maintain and possibly increase populations.

Habitat Needs

During the day, saw-whet owls roost in thick vegetation. These owls favor dense conifers and mixed coniferous deciduous forests, wooded swamps, bogs, moist alder thickets, and dry ponderosa pine slopes. Frequently they can be found next to the trunk of a small tree or in dense shrubby thickets. More typically you will find them near the end of one of the lower branches of a large tree, especially where overhung by another branch. Foraging is done along edges, in forest openings, or wherever perches are available in open habitats.

Northern Saw-Whet owls rely on natural nest sites, or those created by other birds such as Northern Flickers and pileated woodpeckers. These birds will readily accept human-made boxes. Those placed near water seemed to be preferred. In natural and woodpecker cavities, eggs are laid directly onto wood chips or other debris such as gray moss interwoven with small pieces of fibrous bark, a few pine needles, small twigs, and, occasionally, feathers from birds.

Housing Needs for Northern Saw-whet Owls

Box material: Wood
Floor dimensions: 7¾ to 10 inches (19.7–25.4 cm) square
Diameter of entrance hole: 2½ to 4 inches (6.4–10.2 cm)
Box depth below hole: 9 to 12 inches (22.9–30.5 cm)
Mount: At least 14 feet (4.3 m) above the ground
Suggestions: Northern Saw-whet Owls will use a nestbox of the same design as for screech-owls. Place 2 to 3 inches (5.1–7.6 cm) of wood chips or dried grass clippings in the bottom of the box.
Protection: Install predator guards.

Problems

Saw-whet owl nestboxes may be occupied by a wide variety of other animals, among them squirrels, flying squirrels, bluebirds, starlings, and honeybees. All of these are part of the wildlife scene. However, do not hesitate to evict starlings, which have had detrimental effects on cavity-nesting birds. All other birds, with the exception of the House Sparrow and rock dove, are protected by federal law.

Predators, Parasites, and Diseases. Larger owls are frequent predators of the small saw-whet. These include the long-eared, great horned, and barred owls. These species attract the saw-whet by imitating its call. The saw-whet's response to threat is to bob its head up and down and from side to side, shifting from one foot to the other, defecating, occasionally bill snapping, and finally flying away. It may also fluff its body feathers, strike an exaggeratedly upright posture, and emit an insectlike buzz.

Some deaths have been attributed to a bloodsucking fly *(Carnus hemapterus)*. These infestations appear to be severe when the eggs are laid on nests of the European Starling from the previous year. Nestling mortality has been reported from severely bitten individuals. Other insect parasites include chewing lice *(Kurodaia acadica, Strigiphilus* spp.); fleas *(Echidophaga gallinacea, Orchopeas leucopus,* most likely acquired by the owl from its small mammal prey); and Hippoboscidae flies *(Ornithoica vicina, Ornithomyia fringillina, Lynchia americana).*

What You Can Do. Check the nestbox by gently tapping on its side. The owl will peek out of the entrance hole without leaving the box. Females captured on nests before, during, or shortly after egg laying may desert that nest and possibly renest nearby. Individuals captured during late incubation or while brooding young do not appear to desert the nest. If you find a nest then, it is best to wait at least a week before checking its contents.

Nestboxes should be cleaned after all the young have fledged. Cleaned nestboxes have been used in successive years, but not by the same birds. If the hard mat of dried prey remains is not removed from the box, this could make it unsuitable for use for a year or two. It appears that monitoring the nestbox and discarding the starling's nest and its contents is the only solution to the parasite *Carnus hemapterus.* Washing the box with a 10 percent solution of bleach might be of additional help. This might also discourage any parasites introduced to the nestbox from small mammalian prey.

Life Cycle

The increasing day length in late winter stimulates the male saw-whet owl to commence singing in his quest for a mate. Optimum conditions are a clear, calm night with a temperature of about 32°F (0°C) and a bright moon. This song is usually given from a half hour before sunset to just before sunrise from a high but concealed perch. Females are the ones to select nest sites, however.

The first eggs are laid from early spring to as late as mid-March through late April in the northern parts of this owl's range. Usually six eggs are laid, one in the center and the other five around it in a circle. These might be partially buried in the bedding material.

Eggs are laid at intervals of about 2 days. The female remains in the nest cavity during this time, except for one or two short trips to defecate and cough up a pellet. The male will bring food to the female throughout the egg-laying period. Incubation begins with the laying of the first egg and can continue for 21 to 28 days. The young hatch at variable intervals. Newly hatched individuals may be found in the same nest as nearly grown young.

Saw-whet Owl eggs are white, smooth with little or no gloss, and oval to almost spherical.

The young are born blind, helpless, and with a very scanty covering of whitish down. Eyes begin to open between 8 and 9 days of age. By day 16 or 17, the upper parts of the young have become a dark chocolate brown. It is at this age that the owlets begin to snap their mandible (lower jaw) and produce a rasping call when hungry. The young are brooded until the youngest nestling is about 18 days old. Females then leave the nest to roost elsewhere.

Food for the young is generally brought to the nesting cavity by the male and given to the female. Food includes small mammals, birds, insects, and other invertebrates, which may be torn into smaller parts before feeding.

These owls detect their prey by excellent hearing and by good low-light vision. The ears are located asymmetrically, at different levels in the skull, which allows the owl to distinguish sounds originating in the horizontal and vertical

Juveniles are easily recognized by their white facial patch.

planes. Prey is usually swallowed in pieces, starting with the head. Larger prey are usually consumed in two meals, 4 to 5 hours apart. Pellets (1–1½ inches, or 2.5–3.8 cm in length) are produced 4 or 5 hours after the prey has been consumed, usually from either a daytime or a hunting roost. Generally the nest is kept very clean while the female is brooding the young. After the young are no longer brooded, pellets, feces, and excess prey might build up in the nest several inches (cm) thick.

The owlets fledge the nest at between 27 and 29 days of age over a 1- to 2-day period. They tend to stay together outside the nest and continue to be fed by the male for at least 1 month. The young owlets become independent about 6 to 8 weeks after fledging.

Many nestlings die due to starvation. Fledging success for this species is 56 percent of eggs hatched. Many adults are killed by cars. The longest surviving wild bird lived for 7 years, 11 months.

Useful References

Cannings, R. J. "Northern Saw-whet Owl *(Aegolius acadicus)*." In *The Birds of North America,* No. 42 (A. Poole and F. Gill, eds.). Philadelphia and Washington, D.C.: The Academy of Natural Sciences and The American Ornithologists' Union, 1993.

♂

American Kestrel
(Falco sparverius)

See box design on page 153.

Length: 9 to 12 inches (22.9–30.5 cm)

Nest construction: Little or no nesting material is added to the cavity

Eggs per clutch: 3 to 7, usually 4 to 5

Incubation: Mostly by the female, but the male is also capable of incubation

Length of incubation: 29 to 31 days

Age at fledging: 30 to 31 days

Broods per season: 1; sometimes 2

Food: Insects (especially grasshoppers), small mammals (largely mice and voles), small reptiles, small birds including House Sparrows (primarily in winter), and amphibians

Winter range: South to Panama

Description

Formerly known as sparrow hawk, the little American Kestrel is our smallest and most social hawk. It is also our only cavity-nesting hawk. This beautiful raptor is exquisitely patterned and multicolored, as well as remarkably adaptable and widespread in open environments. It is a valuable rodent and insect predator that was once much more common. As with many other cavity-nesting birds, its decline stemmed in part from changes in its habitat, especially the loss of large trees with suitable natural or large woodpecker cavities for nesting. And like other insect-eating birds, kestrels probably suffered from the wide use of persistent pesticides such as DDT during the middle decades of the 20th century.

Fortunately, kestrels readily use nestboxes provided for them. A major project initiated by the Iowa Department of Natural Resources in 1983 in conjunction with that

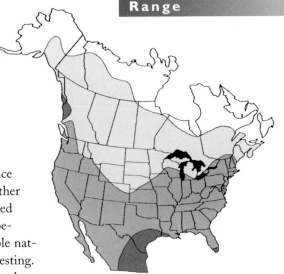

Range

state's department of transportation involved the installation of hundreds of kestrel boxes onto the backs of information signs along interstate highways. Young are raised successfully in about 70 percent of these boxes, and other states have adopted this productive program. Interestingly, mortality due to collisions with vehicles has been lower than expected.

Habitat Needs

Basically a bird of open country, the American Kestrel prefers grasslands, meadows, and abandoned fields with scattered trees or groves. Kestrels will also breed in open woods, orchards, farms and agricultural country, deserts, and unforested mountainsides up to 13,000 feet (4,000 m), avoiding heavily wooded areas. These highly adaptable little hawks are even found in cities and along highway and railroad rights-of-way. They require open habitats for hunting: at the very least 1 acre (.4 ha) of open land near the nestbox.

Kestrels are almost exclusively cavity nesters. For artificial housing they require wooden boxes that are, essentially, large versions of bluebird nestboxes. Situate an *inside* perch 3 inches (7.6 cm) below the entrance hole for the nestlings' use. Painting is generally not recommended, especially not on interior surfaces. The area in front of the box should be clear of vegetation to create a flyway. Place the box within 45 to 90 feet (13.5–27 m) of a tree with dead limbs, a snag, or a pole. The male uses these perches to dismember prey items before passing them to the female.

 Housing Needs for American Kestrels

Box material: Wood
Floor dimensions: 7¾ inches (19.7 cm) square
Diameter of entrance hole: 3 inches (7.6 cm)
Box depth below hole: 9 inches (22.9 cm)
Mount: At least 10 feet (3.1 m), and preferably 12 to 20 feet (3.7–6.1 m), above the ground
Suggestions: Locate the box on a pole, a building, or the main trunk or a vertical branch of a tree; orient it to face away from prevailing weather (usually south, east, or southeast). Place about 1 inch (2.5 cm) of wood shavings or chips (not sawdust or cedar shavings) in the bottom of the box at the beginning of each breeding season.
Spacing: At least 1 mile (1.6 km) apart, but no closer than ½ mile (.8 km)
Protection: Discourage mammalian predators by wrapping a 30-inch (76.2 cm) wide metal sleeve around the supporting pole.

Problems

European Starlings, and (to a lesser extent) especially, screech-owls and other cavity nesters compete with kestrels for nest sites. Gray squirrels also use the boxes.

Predators, Parasites, and Diseases. Larger birds of prey sometimes attack and kill kestrels. Climbing predators including raccoons will consume the eggs and young if able to reach the nest. During their first week, fledglings are vulnerable to mammalian predators such as red foxes and birds of prey.

What You Can Do. You may well need to evict starlings from your kestrel boxes in spring. Discouraging starlings is a difficult proposition. If you find a starling nest, remove it and replace it with a new layer of wood chips. Keep mammalian predators away from nestboxes by wrapping a 30-inch (76.2 cm) wide metal sleeve around the supporting pole (see pages 164–167 for more information about predator guards).

Life Cycle

These most social of our falcons gather into small groups before pair formation begins, which commences about 4 weeks prior to egg laying. American Kestrels breed as yearlings. First-year breeders in Iowa dispersed an average of 5 miles (8 km) from where they hatched. Some older kestrels return to nestboxes that they have used in previous years. Males establish nesting territories and are joined later by the females. Females may move about from one male's territory to those of others prior to choosing one male with which to mate. Copulation peaks just before egg laying.

Eggs range in color from white to pinkish white and occasionally lavender, with brown markings.

Females lay white, pinkish white, or light cinnamon-colored eggs that are rather evenly covered with small dots and spots of various shades of brown. The eggs are laid on alternate days or at intervals of 2 or 3 days. Incubation begins before the last egg is deposited, usually with the laying of the next-to-last egg. Females occasionally sit tight on the eggs; you must lift them bodily to inspect the clutch. After about 1 month of incubation, nearly all of it by the female, the young hatch. Males bring food to their mates during this period. The early stage of incubation is a sensitive time for nesting raptors, and kestrels may abandon their clutches if

These large nestlings are nearly ready to fledge.

Although female kestrels sometimes sit tight during monitoring, nests should not be inspected from the start of egg laying to 2 weeks into the incubation period.

disturbed too often during this phase of the life cycle. *After egg laying begins, do not inspect nests until about 2 weeks into the incubation period.* After this, monitoring may resume.

The nestlings are cared for by both parents; the female does all the brooding and feeding, while the male provides all of the nestlings' food. The male dismembers the prey and then passes the food to his mate for feeding to the young. Initially, the young birds are downy white, but by 3 weeks of age they are well feathered. Even at this stage the sexes can be distinguished by plumage. The nestlings develop rapidly on a diet of insects, often grasshoppers. When they reach 3 weeks of age, their parents begin bringing whole prey, including small mammals, for the nestlings to tear apart. By 4 weeks of age, they are ready to leave the nest.

During the first week after leaving the nest, young kestrels spend nearly all of their time resting on perches with their parents continuing to feed them. This is a vulnerable time for the young, because they are not yet very able flyers and sometimes fall victim to predators. The fledglings begin hunting for themselves during the second week out of the nest cavity. They hunt both from perches and while hovering. All feeding of young by the parents ceases by 22 days after fledging, and the young have dispersed from the area by this time.

Some American Kestrels are resident in their breeding areas all year, while others migrate southward in fall. Kestrels that you see in your region during the winter months may move northward for breeding in spring. They have lived as long as 11 years and 7 months in the wild.

Useful References

Birds of Prey, Part 2. In A. C. Bent. *Life Histories of North American Birds.* Washington, D.C.: United States National Museum, 1938.

Establishing a Nestbox Program for American Kestrels Along an Interstate Highway. Ames: Iowa Department of Transportation, 1992.

Great Crested Flycatcher
(Myiarchus crinitus)

See box design on page 157.

Length: 8 to 9 inches (20.3–22.9 cm)

Nest construction: Female

Eggs per clutch: 4 to 8, usually 5

Incubation: Female

Length of incubation: 13 to 15 days, usually 14

Age at fledging: 13 to 15 days

Broods per season: 1

Food: 93.7 percent animal matter (mostly insects); 6.3 percent vegetable matter (fruit); medium to small insects are fed to the young

Winter range: Most winter in southern Mexico, Central America, and northwestern South America. Some are resident year-round in southern Florida.

Description

The large, colorful, and rather raucous Great Crested Flycatcher is the only cavity-nesting member of its family in eastern North America. Although quite common in open woodland and edge habitats, it is heard more often than seen; its loud *whee-eep* call is unmistakable. This bird is renowned for its habit of using shed snakeskins in nest construction, although it is not the only species to do so. Many aspects of the Great Crested Flycatcher's breeding biology are not fully understood.

As a bird of open woodlands and edges, this flycatcher has actually benefited from forest fragmentation. Its breeding population has expanded in several areas, especially in Canada, while it has decreased in others. It is most common in the southeastern states; less so in the Great Plains states and adjacent Canadian provinces. Although there is no clear population trend, this species' numbers seem to be holding stable at present.

Range

s

s = summer

Habitat Needs

Generally breeding in open deciduous or mixed forests and the edges of clearings, the Great Crested Flycatcher also nests in old orchards, wooded pastures, river corridors, wooded swamps, parks, cemeteries, and other urban areas with large shade trees. It prefers damp to dry woodlands, and does not nest in boreal forests.

Great Cresteds prefer natural cavities to woodpecker holes and artificial cavities, but do regularly use nestboxes. Some studies seem to indicate that these birds choose hanging or swinging nestboxes over those that are fixed, perhaps because starlings never nest in hanging boxes, and perhaps also because suspended boxes may be less vulnerable to predation.

Problems

European Starlings, Tree Swallows, Eastern Bluebirds, Northern Flickers, and red-headed and Red-bellied Woodpeckers compete with Great Cresteds for nest sites. Red Squirrels may also compete for cavities.

Predators, Parasites, and Diseases. Indigo, yellow rat, and corn snakes have been known to eat eggs and young flycatchers, and sometimes incubating females as well. Gray and red squirrels consume their eggs, and sharp-shinned hawks attack the adults.

The tropical fowl mite *(Ornithonyssus bursa)* sometimes causes heavy nestling parasitism. Various fly larvae have also been found in Great Crested Flycatcher nests.

Housing Needs for Great Crested Flycatchers

Box material: Wood
Floor dimensions: 6 inches (15.2 cm) square
Diameter of entrance hole: 2 inches (5.1 cm)
Box depth below hole: 8 inches (20.3 cm)
Mount: At least 8 feet (2.4 m) above the ground
Suggestions: Locate the box fairly close to woodlands; orient it so that the entrance hole is free of obstructing vegetation. Place ¾ to 2 inches (1.9–5.1 cm) of wood chips (but not cedar) in the bottom of the box.
Protection: Discourage snakes and other climbing predators by wrapping a 30-inch (76 cm) wide piece of metal flashing around the tree trunk on which the box is mounted. Place a piece of heavier-gauge metal with a 2-inch (5.1 cm) diameter hole cut in it over the entrance hole to keep squirrels from enlarging this. You can also hang boxes from 3¼- to 3¾-foot (1–1.1 m) long flexible wire or chain 8 to 15 feet (2.4–4.6 m) above the ground.

What You Can Do. To make it more difficult for snakes and other climbing predators to reach nestboxes, attach a 30-inch (76 cm) wide piece of metal flashing around the tree trunk on which the nestbox is mounted. Place a piece of heavier-gauge metal with a 2-inch (5.1 cm) diameter hole cut in it over the entrance hole to keep squirrels from enlarging this.

You can also hang boxes from 3¼- to 3¾-foot (1–1.2 m) long flexible wire or chain at least 8 feet (2.4 m), and up to 15 feet (4.6 m), above the ground.

Life Cycle

After returning to eastern North America from their tropical wintering grounds, the very vocal males call frequently. Females arrive from 7 to 12 days later. Both sexes are capable of breeding during their first year after hatching. Great Crested Flycatchers sometimes select a nestbox that they have used in previous years.

Both sexes inspect potential nest sites, the male doing so initially. The female alone constructs the nest, however, using grasses, leaves, leaf stems, bark fibers, rootlets, trash of various kinds, and often snakeskins. This characteristic habit of incorporating shed snakeskins into the nest was once thought to be a device for scaring off potential predators. It is now thought that the bird is simply attracted to items that have a crinkly texture and/or shiny appearance, as evidenced by the fact that Great Cresteds readily add cellophane wrappers to their nests as well. Two or 3 days is required for completion of most of the nest, while finer items such as feathers are added as a lining during egg laying, incubation, and brooding. The nest cup is often located off center in the nestbox.

Feathers provide a soft, warm lining in many Great Created Flycatcher nests.

One creamy white to creamy or pinkish buff egg, evenly decorated with brown, purple, or lavender blotches or streaks, is laid early each morning until the clutch is complete. Incubation by the female sometimes begins with the laying of the next-to-last egg, and lasts approximately 2 weeks.

Although already similar to the adult, this nestling's bill retains soft yellow corners.

Within a day of hatching, the nestlings begin a constant peeping. The female broods them for about 6 days. The male, meanwhile, is very aggressive in chasing away intruding male flycatchers, as well as potential avian and mammalian predators, especially gray squirrels, from the nest site. Great Cresteds will generally renest within days if their first nest is destroyed.

Both parents feed their nestlings, although the female contributes most of the food, especially early on. Insects, including dragonflies and damselflies, grasshoppers and crickets, butterflies and moths, true bugs, and bees and wasps make up the bulk of the young birds' diet. The adults have three primary methods for catching insect prey: sallying forth from a perch, picking insects off a leaf or bark surface while hovering, and dropping to the ground from a perch. A small amount of wild fruit may also be fed to the young.

The young are ready to leave the nestbox after about 2 weeks, although they may fledge prematurely at 8 or 9 days of age, especially if disturbed. Therefore, after the nestlings are 1 week old, monitoring should be done very cautiously. The adults continue to bring food to nestlings that have not yet fledged. Once out of the box, they are fed by their parents for up to 3 weeks, albeit with decreasing frequency.

The longest recorded life span of a banded bird is 13 years, 11 months.

Adults continue to bring food to nestlings that have not yet fledged.

Useful References

Lanyon, W. E. "Great Crested Flycatcher *(Myiarchus crinitus)*." In *The Birds of North America*, No. 300 (A. Poole and F. Gill, eds.). Philadelphia and Washington, D.C.: The Academy of Natural Sciences and The American Ornithologists' Union, 1997.

Taylor, W. K., and M. A. Kershner. "Breeding Biology of the Great Crested Flycatcher in Central Florida." *Journal of Field Ornithology* 62:28–39, 1991.

Ash-throated Flycatcher
(*Myiarchus cinerascens*)

See box design on page 157.

Length: 7 ½ to 8 ½ inches (19–21.6 cm)

Nest construction: Both sexes

Eggs per clutch: 3 to 7, usually 4 to 5

Incubation: Female

Length of incubation: 15 days

Age at fledging: 14 to 16 days

Broods per season: Presumably 1

Food: 92 percent animal, including large flying insects such as wasps, true bugs, moths (including caterpillars), flies, grasshoppers, and beetles; 8 percent vegetable, including small fruits such as elderberries and mistletoe

Winter range: From southwestern Arizona and extreme southeastern California south to northeastern Costa Rica

Description

Surprisingly little is known about this common western species, which is believed to be closely related to the eastern Great Crested Flycatcher and the southwestern brown-crested flycatcher. The Ash-throated is believed to fill the same ecological niche in the West that the Great Crested fills in the East. Its nesting biology seems to differ little from that of its close relative, although many details of its life history have yet to be studied.

The Ash-throated Flycatcher, like the Great Crested, displays traits that seem to indicate it is still evolving as a cavity nester. For instance, it lays streaked (camouflaged) eggs and builds a nest within the cavity, just like most non-cavity-nesting songbirds.

Range

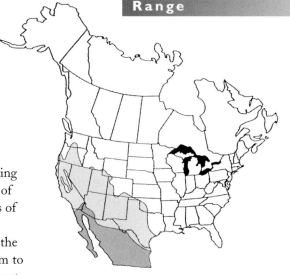

Habitat Needs

For the most part birds of arid, brushy lands, these flycatchers breed in areas intermediate between woodland and open range. They nest in open woodland, piñon-juniper woodland, chaparral, oak canyons, streamside groves, and desert washes. Examples of their broad range of habitats include the southern Sierra Nevada Mountains, up to 9,000 feet (2,769 m), and — in sharp contrast — California's Death Valley.

Ash-throated Flycatchers use artificial nestboxes quite frequently in some areas, but they generally use natural cavities or those created by woodpeckers. Nest locations have also included such atypical sites as a drainpipe, an abandoned cactus wren nest, behind loose bark, in an empty mailbox, and even in the exhaust pipe of a derelict engine.

Problems

Ash-throated Flycatchers sometimes usurp nesting cavities from smaller species of woodpeckers, and they probably vie with Mountain and Western Bluebirds for nest sites, too. Competition for a nestbox in south-central Oregon between an Ash-throated Flycatcher and a smaller Plain (now Juniper) Titmouse has been recorded. In this instance, the flycatcher drove off the titmouse, which had already laid five eggs in a box occupied the previous year by the flycatcher.

Predators, Parasites, and Diseases. Bird-eating hawks presumably prey upon this species.

What You Can Do. Be sure to follow general guidelines for mounting nestboxes. Because Ash-throated Flycatchers do not face competition from European Starlings or House Sparrows, protection from heat and climbing predators are probably your chief concerns.

Housing Needs for Ash-throated Flycatchers

Box material: Wood
Floor dimensions: 6 inches (15.2 cm) square
Diameter of entrance hole: 1¾ to 2 inches (4.4–5.1 cm)
Box depth below hole: 8 inches (20.3 cm)
Mount: 4½ to 8 feet (1.4–2.4 m), preferably 6 to 8 feet (1.8–2.4 m) above the ground
Suggestions: Boxes have successfully been mounted on juniper trunks and scrub oaks. Floor dimensions of 5 inches (12.7 cm) square, with entrance holes 6 to 7 inches (15.2–17.8 cm) above the floor, have also been successful.
Protection: For tree mounting, affix a 30-inch (76.2 cm) wide piece of sheet metal below box, to discourage climbing predators.

Life Cycle

Migratory over most of their North American range (except in southern Arizona and extreme southeastern California), these birds return to their breeding range from Mexico and northern Central America in spring. After mating, the female gathers nesting material, while the male sings and vigorously defends the nesting territory. In a manner reminiscent of the kingbirds, Ash-throateds will harass potential predators as large as ravens and red-tailed hawks.

The nest, which is built to fill the cavity at hand, is constructed of dried forbs, grass, rootlets, bits of manure, and sometimes shed snakeskins, although not as frequently as in the case of the Great Crested Flycatcher. The inner cup, which holds the eggs, is often situated in one corner of the box. The cup is generally lined with a soft mass of hair and fur. In southeastern Arizona these flycatchers used deer, rabbit, and squirrel hair. The female usually lays four or five creamy white eggs that are speckled, spotted, or blotched with browns and purples.

The eggs hatch after just over 2 weeks of incubation by the female. Both parents feed soft insect material to the nestlings. At first the food is regurgitated; later the young are fed whole insects. In south-central Oregon, nestlings were fed a diet composed primarily of young (non-flying) grasshoppers. This bird does most of its hunting in low vegetation. Ash-throated

Ash-throated Flycatchers lay heavily marked eggs, just like their eastern relatives.

The nest's inner cup, lined with a mass of hair and fur, insulates the nestlings.

Flycatchers tend to be more proactive than Great Cresteds in their pursuit of prey: Rather than waiting for insects to happen by their perch, Ash-throateds tend to go looking for them over a wide area. They will sometimes also take prey from bark, leaves, and the ground. Nestlings develop the ability to give their species' two most characteristic calls, *ha-whip* and *ha-wheer*, by the time they are ready to leave the nest.

After approximately 16 days, the young fledge. They follow the adults around for a time, learning the art of catching insect prey from their parents. Adult Ash-throated Flycatchers have been seen releasing slightly injured insects in front of their young in an apparent attempt to induce the fledglings to capture their own flying prey. Banding data indicate a current longevity record of 9 years.

Useful References

"Flycatchers, Larks, Swallows, and Their Allies." In A. C. Bent. *Life Histories of North American Birds*. Washington, D.C.: United States National Museum, 1942.

European Starling
(*Sturnus vulgaris*)

Length: 7½ to 8½ inches (19–21.6 cm)
Nest construction: Both sexes
Eggs per clutch: 4 to 8, usually 4 to 5
Incubation: Both sexes
Length of incubation: 11 to 14 days, usually 12
Age at fledging: 18 to 25 days, usually 21 to 22
Broods per season: Typically 2, occasionally 3
Food: An extremely diverse diet of insects (42 percent), and other invertebrates, cultivated and wild fruits, grains, and seeds

Description

The European Starling, whose North American population is now over 200 million strong, is arguably the most "successful" avian introduction ever on this continent: Successful to the extent that those 200-plus million individuals are all descended from 100 birds introduced in New York City's Central Park during 1890 through 1891. This species was not accidentally introduced, but rather deliberately liberated by one Eugene Scheifflin, who sought to introduce all the bird species mentioned by Shakespeare in his writings. Conditioned as they were by centuries of living in European cities, starlings found North American cities to be fertile ground indeed. By 1942, starlings had spread all the way across the continent to the Pacific shore. In many areas, European Starlings are now the most abundant bird species. They may be increasing along southern and northern edges of their range, but overall the population seems to have stabilized. The history of the starling in North America serves as an archetypal example of what can happen when exotic species find their way into ecosystems not equipped to deal with them.

Starlings, of course, are despised by birders and those who seek to encourage cavity-nesting birds because, as secondary cavity nesters themselves, aggressive starlings regularly

evict native species and appropriate their nest sites. This has led at least to decreases in local populations of some species, such as the Purple Martin and red-headed woodpecker, to name just two.

Habitat Needs

The European Starling is a generalist that thrives in a wide variety of human-altered habitats, including cities, towns, parks, farms, ranches, fields, and open country. They are usually absent from deep forests. Starlings have even reached areas above 6,000 feet (1,830 m) in elevation.

Starlings will nest in virtually any cavity, natural or artificial, that has an opening large enough to admit them (larger than 1½ inches, or 3.8 cm). This includes empty buildings, nooks and crannies of structures, natural tree cavities, woodpecker holes, and, of course, nestboxes with suitably sized entrances.

Problems

The European Starling competes with virtually all native cavity-nesting birds, especially the Northern Flicker but also the red-headed woodpecker, Eastern Bluebird, Purple Martin, Tree Swallow, and Wood Duck. To some extent starlings also affect the Great Crested Flycatcher, screech-owls, American Kestrel, and House Wren. Perhaps ironically, starlings also compete with that other hated exotic, the House Sparrow.

Predators, Parasites, and Diseases. Bird-eating hawks such as the sharp-shinned, Cooper's, and peregrine falcons prey upon adults, as do owls, weasels, rats, dogs, and cats. Gray and red squirrels eat starling eggs and young.

European Starlings have been found to harbor mites (the northern fowl and red mites), ticks, and lice.

What You Can Do. Excluding starlings from nestboxes is a major preoccupation of nest monitors, especially those erecting boxes for larger species that require entrance holes greater than 1½ inches (3.8 cm). Especially vulnerable to starling takeover are boxes meant for the Northern Flicker, Purple Martin, Red-bellied and red-headed woodpeckers, and Great Crested Flycatcher. Make sure that nestboxes designed for bluebirds, swallows, and smaller species have entrance holes with a diameter no greater than 1½ inches (3.8 cm)!

To control starlings, trapping and elimination may be necessary; some would say absolutely essential. Another approach to disrupting their nesting is to remove the starlings' eggs and replace them with marbles. In any case, failure to deter starlings from taking over a martin house or flicker box is cause to remove that house rather than adding to the already astronomical size of the European Starling population.

Life Cycle

Male starlings begin to investigate suitable nest cavities in late winter. Once they have chosen a nesting territory (which extends only 20 inches, or 50.8 cm, beyond the cavity opening) they advertise to prospective mates by shaking their wings, often while singing; starlings are very adept mimics capable of imitating 20 species. Females choose among these advertising males, which then begin depositing nesting material in the chosen cavity. (About one-third of adult females return to the same cavity that they used in previous years.) Since there are almost always more starlings than cavity sites available, roving bands of nonbreeding adults are common. During the breeding season, starlings can be distinguished by the color of the base of their lower bills. In males it is dark blue, in females pink.

Starling eggs, like these in a bluebird nest-box, should be removed immediately.

Actual nest construction, although conducted by both birds, is accomplished mostly by the female and takes place after pairs are formed. Males characteristically place green sprigs of vegetation in the cup. A family member of ours residing in Chicago described to us how she witnessed a starling plucking sacred basil leaves from her garden one spring, and carrying the aromatic herb to its nest behind the garage eaves. The cause for such behavior is not fully known, but the vegetation may well serve as a deterrent to nest parasites.

Regular monitoring is required to prevent starling eggs from becoming nestlings.

Females generally lay four or five pale bluish or greenish, unmarked eggs, one each morning, in a 3-inch (7.6 cm) diameter cup of fine plant materials and feathers. This cup is surrounded by a mass of twigs, grass, and assorted trash sized to fit the cavity. Starlings are very social birds and will nest in loose colonies as well as singly. Incubation, mostly by the female, begins in earnest when the last or next-to-last egg is laid. The young emerge after about 12 days of incubation.

Both sexes feed and care for the young for the first week, after which the female may do most or all of the feeding. Insect larvae make up the nestlings' primary diet. Starlings tend to be ground feeders and are especially suited to foraging for insects in short grass: They possess powerful jaw muscles that enable them to insert their closed and pointed bills into the turf and then, by spreading their beaks apart, uncover beetle grubs and other hidden prey. They are also able to find dormant insects under snow, a valuable survival skill. The fact that they consume large quantities of injurious insects is their one redeeming quality.

Brooding occurs for 1 week after hatching, and the young birds' eyes open by the end of this first week. Body feathers emerge by day 7, flight feathers by day 10. By 13 days of age, the well-feathered nestlings are able to regulate their own body heat. If one of the adults dies, the other is usually capable of successfully raising the young. By 15 to 21 days, they are fully feathered. The young leave the nest cavity after about 21 days, and forage with their parents within 1,500 feet (458 m) of the nest site. The total cycle from nest building to fledging generally lasts 40 days. Juvenile starlings are gray-brown in color, very unlike their iridescent, speckled parents.

South of the latitude of 48 degrees north, most European Starlings initiate a second brood almost immediately after their first brood fledges. Males again select the nest sites.

Starlings forage in flocks throughout the year, but especially from late summer through winter. Those living south of the latitude of 40 degrees north rarely migrate. Birds of the Great Lakes region and U.S. midwestern regions are most likely to move southward in fall. European Starlings have lived up to 17 years, 8 months in North America.

Useful References

Cabe, P. R. "European Starling *(Sturnus vulgaris)*." In *The Birds of North America*, No. 48 (A. Poole and F. Gill, eds.). Philadelphia and Washington, D.C.: The Academy of Natural Sciences and The American Ornithologists' Union, 1993.

House Sparrow
(Passer domesticus)

Length: 5¾ to 6½ inches (14.6–16.5 cm)

Nest construction: Both sexes

Eggs per clutch: 1 to 8, usually 4 to 6

Incubation: Female

Length of incubation: 10 to 13 days, usually 12 days

Age at fledging: 12 to 24 days, usually 14 to 18, depending upon region

Broods per season: Normally 2, often 3, and as many as 4

Food: Adults consume 96.7 percent vegetable matter (weed seeds, grass and forb seeds, grains, livestock feed, fruit, and blossoms) and 3.3 percent animal matter (insects and spiders). Young are fed mostly insects.

Description

The House Sparrow is not a true sparrow at all, but rather an Old World weaver finch originally native to the Mediterranean region. As in the case of our other alien pest species, the European Starling, the first House Sparrows were purposely released in the New York City area during the nineteenth century, this time in a misguided attempt to control insect pests. Between late 1851 and early 1852, 100 birds were liberated in Brooklyn. By 1886, they had spread beyond the Mississippi River; four years later, House Sparrows reached the Rocky Mountains. Additional releases were made elsewhere between 1861 and 1875 in the East, in numerous Midwestern locations, and in the West. This exotic species successfully colonized the continent within only 60 years.

In the early part of the 20th century, it was the most abundant bird in the United States. Although still exceedingly numerous, the House Sparrow has undergone a general population decrease, especially in the Maritime Provinces and the eastern and

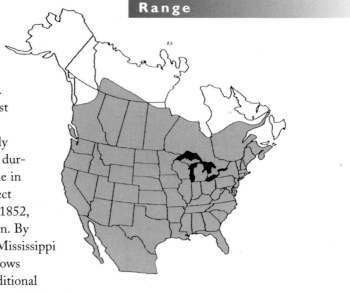

Range

central United States. After the decline of horse transportation in cities (the species fed on the undigested grain in horse manure), House Sparrow abundance shifted to rural areas. In time, however, changes in agricultural practices, such as the rise of larger farms specializing in just one crop, caused a continentwide decline in the sparrow population.

House Sparrows thrive near, and indeed require, human settlement. At virtually every fast-food restaurant on the continent, flocks of House Sparrows patrol the parking lot for food scraps. House Sparrows are so despised because they aggressively appropriate the nest sites of native, cavity-nesting songbirds, often killing the incubating or brooding adults and their young in the process.

Habitat Needs

House Sparrows live in cities, towns, suburbs, parks, farms, ranches, and agricultural areas, always in close proximity to humans. They are not found in densely forested areas, extensive grasslands, or alpine or desert environments.

This highly adaptable species will nest almost anywhere an artificial or natural cavity exists. They also sometimes construct nests in trees.

Problems

Virtually every native cavity-nesting species is vulnerable to the aggressive House Sparrow, but especially bluebirds, wrens, Tree Swallows, and Purple Martins. It is estimated that 20 percent of all martin house compartments are occupied by House Sparrows. These Sparrows are known to have attacked 70 species of North American birds, mostly at nest sites. They can also wreak havoc on a bluebird trail, as many a nest monitor knows.

Predators, Parasites, and Diseases. Hawks, including the American Kestrel, merlin, and sharp-shinned and Cooper's hawks, eat House Sparrows, as do owls and loggerhead shrikes. House cats, dogs, raccoons, and black (pilot black) rat snakes also prey upon them.

Blowflies, fleas, and mites occur in House Sparrow nests.

What You Can Do. Although there is no such thing as a truly sparrow-proof nestbox, some designs are apparently less popular with the species. To discourage House Sparrows, build boxes that are shallow and have a 3-inch × ⅞-inch (7.6 cm × 2.2 cm) entrance; mount them low to the ground, remembering to add a baffle against predators. Sparrow-inhibiting designs have been developed (one uses 4-inch, or 10.2 cm, diameter PVC plastic sewer pipe), but many of these also discourage the bluebirds and other desirable cavity nesters for which they were erected in the first place.

In addition to nestbox design, location is important. Do not place boxes near farmyards, barns, feedlots, houses, or outbuildings, because House Sparrows frequent these areas.

It may be advantageous to leave your nestboxes open after you clean them, or to plug their entrance holes, until the desired species arrive back in spring to claim nest sites. This eliminates having House Sparrows use them earlier for nesting or roosting.

If you feed birds, use only sunflower and/or safflower seeds, because House Sparrows prefer millet, cracked corn, wheat, and other less expensive feed. If House Sparrows are your primary feeder patrons, you should seriously consider moving your feeder or taking it down altogether. The prime objective is to diminish the size of the sparrow population, not to increase it.

Outright House Sparrow control may also be necessary. Be diligent in removing sparrow nests from the nestboxes you monitor. This must often be done again and again. You may also have to take more drastic action when dealing with this species, namely trapping and elimination. If you are unwilling or unable to capture and eliminate House Sparrows (like starlings, they are not protected by law), and they continue to be a problem, you should definitely remove your nestboxes or martin houses rather than create more problems for native cavity nesters.

Life Cycle

House Sparrows are resident year-round near their breeding colonies. They nest earlier than many returning cavity nesters, as well as late into the season, and will forcibly evict native species from the latter's chosen nest sites. House Sparrows are monogamous and usually remain paired through the breeding season, as well as between breeding seasons. If a male is removed from an area, his mate will desert the nest; if a female is removed, the remaining male will seek a new mate.

House Sparrows are quite social and nest in small colonies or loose associations of pairs. Nest sites are chosen both before and after mating has occurred. Males vigorously defend a small territory centered on the nest. Both sexes work to construct the nest of dried grass and other plant materials and a wide assortment of trash. Nests often contain feathers (which Tree Swallows also regularly use). Nests are sometimes reused during a season and in consecutive seasons. House Sparrows are persistent renesters if their nest is destroyed.

House Sparrow nesting material and eggs should be removed at once.

The female lays four to six white to greenish or bluish white eggs that are speckled around the larger end with grays or browns. Eggs are laid one per day, and incubation begins when the next-to-last is deposited. After about 11 days of incubation by the female, the eggs hatch. Males sometimes spend brief periods of time on the eggs but do not actually incubate them.

Young sparrows open their eyes at 4 days of age, and at 6 days they are beginning to generate their own body heat. The female usually broods the young overnight. Both parents feed the young a diet of regurgitated insects. After about 2 weeks in the nest, the young are ready to fledge. They remain with the adult male for several days thereafter, then assemble into foraging and roosting flocks with other young House Sparrows. Within 110 days of leaving the nest, the young are on their own. The entire cycle from nest building to fledging of young usually spans 5 weeks. The current longevity record for a House Sparrow in the wild is 13 years, 4 months.

Useful References

Lowther, P. E., and C. L. Cink. "House Sparrow." In *The Birds of North America,* No. 12 (A. Poole, P. Stettenheim, and F. Gill, eds.). Philadelphia and Washington, D.C.: The Academy of Natural Sciences and The American Ornithologists' Union, 1992.

Females lack the black bib, white cheeks, and chestnut nape of the male.

Nestbox Designs

At one time or another, we've all seen decorative birdhouses that rival dollhouses in their level of detail. Though they may be nice to look at, these designer birdhouses do little for birds. In fact, the human urge to make birdhouses more aesthetically pleasing is generally misguided and counterproductive. The nestbox designs in this book are devoid of exterior perches that invite predation, a feature common to some commercially available birdhouses. Novelty birdhouses also are often undersized; have entrance holes that are too large or too small; are sealed shut, allowing no access to the interior for monitoring or cleaning; lack vent and drain holes; are constructed of wood that is much too thin; or lack other features crucial for success.

A well-designed and constructed nestbox, on the other hand, is beautiful in a utilitarian way. Underlying the box's simple exterior are a host of special design features that have taken many years of trial-and-error experimentation to discover. All cater to the needs of the particular species. "Amenities" that birds most need are a correctly sized entrance hole, a sufficient interior floor size to accommodate eggs and nestlings, and sufficient depth below the entrance hole to help thwart potential predators. Drainage holes, drip edge, and roof overhang to shed water and ventilation holes to prevent temperatures from exceeding safe levels are among the other, more subtle features that will contribute to a successful nesting season in your box. In addition, the nestbox designs included here all open from the side at least and some also open from the top, to allow for convenient, less obtrusive monitoring.

These are basic designs. Remember that there is always room for experimentation, but once you find a design that works for your target species, stick with it — and enjoy. Few things are more satisfying than watching a pair of our native songbirds going about the business of rearing the next generation in a nestbox that you built!

Getting Started

Now that you're ready to begin constructing a nestbox, review the eight basic nestbox plans provided here, and select the one designed for the species that you want to attract. (Remember to consider available habitat when making this decision.) All nestboxes can

◄ Although tree mounting is convenient, such nestboxes are easily reached by climbing predators and so should be fitted with predator guards.

be constructed with simple hand tools, but the job may be less time-consuming and perhaps more efficient if you use power tools. For best results, read all instructions carefully before beginning your work. Then, follow the step-by-step cutting and assembly directions, using the illustrations as a guide. Most importantly, be sure to follow this valuable piece of woodworking advice at every turn — "measure twice and cut once."

Choosing Lumber for Your Nestbox

Before selecting wood for your nestbox, read this section carefully. Treated woods and wood preservatives, though beneficial in maintaining the wood, are almost always harmful to birds.

Cedar. Western red cedar is an attractive, light, sturdy, and very long-lasting wood excellently suited for nestbox construction. One-inch cedar lumber is usually rough cut (unplaned) on one side, smooth (planed) on the other, and actually ⅞-inch (2.2 cm) thick. Grade 3 is fine for this purpose. Cedar is also available as ¾-inch (1.9 cm) thick planed lumber. Because cedar may split when nailed, it should be predrilled (use a drill bit slightly narrower than the nail). Cedar is quite expensive but lasts far longer than most other woods. *Note:* Do not use cedar shavings as nesting material, because the oils they contain can irritate nestlings.

Pine. Pine lumber is light, easily worked, and fairly well suited for nestbox construction. It will warp and crack over time. Rough-cut pine is rough on both sides, usually 1 inch (2.5 cm) thick, and makes quite serviceable nestboxes. Planed 1-inch pine lumber is actually only ¾ inch (1.9 cm) thick. Pine is abundant and inexpensive in comparison to cedar. Grade 2 pine has knots and may be fine for this purpose. A well-constructed, unpainted nestbox made of pine will last 10 years in most climates.

Fir. Fir is probably the best alternative to cedar for nestbox construction. It weathers better than pine, but is as easily worked as that wood. It may be less available than pine, however, and somewhat more costly.

Exterior Plywood. Although some books offer nestbox plans that call for ⅝-inch (1.6 cm) thick exterior-grade plywood, we do not recommend it for nestbox construction because it is treated with the carcinogen formaldehyde. Using exterior plywood for box roofs only may be fine; it resists warping and cracking, and the birds do not generally come into contact with it.

Pressure-Treated Lumber. Pressure-treated wood has a greenish hue because it is impregnated with chromated copper-arsenate, a highly toxic substance. Treated 4 × 4 inch (10.2 cm × 10.2 cm) posts are a viable alternative to cedar, but under no circumstances should they be used to construct the nestbox itself. Nor should treated wood posts be used for in-water installation. Take precautions when working with pressure-treated lumber. *Note:* New long-lasting alternatives to pressure-treated lumber include wood-plastic composites and wood treated with alkaline copper quat (ACQ).

Redwood. Although resistant to rot, most redwood lumber is prone to splitting and cracking, and therefore not well suited for nestbox construction. It is fine for use as support posts. Redwood is also expensive.

Cypress. Cypress, like redwood, is rot resistant but not terribly well suited for nestbox construction because it is difficult to nail. It is also expensive and usually less available than cedar. Like redwood, it may be used for supporting posts.

Actual Sizes of Finished Lumber

Given Size (English)	Actual Size (English)	Given Size (Metric)	Actual Size (Metric)
1" × 4"	¾" × 3½"	2.5 cm × 10.2 cm	1.9 cm × 8.9 cm
1" × 6"	¾" × 5½"	2.5 cm × 15.2 cm	1.9 cm × 14 cm
1" × 8"	¾" × 7½"	2.5 cm × 20.3 cm	1.9 cm × 19.1 cm
1" × 10"	¾" × 9¼"	2.5 cm × 25.4 cm	1.9 cm × 23.5 cm
1" × 12"	¾" × 11¼"	2.5 cm × 30.5 cm	1.9 cm × 28.5 cm
2" × 4"	1½" × 3½"	5.1 cm × 10.2 cm	3.8 cm × 8.9 cm
4" × 4"	3½" × 3½"	10.2 cm × 10.2 cm	8.9 cm × 8.9 cm

Note: Most lumber can be obtained in lengths of 8' (2.4 m), 10' (3.1 m), and 12' (3.7 m); 4 × 4 posts can usually be purchased in 8' (2.4 m), 10' (31. m), and 16' (4.9 m) lengths.

Choosing Nails

Most nails are measured in ½-inch (1.3 cm) increments and designated in "penny sizes." Twopenny (2d) nails are 1 inch (2.5 cm) long, fourpenny (4d) nails are 1½ inch (3.8 cm) long, sixpenny (6d) nails are 2 inches (5.1 cm) long, and eightpenny (8d) nails are 2½ inches (6.4 cm) long.

In general, you should use nails that are at least twice as long as the thickness of wood that you choose. For example, use a 2-inch-long (6d) nail for 1-inch-thick lumber. Be sure, of course, that nails do not protrude into the box cavity.

Choose galvanized nails or electrogalvanized nails for nestbox construction. Galvanized nails are tumbled in molten zinc to produce a uniform coating that resists weathering; electrogalvanized nails are coated with a thin film of zinc that leaves them less corrosion resistant than those covered with molten zinc.

In cold climates, where temperatures regularly fall well below freezing, it is better to use ring-shank nails, which are ribbed, than smooth ones; over time, smooth nails will work loose. Small-head finishing nails are used as pivots in designs that feature swing-out doors.

Choosing Screws

Diameters of wood screws are designated by numbers such as #6 or #8; the larger the number, the greater the diameter. Their lengths are indicated in inches (cm). A typical screw, then, might be a #6 × 1½ inches (3.8 cm).

Screws are manufactured with flat, round, and pan heads. Pan-head screws have rounded, slightly flatter tops than round-heads. Flat-head screws should be countersunk (drill a shallow depression to hold the head so that it is flush with the wood surface) for a better, more attractive fit.

Screws also are either standard-head or Phillips-head; this refers to the type of screwdriver you need to drive them. Phillips-head screws provide a better grip for the screwdriver and are usually less apt to be removed by vandals, who rarely carry Phillips-head screwdrivers.

Brass wood screws do not corrode; galvanized wood screws retard corrosion. Brass screws will tarnish and stain raw wood, but that is of no concern in nestbox construction. Galvanized screws are less expensive. You should use washers to prevent the screw head from gouging the wood in situations that require frequent loosening and tightening.

Drywall screws are fine for nestbox construction. They do not corrode and come in several lengths, including 1¼ inches (3.2 cm), 1⅝ inches (4.1 cm), and 3 inches (7.6 cm). The 1⅝-inch length is fine for use with ¾-inch (1.9 cm) thick (planed) lumber. For rough-cut lumber, which is 1 inch (2.5 cm) thick, it is best to use longer screws or ring-shank nails.

You can use chrome-plated right-angle screws (hooks) as a convenient means of holding cleanout doors (sides) in place.

Choosing Lag Screws and Bolts

Use 2½- to 4½-inch (6.4–11.4 cm) long lag screws, depending upon the size and weight of the nestbox, to attach it to wooden supporting posts and trees. Use lag bolts and nuts to attach boxes to metal or PVC (polyvinyl chloride) plastic pipes. For Wood Duck and Hooded Merganser boxes, for instance, use ⁵⁄₁₆ × 4½ inch (.8 × 11.4 cm) lag bolts. Bolts and screws should be fitted with metal washers to protect the wood.

Safety Tips

- Always wear safety goggles when sawing, drilling, chiseling, or driving nails.
- Wear a dust mask over your face when using power saws or sanders.
- Use care when driving nails, and hammer away from your body.
- Use ear protection when operating noisy power tools.
- Wear gloves when handling rough-cut and pressure-treated lumber to avoid picking up splinters.
- Make sure that your saws are sharp: Dull blades are less efficient and more dangerous.
- Keep your fingers away from the blade of a table saw by using a push stick to guide the wood.
- Make sure that you have proper ventilation when working with paints, stains, and glues.
- Be careful with ladders: Plant them on firm ground, and do not stand above the recommended height indicated on the ladder.
- Be mindful of utility lines, tree limbs, and other obstructions when using long ladders to mount nestboxes.
- Make sure copper sulfate (used in treating Purple Martin gourds) is stored out of reach of children and pets. Dispose of spent chemicals properly.

Bluebird/Swallow Nestbox

No other species (with the possible exception of the Purple Martin) has been studied so extensively with regard to nestbox design as the Eastern Bluebird. Several basic wooden box designs as well as many variations on the basic plans have been developed. Indeed, new variations appear in the literature on a regular basis. The design here is patterned on the standard or Zeleny plan, although some bluebirders, especially in certain parts of the continent, prefer the Peterson or slant-box. (See pages 135–137 for a discussion of this alternative design and its advantages and disadvantages). Another design, the open-top box, was found to increase bluebird productivity in Wisconsin. Its top has a 3⅛-inch (8 cm) diameter hole covered with wire mesh.

This standard bluebird/swallow box features a combined top- and side-opening design. Top opening permits less obtrusive monitoring, while side-opening capability allows for easy cleaning.

Materials

- ⅞" x 10" x 50" (2.2 cm x 25.4 cm x 1.27 m) rough-cut (unplaned) cedar. Or, use 1" (2.5 cm) rough-cut pine lumber. Roofs should be cut from cedar rather than other woods to prevent cracking.
- ½" x 6" (1.3 cm x 15.2 cm) maple dowel (optional)
- Sixteen 6d (2", or 5.1 cm) long galvanized ring-shank siding nails
- Three 2d (1", or 2.5 cm) galvanized finishing nails, or wood screws to attach dowel (optional)

- Two galvanized #6 x 1½" (3.8 cm) pan-head screws and washers
- Eyelet screw (optional)
- If using planed lumber, 2" x 4" (5.1 cm x 10.2 cm) piece of ¼" (.625 cm) galvanized wire mesh hardware cloth. Attach inside of front, and turn down sharp edges, to aid fledging. Or, route or score inside front to provide a grip.
- Heavy-duty staples or ¾" (1.9 cm) 18-gauge wire brads to attach hardware cloth

NOTE: *For nestboxes with a 5" x 5" (12.7 cm x 12.7 cm) floor, use ⅞" x 12" x 51" (2.2 cm x 30.5 cm x 1.3 m) or ⅞" x 10" x 60" (2.2 cm x 25.4 cm x 1.5 m) lumber.*

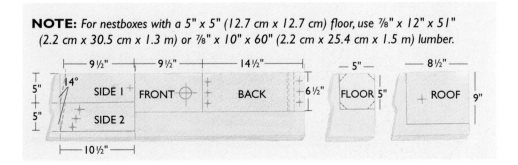

Tools

- Table saw, saber saw, jigsaw (bevel cuts are required), or carpenter's handsaw and miter box
- Power or hand drill
- 1½" (3.8 cm) diameter keyhole saw or expansion bit
- ³⁄₁₆" (.469 cm) and ¼" (.625 cm) drill bits
- Standard or Phillips-head screwdriver, or power drill fitted with screwdriver bits
- Claw hammer
- Tape measure or yard (meter) stick
- Carpenter's square
- Pencil
- Staple gun (optional)
- Sandpaper (optional)
- Light-colored exterior latex house paint (optional)
- Paintbrush (optional)

Cutting and Preparation Notes

Be sure to allow for the width of the saw blade when measuring. The wood grain should run longitudinally to minimize warping and cracking. You may want to sand the exterior surfaces of rough-cut lumber to touch. Drill a centered 1½" (3.8 cm) diameter hole, with its upper edge situated 1" (2.5 cm) below the top of the front.

Eastern Bluebirds will readily use wooden nestboxes with either a 4" (10.2 cm) or a 5" (12.7 cm) square floor. Mountain Bluebirds and swallows tend to have larger clutches, so a 5" (12.7 cm) square floor is recommended for them. For Eastern Bluebirds and swallows, the diameter of the entrance hole must not exceed 1½" (3.8 cm); the bottom of the entrance hole must be located at least 6" (15.2 cm) above the floor. For Western and Mountain species, the entrance hole should be 1⁹⁄₁₆" (3.9 cm) in diameter.

Cutting Diagram

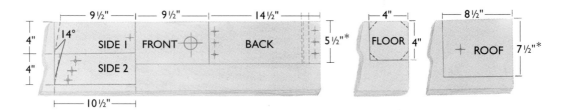

*Measurements for ¾" thick lumber. If using 1" thick lumber, width of front and back must be 6"; width of roof must be 8".

1. Cut ⅝" (1.6 cm) off each corner of the floor to create drainage holes. Nail the *floor* to the *back*, recessing it ¼" (.6 cm) from the bottom to create a drip edge.

2. Screw or nail *side 1* to the joined back and floor, leaving a ¼" (.6 cm) wide gap at the top for ventilation.

3. Screw or nail the *front* to the joined *floor* and *side*, again being sure to leave a ¼" (.6 cm) recess at the bottom.

4. Attach *side 2* (clean-out door) only at the top, using two 4d galvanized finishing nails to create a pivot. *Important:* The pivot nails must be exactly opposite each other for proper opening. Using predrilled holes will help you properly locate these. Be sure to leave the necessary ventilation gap on this side as well. Add a centered galvanized #6 × 1½" (3.8 cm) pan-head screw and washer near the bottom of this side to line up with the recessed floor in order to secure the side in place. Alternatively, use a right-angle screw.

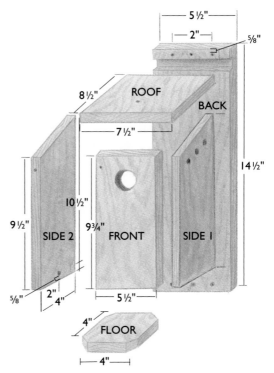

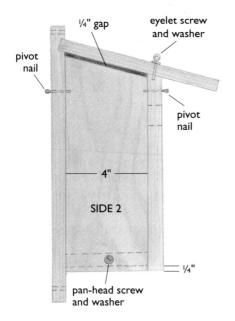

5. Fit the *roof* into the angled slot cut in the *back* and hold it there by placing a single centered #6 pan-head screw and washer through the top into the top edge of the front. You can also use an eyelet screw and washer; this eliminates the need for a screwdriver each time you open the box.

NOTE: *If you have not cut a 14-degree angled slot into the back of the box near the top for the insertion of the angle-cut roof, you must nail or screw an additional 5½" x ½" (14 cm x 1.3 cm) maple dowel to the back above the roof to act as a support. Drill three ³⁄₁₆" (.5 cm) holes spaced 1" (2.5 cm) apart in a horizontal row across the top of the backboard prior to mounting with either wire, screws, or nails. The hole diameters, of course, depend upon your mounting method.*

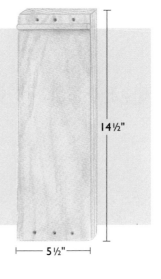

Painting/Staining

Boxes need not be painted, but if you decide to do so, be sure to paint only the outside surfaces of the box. Also, do not use paints or stains that contain lead or toxic wood preservatives. Exterior latex house paint is fine. Use only light colors so that the boxes do not heat up unnecessarily when exposed to bright sunlight.

Location

For bluebirds, place boxes in semi-open country with scattered trees. Keep them away from forest edges and shrubby growth (at least 120 feet, or 37 m, if possible) where House Wrens may be a competitor. A minimum of 2 acres (.8 ha) of suitable habitat is usually required per nesting pair. Mounting paired boxes 15 to 25 feet (4.6–7.6 m) apart can alleviate competition between swallows and bluebirds. Bluebirds generally require short-grass areas for finding insect prey. Paired (or single boxes where swallow competition is not an issue) should be spaced no closer together than 300 feet (91.5 m). Avoid areas where House Sparrows are common.

Tree and Violet-green Swallows prefer to nest and forage in open areas near water.

Mounting

Boxes may be mounted in a number of different ways, depending on the type of support you have available. Boxes can be nailed, bolted, screwed, or wired to fence posts, iron pipes, electrical conduit (fitted with steel reinforcing rod), wooden posts, or dead trees with sound wood. A pipe flange attached to the bottom of the box allows attachment of ¾-inch (1.9 cm) or 1-inch (2.5 cm) galvanized pipe. Plumber's hanger iron (perforated galvanized steel), pipe clamps, or wire can also be used to attach boxes to posts or pipes. Using screws or bolts rather than nails allows for easier removal of the box for repairs or relocation (see pages 161–164 for mounting options).

Boxes should be placed between 4½ and 5½ feet (1.4–1.7 m) above the ground to facilitate monitoring. Boxes placed less than 4 feet (1.2 m) above the ground may be more vulnerable to predation. On fence posts along active pastures, mount the box on the outside of the post, away from livestock: Cattle and horses have been known to use nest-boxes as scratching posts. In general, face boxes toward open country, away from roads, and in directions that aid monitoring.

Western Bluebirds have successfully used hanging boxes in California and Oregon. A specially designed pole has been developed to lift the boxes onto their support hooks (see Hanging Nestboxes on page 164).

In most areas, the use of a predator guard is crucial. For information about the fabrication and installation of predator guards, see pages 164–167.

Peterson Nestbox
for Bluebirds

This unique design was developed by Dick Peterson as an alternative to the conventional rectangular bluebird nestbox. Not only does it employ a totally different triangular shape, but it also has a unique 1⅜ × 2¼ inch (3.5 cm × 5.7 cm) oblong entrance hole. It has been so successful that it has virtually supplanted the more traditional design in the north-central United States.

Among the advantages of the Peterson box are easy feeding and nest sanitation by the adult birds due to the oblong entrance, easier monitoring and cleaning by humans, a roof that is steeply angled so that climbing predators have a difficult time standing on it, and an angled front panel that makes it more difficult for predators to hang on (and conversely easier for the nestlings to fledge). The front panel is also easily removed and replaced.

On the downside, this design readily admits starlings. But because these boxes are relatively shallow and have a small floor, starlings tend not to nest in them.

This box is more difficult to construct than more conventional designs. Power tools are not absolutely necessary, but make the job considerably easier and produce better results.

Materials

- ¾" x 12" x 27½" (1.9 cm x 30.5 cm x 70 cm) planed cedar or pine (Alternatively, you can use hardboard lap siding. If you are building the rest of the box from pine, make the roof from cedar.)
- ⅞" x 3½" x 12½" (2.2 cm x 8.9 cm x 31.8 cm) unplaned cedar for the front
- One standard 2" x 4" board (this is actually 1½" x 3½", or 3.8 cm x 8.9 cm) that is 36" (86.4 cm) long
- Sixteen 1⅝" (4.1 cm) drywall screws or 2" (5.1 cm) ring-shank wood siding nails
- Two 4d (1½", or 3.8 cm) galvanized finishing nails
- One right-angle screw

Tools

- Table saw, saber saw, jigsaw (seven bevel cuts are required), or carpenter's saw and miter box
- Power or hand drill (a drill press is best for cutting the oblong entrance hole)
- ⅛" (.313 cm) and ¾" (1.875 cm) drill bits
- 1⅜" (3.5 cm) diameter keyhole saw, expansion bit, or Forstner bit
- Rasp or wood chisel
- Claw hammer (if using nails)
- Phillips-head screwdriver or power drill fitted with screwdriver bit
- Tape measure or yard (meter) stick
- Pencil
- Sandpaper (optional)
- Light-colored exterior latex house paint (optional)
- Paintbrush (optional)

Cutting and Preparation Notes

Be sure to allow for the width of the saw blade when measuring. The wood grain should run longitudinally to minimize warping and cracking. The inside surface of the front should be rough to help the young birds get a grip when fledging.

Create the entrance hole by drilling two overlapping 1⅜" (3.5 cm) diameter holes, then chiseling or rasping out the protruding sections in order to form a uniformly oblong hole 2¼" (5.7 cm) long (see the cutting diagram; with a Forstner bit you can bore an oblong hole). The top of the entrance hole should be located 1" (2.5 cm) below the top of the front panel. The top end of the front must be cut at a 45-degree angle. Both ends of the roof are bevel-cut at 65 degrees. Drill two ¾" (1.9 cm) diameter ventilation holes near top of each side. The inner roof must be cut at 45 degrees at one end, 65 degrees at the other. The floor must be cut at 65 degrees at one end; bevel the top of the backboard at 65 degrees also.

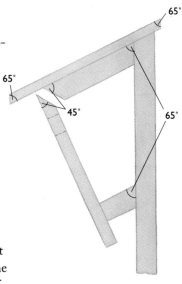

NOTE: *Cedar may split, so you should predrill nail holes.*

Cutting Diagram

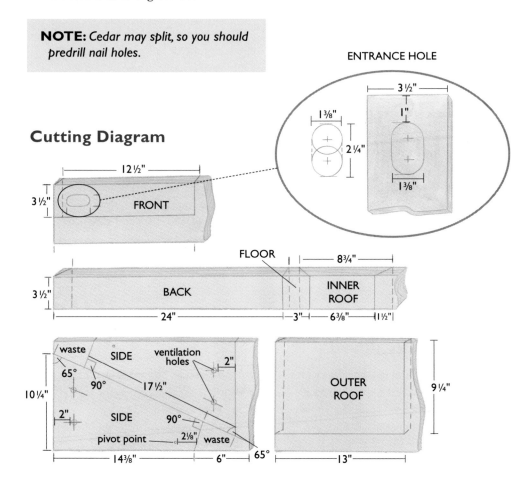

ENTRANCE HOLE

136 Nestbox Designs

Assembly

1. Screw or nail the *inner roof* to the *back*. Make sure they fit flush.

2. Screw or nail the angled edge of the *floor* to the *back*, 10½" below the inner roof's top edge.

3. Attach one *side* to the frame, being sure that all edges fit flush.

4. Now screw or nail the other *side*.

5. Next, attach the *front*, which is hinged at the bottom, with two 4d galvanized finishing nails; predrill guide holes. *Important:* The pivot nails must be exactly opposite each other for proper opening. Insert the right-angle screw in a predrilled hole through the side of the box to secure the front (see the diagram).

6. Finally, screw or nail on the *outer roof.*

Painting/Staining

Cedar does not require painting; applying two coats of a light-colored exterior latex house paint will prolong its life, however.

Location

See pages 19–20 for information about where and how high to place your bluebird box(es).

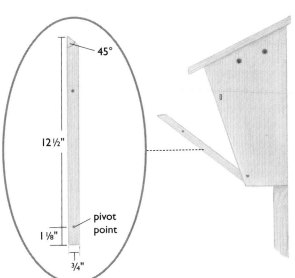

Mounting

The 2 × 4 inch (actually 1½" × 3½") board that forms the back of the box can be attached directly to a wooden pole or fence post with 3-inch (7.6 cm) lag screws, or attached to a metal pipe with two or three pipe clamps (see pages 161–164 for mounting methods).

Be sure to install a predator guard of some type to the support (see pages 164–167 for information).

Purple Martin House

This design is different from the traditional martin apartment house in that it joins four separate double-decker units into one structure, creating an eight-unit box. It was developed by Kip Sorlie and Richard Schinkel.

It incorporates a feature that may be advantageous to martins: entrance holes located 2 inches (5.1 cm) above the floor. Nestlings may be less likely to fledge prematurely, and a higher entrance hole also eliminates egg loss due to eggs being inadvertently brushed out by exiting adults. Compared to more traditional designs, this house plan is rather straightforward and easy to construct.

Materials

- ¾" x 10" x 14' (1.9 cm x 25.4 cm x 4.3 m) cedar (planed)
- ¾" x 6" x 10' (1.9 cm x 15.2 cm x 3.1 m) cedar (planed)
- 112 (½ lb., or 227 g) 6d (2", or 5.1 cm) galvanized ring-shank wood siding nails, or 1⅝" (4.1 cm) drywall screws
- Eight 4d (1 ½", or 3.8 cm) galvanized finishing nails
- Four right-angle screws
- White exterior latex house paint

Tools

- Table saw, saber saw, jigsaw (12-degree bevel cuts are required), or carpenter's saw and miter box
- 2" (5.1 cm) diameter keyhole saw or expansion bit
- ⅜" (.95 cm) drill bit
- ⅛" (.3125) drill bit
- Power or hand drill (brace)
- Claw hammer
- Standard screwdriver
- Phillips-head screwdriver (if using drywall screws)
- Tape measure or yard (meter) stick
- Carpenter's square
- Pencil
- Resorcinol wood glue
- Paintbrush
- Sandpaper (optional)

Cutting and Preparation Notes

Be sure to allow for the width of the saw blade when measuring. The grain of your board lumber should run lengthwise to prevent warping and cracking. *Note:* The cutting diagram shown is for one double-decker unit. Cut four of each piece to construct the 8-unit house.

Cut ⅝" (1.6 cm) off the corners of each floor to create drainage holes. The four clean-out doors (sides) must be cut ¼" (.6 cm) shorter at the top to create easy pivot and for ventilation. Make 12-degree bevel cuts on the top and bottom edges of the fronts, the back edges of the roofs, and both top and bottom edges of the backs.

Drill two 2" (5.1 cm) diameter entrance holes in each of the four front boards. Drill three ⅜" (.95 cm) ventilation holes into each of the four sides in a horizontal row 1½" (3.8 cm) below the midpoint of the board (see the diagram); use a carpenter's square to locate the midline on each side.

NOTE: *Cedar may split, so you should predrill nail holes. A weather-tight box is very important for martins; therefore, you should run a bead of resorcinol wood glue along the edges of lumber to be joined, in addition to nailing or screwing pieces together. Do not use yellow wood glues, which are not waterproof.*

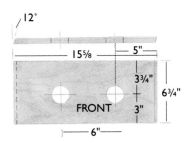

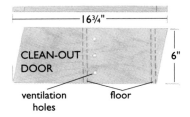

Cutting Diagram

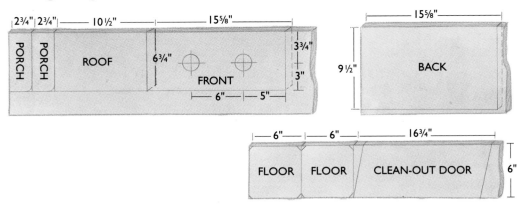

Assembly

1. Nail or screw the four *back* pieces together at right angles as shown in the diagram (top view); the 2" (5.1 cm) square space created in the center will be used to mount the house.

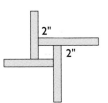

2. Nail or screw the eight *floor* pieces at their appropriate positions to the four *back* pieces already joined. Measuring down from the top of the back, place tops of floors at 8" (20.3 cm) and 14" (35.6 cm).

3. Set the *clean-out door* in place, flush with the bottom edge of the back. Now place the *front* piece flush with the bottom edge of the *clean-out door*. With a pencil, mark the location where the two *floors* will attach to the *front*. Do this for each of the four units. Do not attach any of these yet.

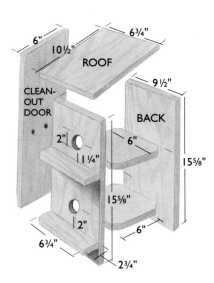

4. From the inside of the front, nail or screw two *porch* pieces to each front, so the top of each is ¾" (1.9 cm) above the point where the *floor* pieces will join.

5. Now attach the four *fronts* to their respective *floors*.

6. Next, return the *clean-out door* to its correct position, flush with the bottom edges of the *back* and *front*. Make sure that the door is ¼" (.6 cm) shorter at the top; this will enable it to pivot out easily and also will create a ventilation space.

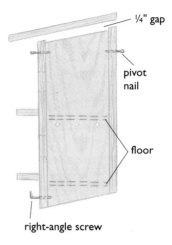

¼" gap

pivot nail

floor

right-angle screw

7. With the carpenter's square, mark the locations of the two galvanized finishing nails that will act as pivots (see the diagram). Drill guide holes and install two 4d (1½", 3.8 cm) nails in each unit. Note that these must be exactly opposite each other. Repeat for other three units.

8. Drill a third guide hole near the edge of each *front* at the bottom, on the *clean-out door* side (see the diagram); insert right-angle screws. These will hold the clean-out doors in place.

9. Finally, nail or screw the *roof* to the *back* and *front* boards. Repeat with the other three units to complete the house.

Painting/Staining

To decrease the nestbox's interior temperature, the exterior must be painted white or another light shade. Use several coats of exterior latex house paint.

Location

Purple Martins prefer open country near water. In some areas, houses or gourds are mounted on poles directly over the water, with great success. Open space around nest sites is important; locate any house or group of gourds a minimum of 30 feet (9.2 m) from buildings or tree limbs. Martins do require a good selection of perches on or near the nest site.

Mounting

Houses should be erected on sturdy posts or pipes, and gourds should be suspended from wire hooks and hung in groups. The house plan included here is designed to be mounted on a pipe or telescoping pole. Be sure to put a cap on the top of the pipe. (See page 163 for information on constructing a telescoping pole.) If you choose not to use a telescoping pole, a tall ladder will be required for monitoring. Ideally, houses should be capable of being raised by means of a winch (telescoping pole) system.

Install houses or gourds 12 to 20 feet (3.7–6.1 m) above the ground. On land, martins generally will not nest in houses less than 8 or 9 feet (2.4–2.7 m) high. Be sure to safeguard the house with a predator guard (see pages 164–167 for options).

For information about obtaining, preparing, and hanging calabash gourds for martins, see pages 141–142. It is important to remove the house and/or gourds at the end of the nesting season. This will lessen the effects of the elements on them, and allow you to thoroughly clean and refurbish them as necessary.

Gourds as Nest Cavities for Purple Martins

Large calabash gourds have been used as Purple Martin nest cavities, especially in the southern United States, with good results. You can purchase them or even grow them yourself, if the growing season in your area is sufficiently long (see the appendix for suppliers of gourds and seeds). In the latter case, do not pick gourds until the vine is dead. Gourds must be turned frequently during the three to four weeks they require for drying.

The advantages of using gourds are that they offer martins deep cavities and larger compartment sizes than nearly all aluminum or wooden apartment houses. They may give martins greater protection from predators, and can also be less costly. Gourds may be hung in conjunction with and even from martin houses, or situated by themselves in groups. One disadvantage is that they lack porches for the emerging young to use.

Materials
- Gourds 8"–10" (20.3–25.4 cm) in diameter; start with at least 4 or 8
- 1 ½ lbs. (680 g) copper sulfate (toxic; use caution)
- White oil-based primer
- White enamel paint
- 1' (30.5 cm) rigid wire (or coat hanger wire) per gourd
- Textured aluminum or flexible plastic: one 6" x 2 ½" (15.2 cm x 6.4 cm) sheet for each gourd, to serve as a canopy over the entrance hole (optional)
- Silicone caulking, white (optional)

Tools
- Wire brush
- Sandpaper
- 2" (5.1 cm) diameter keyhole saw or expansion bit
- Serrated knife
- Power or hand drill
- ¼" (.625 cm) and ⅜" (.938 cm) drill bits
- Compass, to draw 2" (5.1 cm) diameter circle
- Pencil
- Wire cutters
- Tin snips, for cutting canopies (optional)
- Container(s) for soaking gourds
- Paintbrush
- Paint thinner
- Rubber gloves, for soaking gourds

NOTE: *Preparing raw gourds for use by martins is a laborious and time-consuming process that is not necessarily easier than constructing your own martin house.*

Preparation and Assembly

1. Clean the outside of each gourd with a wire brush and sandpaper.

2. Cut a 2" (5.1 cm) diameter entrance hole in each gourd with the keyhole saw or expansion bit. Be sure to locate the hole in the approximate center of the gourd. A colleague of ours takes his gourds to a dentist, who volunteers his time and equipment to neatly cut the entrance holes.

3. Through the new entrance hole, use a serrated knife to break up the hard mass of pith and seeds inside; thoroughly remove this material.

4. Drill ¼" (.6 cm) diameter holes through both sides of the "handle" end of the gourd to permit insertion of wire for hanging. Drill five ⅜" (1 cm) holes in the gourd's bottom for drainage.

5. Wearing rubber gloves, dissolve the copper sulfate in 7½ gallons (28.4 L) of water. Soak the gourds in the copper solution for 15 minutes, in order to protect them from mold and rot by fungus. Allow them to dry.

6. You may wish to add a metal or plastic canopy above each gourd's entrance hole; cut these to size (see the diagram) and attach with silicone caulking. Let dry.

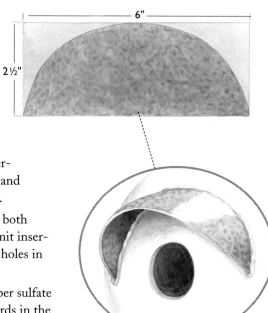

Painting/Staining

Paint the outside surfaces of your gourds with one coat of white oil-based primer and three coats of white enamel paint. This is especially important in hot climates.

Location

Mount these gourds in the same areas as martin houses; open fields, nearby water, and an adequate number of perches are desirable. Make sure the gourds are at least 30 feet (9.2 m) from buildings or tree limbs. Gourds may also be hung directly over water.

Mounting

Suspend gourds from wires attached to eye bolts secured near the top of two or more wooden posts or metal poles, or hang them from special gourd racks attached to single poles or pipes. As with martin houses, a telescoping pole is usually necessary to permit convenient monitoring (see page 163). Be sure to add an appropriate predator guard to the support post or pipe (see pages 164–167 for options).

Wren/Chickadee Nestbox

The wren/chickadee box plan is almost identical to that for the Eastern Bluebird — a dual side- and top-opening box with a 4 × 4 inch (10.2 cm × 10.2 cm) floor (see page 131 for the box plan). The one exception is the size of the entrance hole. To make this box suitable for only the three species of wrens and two species of chickadees included in this book, and at the same time exclude the House Sparrow (which requires a 1¼-inch, or 3.2 cm, diameter hole) — drill the following entrance hole sizes:

• **Carolina Wren.** The largest of our cavity-nesting wrens requires at least a 1⅛-inch (2.9 cm) diameter entrance hole.
• **Bewick's Wren.** This intermediate-size wren can enter an entrance hole of 1 inch (2.5 cm) or larger.
• **House Wren.** The most common of the three nestbox-using wrens and the smallest, this species finds a 1-inch (2.5 cm) diameter hole large enough.
• **Black-capped Chickadee.** One of the most familiar birds in wooded portions of North America, this chickadee requires a 1⅛-inch (2.9 cm) diameter entrance hole.
• **Carolina Chickadee.** This southeastern counterpart of the Black-capped is slightly smaller, but also uses a 1⅛-inch (2.9 cm) diameter entrance hole.

Of course, all three wrens and both chickadees are accommodated by a 1⅛-inch (2.9 cm) or larger diameter entrance. In general, however, size the entrance hole as small as possible in order to exclude birds other than your target species. If the House Sparrow is not a problem, you may want to consider a larger entrance hole, because male House Wrens especially seem to have an easier time bringing sticks into a box with a larger opening.

Location

Other than the sizing of the entrance hole, siting the nestbox in appropriate wren or chickadee habitat is the other important factor that determines the species your box will attract. Wrens are birds of thickets and woodland edges; thus, you should locate wren boxes in semi-open habitats near cover such as shrubbery and trees. Their habitat requirements are somewhat intermediate between bluebirds, which prefer more open sites, and chickadees, which will nest in both woodland and edge situations. Place boxes meant for chickadees adjacent to woodland edges, as well as in woodland clearings, where they will receive sunlight 40 to 60 percent of the day.

Mounting

Mount these boxes as you would a bluebird nestbox, and from 4½ to 10 feet (1.4–3.1 m) above the ground. Be sure to attach a sheet metal cone, stovepipe, PVC plastic, or other baffle to the support pipe, post, or tree (for more about predator guards, see pages 164–167).

House Wrens will readily nest in hanging boxes as well. Place 1 inch (2.5 cm) of wood chips or shavings into any chickadee box.

Titmouse/Nuthatch Nestbox

The titmouse/nuthatch box plan is nearly identical to that for the Eastern Bluebird; again, you will make a dual side- and slant-top–opening box with a 4 × 4 inch (10.2 cm × 10.2 cm) floor (see page 131 for the box plan). The one exception is the diameter of the entrance hole. To tailor this box for the titmice and nuthatch included in this book, drill a 1¼-inch (3.2 cm) diameter entrance hole in the front. Note that this is also large enough to admit House Sparrows.

Location

Siting the nestbox in appropriate habitat is, of course, as important as the correct sizing of the entrance hole. Titmice and nuthatches are essentially woodland and woodland edge birds.

• **Tufted Titmouse.** These birds inhabit mostly deciduous and mixed deciduous-evergreen woodlands with a large variety of tree species that create a dense canopy. In eastern and southern Texas, they also occur in riparian and mesquite habitats. Situate the box in an area with a variety of trees as well as open space. Place the box 5 to 15 feet (1.5–4.6 m) up on a tree or post, and in semishade.

• **Bridled Titmouse.** These birds are essentially mountain dwellers that prefer oak and oak-pine woodlands, but they will also use streamside groves for nesting. Mount the nestbox 6 to 15 feet (1.8–4.6 m) above the ground in a tree.

• **Oak Titmouse.** Favors Live Oaks, but also uses various types of deciduous woodland. Locate the box in an area with a variety of tree species and adjacent open areas. Mount the box on a tree or post 5 to 10 feet (1.5–3.1 m) above the ground.

• **Juniper Titmouse.** Prefers mixed piñon pine-juniper-oak woodlands. Situate the box in an area with a variety of trees and open spaces nearby. Mount the box on a tree or post 5 to 10 feet (1.5–3.1 m) up.

• **White-breasted Nuthatch.** Mature deciduous and mixed deciduous-evergreen forests are this bird's haunt, although it prefers to nest along forest edges. An area that also contains fields, water, and orchards is often favored. Locate the box in a mature forest near a cleared area, 12 to 20 feet (3.7–6.1 m) above the ground.

Mounting

Place boxes on trees for the White-breasted Nuthatch and Bridled Titmouse, and on trees or posts for the other titmice species. Be sure to use baffles: Wrap 30-inch (76 cm) wide pieces of sheet metal around tree trunks, or wrap sheet metal cone, stovepipe, or PVC plastic baffles around poles to prevent climbing predators from raiding the nest (see pages 164–167 for more about predator guards).

NOTE: For Tufted, Oak, and Juniper Titmice, place hair, fur, feathers, or thread no more than 3 or 4 inches (7.6–10.2 cm) long near the box as nesting material.

Northern Flicker/Red-bellied Woodpecker Nestbox

Suitable for the Northern Flicker or the smaller Red-bellied Woodpecker, this design is essentially a larger and deeper version of the standard, slant-top, side-opening bluebird nestbox. It can be attached directly to a tree or post, but must be packed with wood shavings and/or sawdust to entice woodpeckers to use it.

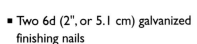

Materials

- ⅞" x 9" x 10' (2.2 cm x 22.9 cm x 3.1 m) rough-cut (unplaned) cedar. Rough-cut or planed pine may be substituted, but has shorter life span.
- ½" x 9" (1.3 cm x 22.9 cm) maple dowel (optional)
- Twenty 1⅝" (4.1 cm) drywall screws or 2" (5.1 cm) galvanized ring-shank wood siding nails. If using thicker rough-cut lumber, use 2" ring-shank siding nails.
- Two 6d (2", or 5.1 cm) galvanized finishing nails
- Four 2d (1", or 2.5 cm) galvanized finishing nails (optional)
- One right-angle screw
- Heavy-duty staples, or ¾" (1.9 cm) 18-gauge wire brads (optional)

> **NOTE:** *If finished (planed) lumber is used, staple or nail a 3" x 16" (7.6 cm x (40.6 cm) piece of ¼" (.625 cm) galvanized wire mesh (hardware cloth) to the inside of the front, below the entrance hole; be sure to bend the sharp edges under. Alternatively, the inside front can be routed or scored with a sharp tool such as an awl or rasp to provide nestlings with a grip.*

Tools

- Table saw, saber saw, jigsaw (two bevel cuts are required), or carpenter's hand-saw and miter box
- 2½" (6.4 cm) diameter keyhole saw (2", or 5.1 cm, diameter for Red-bellied Woodpecker) router, or expansion bit to cut entrance hole
- Power or hand drill
- ⅛" (.313 cm), ¼" (.625 cm), and ⅜" (.938 cm) drill bits
- Claw hammer
- Phillips-head screwdriver or power drill fitted with screwdriver bits
- Tape measure or yard (meter) stick
- Carpenter's square
- Pencil
- Awl or rasp (optional)

Cutting and Preparation Notes

Be sure to allow for the width of the saw blade when measuring. The grain of the lumber should run longitudinally to prevent warping and cracking. Cedar resists warping, and you may want to use it for the roof if you are building your box of pine. Do not sand either the exterior or the interior of the box, nor paint it. The more the box mimics a natural cavity, the more likely a woodpecker pair is to nest in it.

This wooden box has a 7¼-inch (18.4 cm) square floor. The bottom of the entrance hole should be located at least 16 inches (40.6 cm) above the floor. When drilling the 2½-inch (6.4 cm) diameter hole for flickers, or the 2-inch (5.1 cm) hole for Red-bellies, be sure to take into account the width of the floor and the fact that it is recessed ¼ inch (.6 cm) to create a drip edge. Cut ⅝ inch (1.6 cm) off each corner of the floor to create drainage holes; alternatively, drill four ¼-inch (.6 cm) diameter drainage holes into the floor.

Drill three ⅜-inch (1 cm) diameter holes in a line 1½ inches (3.8 cm) apart near the top of the nonpivoting side for ventilation. The back edge of the roof and the top edge of the front will fit better if cut at a 5-degree angle. Alternatively, you may nail a ½" (1.3 cm) diameter maple dowel where the roof and the back meet to prevent rain seepage.

> **NOTE:** *Cedar may split, so predrill nail holes.*

Cutting Diagram

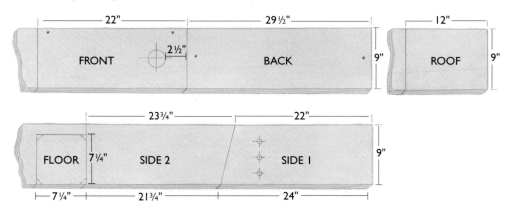

An Alternative Flicker Box

Allen Bower in Michigan has had better success than most in attracting Northern Flickers to his nestboxes. His boxes, which weigh 25 lbs. (11.4 kg), are made of planed 2" x 10" lumber. Box dimensions include a 6¼" x 7¼" (15.8 cm x 18.4 cm) floor; a height of 24" (61 cm); a distance of 18" (45.7 cm) from the entrance hole to the floor; and a vertical-oval entrance hole measuring 3¼" x 2½" (8.2 cm x 6.4 cm). He mounts them 14' (4.3 m) up on a metal post in partial shade. He roughs up the interiors with saw cuts (kerfs), and nails 45-degree pieces of 2" x 4" lumber into the corners to make the cavity rounder. All this to better simulate flicker-excavated cavities.

Assembly

1. Screw or nail the box's longer side *(side 1)* to the *back* of the box. Note that the shorter side *(side 2)* will be hinged at the top with two galvanized finishing nails.

2. Screw or nail the *front* to *side 1*. A finished (smooth) lumber front must be fitted with a galvanized ladder on the inside, or be roughened up with a rasp, for the nestlings.

3. Attach the *floor*, being careful to recess it ¼" (.6 cm).

4. Now attach the shorter *side 2*, using two pivot nails lined up exactly opposite each other (measure first with a carpenter's square). Note that this side is ¼" (.6 cm) shorter, to enable it to pivot properly. When it is not open, this side is secured with a right-angle screw; drill a ⅛" (.3 cm) guide hole for this in the bottom of the *front*.

5. Finally, attach the *roof*, and add the dowel if necessary.

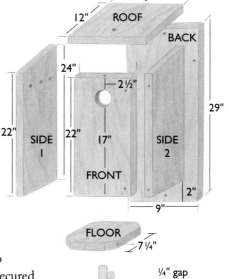

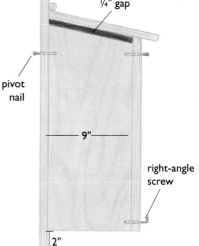

Painting/Staining

Woodpecker nestboxes should not be painted or stained. In fact, adding wood slabs with bark to the outside of the box may make it more attractive to woodpeckers. Be careful that the nails you use to attach the slabs do not penetrate the box's interior.

Location

Place the nestbox in semi-open country and in a generally sunny, easily seen (by the woodpeckers) location. For the Northern Flicker, mount 6 to 20 feet (1.8–6.1 m) high; for the Red-bellied Woodpecker, between 8 and 20 feet (2.4–6.1 m) up.

Mounting

The box may be attached to a dead tree (make sure the wood is sound), a 4 × 4 inch (10.2 cm × 10.2 cm) cedar post, a 1½-inch (3.8 cm) diameter galvanized pipe, or another suitable support. Face the box away from prevailing storms, usually southeasterly. Use two 3-inch (7.6 cm) long lag screws, or bolts with washers centered at the top and bottom ends of the backboard. Predrill holes. Galvanized nails are an alternative, but moving the box will be much more difficult if you decide to do so.

When using a post, bury its end 2 to 3 feet (.6–.9 m) into the ground for stability. Be sure to consider this added length when you purchase materials. See pages 161–164 for more about mounting methods.

It is important to fabricate a predator guard from a 30-inch (76 cm) wide piece of aluminum sheeting and attach it to the support at least 6 feet (1.8 m) above the ground with galvanized or brass screws. For more information about predator guards, see pages 164–167.

Red-bellied Woodpeckers will also use nestboxes that are hung from a flexible wire or chain.

To improve your chances of luring a pair of flickers or red-bellieds to your box, be sure to pack the box tightly from top to bottom with wood chips, shavings, or sawdust (other than cedar).

Wood Duck/Hooded Merganser Nestbox

This is the largest box to use the traditional slant-top design. One variation that distinguishes it from boxes for songbirds is its oval entrance hole. This wooden box may be mounted directly over water on a cedar post, or attached to a tree near the shore of a permanent water body. A predator guard is essential. Three inches (7.6 cm) of wood shavings must be placed in the bottom prior to each nesting season.

The box has a 10 × 10 inch (25.4 cm × 25.4 cm) interior floor dimension. It is 17 inches (43.8 cm) deep from the bottom edge of the entrance hole to the floor.

Materials

- 1" x 12" x 11' (2.5 cm x 30.5 cm x 3.3 m) rough-cut (unplaned) grade 3 cedar. Rough-cut pine can also be used, but has a shorter life span.
- 1" x 2" (2.5 cm x 5.1 cm) piece of lumber, for door stop
- Thirty 1⅝" (4.1 cm) drywall screws or 2" (5.1 cm) galvanized ring-shank wood shingle nails. These anchor or grip wood; smooth nails loosen over time. For thicker, rough-cut lumber use 2" ring-shank nails.

- Galvanized hardware cloth, ¼" (.625 cm) mesh, 4" x 16" (10.2 cm x 40.6 cm). Be sure to bend sharp edges away from inside of box before attaching.
- #5 staples, or ¾" (1.9 cm) 18-gauge wire brads
- 3" (7.6 cm) brass cabinet hinge
- Six brass or galvanized flat-head wood screws for hinge
- One piece of rigid plastic ⅛" x 1" x 2½" (.313 cm x 2.5 cm x 6.4 cm), for latch
- One brass #8 x ¾" (1.9 cm) round-head wood screw, to secure latch

Tools

- Table saw, sabersaw, jig saw (two bevel cuts are required), or carpenter's hand saw and miter box
- 3" (7.6 cm) expansion bit or keyhole saw, to cut entrance hole (you can also use a band saw or router; see the diagram)
- Power or hand drill
- 1" (2.5 cm) diameter keyhole saw or expansion bit

- ⅛" (.313 cm), ¼" (.625 cm), and ⅝" (.938 cm) drill bits
- Claw hammer
- Phillips-head screwdriver, or power drill fitted with screwdriver bit
- Tape measure or yard (meter) stick
- Carpenter's square
- Pencil
- Staple gun
- Rasp or awl

Cutting and Preparation Notes

Be sure to allow for the width of the saw blade when measuring. The grain of the lumber should run longitudinally to prevent warping and cracking. Exterior plywood resists warping, and you may want to use it for the roof if your box is built of pine.

Cut ⅝" (1.6 cm) off each corner of the floor to create drainage holes. Alternatively, drill four or five ¼" (.6 cm) drainage holes in the floor. The back edge of the roof will fit better if beveled at a 5-degree angle.

> **NOTE:** *Cedar may split, so predrill nail holes. Make sure the seams are tight.*

Cutting Diagram

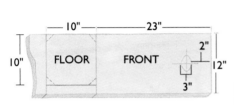

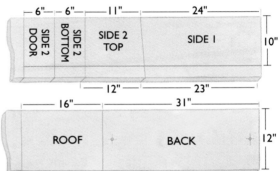

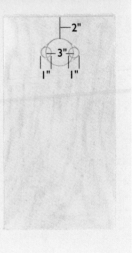

Entrance Hole

The horizontal elliptical entrance hole is 4" x 3" (10.2 cm x 7.6 cm) in size. This is designed to exclude all but the smallest adult raccoons. There is some evidence that Hooded Mergansers favor a 4" x 5" (10.2 cm x 12.7 cm) entrance hole.

To locate the hole, draw a 3" (7.6 cm) diameter circle, centered 3½" (8.9 cm) down from the top of the front. Be sure to do this after the top of the front has been beveled down ⅛" (.3 cm). Now draw two 1" (2.5 cm) diameter circles centered on opposite edges of the 3" (7.6 cm) circle. Cut out these two holes with the keyhole saw or expansion bit. Then cut out the center 3" (7.6 cm) hole with the expansion bit, keyhole saw, or band saw. Use a rasp to smooth off the four edges you have created, until you have a symmetrical ellipse.

Assembly

1. Screw or nail *side 1* (the one without the access door) to the *floor*.

2. Screw or nail *back* to the joined *side* and *floor*. Allow for 3" (7.6 cm) of the backboard to extend beyond the top and bottom of the box (for use in mounting).

3. Make sure that the hardware cloth has already been centered on the inside of *front* and stapled below the entrance hole (use wire brads if you lack a staple gun). Then attach the *front*, making sure that its top is flush with the top of *side 1*. Also, attach the *door stop* 8" (20.3 cm) up from the bottom of the *front* (see diagram). Allow for the thickness of the door.

4. Now nail or screw the the *top of side 2* (largest portion) to the *back* and *front*.

5. Fit the access door for size; do not attach it now, because it will be hinged at one end. Mark the bottom edge on the front and back with a pencil.

6. Screw or nail the *bottom of side 2* to the *front*, *back*, and *floor* of the box, making sure that there is a snug fit, but that the hinged section above it will open and close freely.

7. Attach the *roof*, making sure that the top of the front and the roof are flush. The back edge of the roof and the backboard should also be flush.

8. Finally, attach the *door* by means of the hinge and ¾" (1.9 cm) brass or galvanized screws, then use the latch, held in place by a brass round-head screw, to secure it.

Painting/Staining

Painting is not necessary, but if you do wish to paint your box, do so only on the outside with a light-colored exterior latex house paint.

Location

Mount boxes in shallow, freshwater wetland areas no more than ½ mile (.8 km) from water, preferably closer than ¼ mile (.4 km). Optimum habitat includes nut- and berry-producing hardwood trees and shrubs bordering permanent streams, ponds, swamps, and lakes. Site the box over water, if possible, or 30 to 100 feet (9.2–30.5 m) from shore, rather than immediately along shore, where the

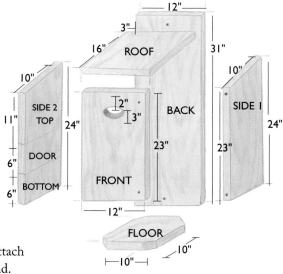

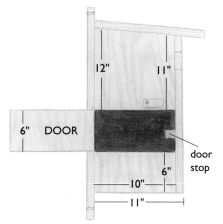

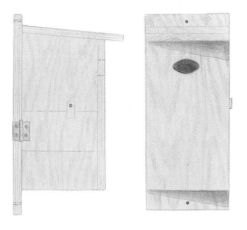

An alternative design that may be useful for direct-mounting on trees, without the use of additional predator guards, consists of constructing a 5¾" x 5½" x 8" (14.6 cm x 14 cm x 20.3 cm) wooden tunnel, which is affixed over the entrance hole with wooden blocks or four L-brackets.

box may be more prone to raccoon predation. The front of the box should be free of foliage or other obstructions. Heights of 12 to 30 feet (3.7–9.2 m) are recommended by some authors, but these can make maintenance very difficult.

The box must be at least 4 feet (1.2 m) above the normal waterline, and at least 2 feet (.6 m) above the high-water (annual flood) line. When mounting on land, it should be at least 5½ feet (1.7 m) above the ground.

Boxes can be spaced as close together as 50 feet (15.3 m).

Mounting

The box may be attached to a dead tree (make sure the wood is sound), or mounted on a 4 × 4 inch (10.2 cm × 10.2 cm) cedar post, or atop a 1½-inch (3.8 cm) diameter galvanized pipe; 4-inch (10.2 cm) diameter PVC plastic pipe may also be used for in-water mounting. Be careful not to mount the box with a backward slant, as this admits rainwater. Mount it level or with a slight downward tilt.

Another mounting option over water is to use two 4 × 4 inch (10.2 cm × 10.2 cm) cedar posts fitted with a horizontal board, upon which the nestbox is carriage-bolted. Both posts must be fitted with cone-type predator guards.

Wooden mounting posts should be 16 feet (4.8 m) long. Use two 4½-inch (11.4 cm) lag screws (top and bottom) with ⁵⁄₁₆-inch (.8 cm) washers; predrill guide holes. Loosen the lag screws slightly each spring if you are mounting on a live tree.

If you are mounting atop a 1½-inch (3.8 cm) galvanized metal post, use a threaded pipe flange to attach the pipe to the box. Screw the flange to the bottom of the box first. Do not use pipe strapping as added support where climbing snakes are a problem.

When mounting on a tree, attach a 30-inch (76 cm) wide metal sheet (or flexible fiberglass wrap) to the trunk to keep predators from reaching the box. The sheet must be loosened annually as the tree grows. You may also attach a wooden tunnel over the entrance. (For more about predator guards, see pages 164–167.)

It is important to put 3 to 4 inches (7.6–10.2 cm) of wood shavings in the box when you clean and refurbish it prior to the nesting season. This should be done in mid- to late winter.

American Kestrel/Screech-Owl/Northern Saw-whet Owl Nestbox

Nearly all kestrel boxes follow the same basic design: that of an enlarged standard bluebird box. Dimensions vary, however, from plan to plan. The design presented here has been recommended by Kestrel Karetakers, a Virginia-based organization dedicated to helping the American Kestrel (see the appendix). In addition to different dimensions, some kestrel boxes, as with bluebirds, are side opening, while others are top opening. The design presented here is side opening. This should make the box easier to monitor and clean, given the heights at which it will be mounted.

Materials

- ⁷⁄₈" x 9³⁄₄" x 8' (2.2 cm x 24.8 cm x 2.4 m) rough-cut cedar board. Rough-cut or planed pine may also be used, but has a shorter life span.
- ½" (1.3 cm) maple dowel (optional)
- Twenty-six 1⁵⁄₈" (4 cm) long drywall screws or 2" (5.1 cm) galvanized ring-shank wood siding nails (use the latter with thicker rough-cut lumber)
- Two galvanized 6d, 2" (5.1 cm) finishing nails, for pivot
- One brass or galvanized #6 x 1½" (3.8 cm) flat-head wood screw, to hold inside perch
- One brass or galvanized #6 x 2" (5.1 cm) pan-head wood screw
- One washer to fit pan-head screw
- Heavy-duty staples, or ten ¾" (1.9 cm) 18 gauge wire brads

NOTE: *If you use finished lumber, staple or nail a 3" x 6" (7.6 cm x 15.2 cm) piece of ¼" (.625 cm) galvanized wire mesh (hardware cloth) to the inside of the front, below the inside perch to enable the young to climb to the entrance; be sure to bend sharp edges away. Alternatively, you can rout or score the front inside with a sharp tool such as a rasp or awl to provide a grip for the young.*

Tools

- Table saw (two angle cuts are required), or carpenter's handsaw and miter box
- 3" (7.6 cm) keyhole saw or expansion bit, for cutting entrance hole; 2½" (6.4 cm) keyhole saw or expansion bit for Northern Saw-whet Owl
- Power or hand drill
- ³⁄₁₆" (.469 cm), ⅛" (.313 cm), ¼" (.625 cm), and ⅜" (.938 cm) drill bits
- Claw hammer
- Phillips-head screwdriver, or power drill fitted with screwdriver bits
- Carpenter's square
- Tape measure or yard (meter) stick
- Pencil
- Rasp or awl (optional)
- Staple gun (optional)
- Sandpaper (optional)
- Light-colored exterior latex house paint, for pine boxes (optional)
- Paintbrush (optional)

Cutting and Preparation Notes

Be sure to allow for the width of the saw blade when measuring. The grain of the wood should run longitudinally, to minimize warping and cracking. If you use pine lumber, consider using cedar for the roof. You may wish to sand the exterior surfaces, but be sure to leave the inside surfaces rough, to enable the young birds to get a grip when fledging.

This wooden box has a 7¾" (19.7 cm) square floor, although some boxes have floors as large as 8" × 9" (20.3 cm × 24.2 cm). All designs have a 3" (7.6 cm) diameter entrance hole (the Northern Saw-whet Owl requires only a 2½-inch, or 6.4 cm, diameter hole; the screech-owl a 2¾-inch, or 7 cm, hole). The bottom of the entrance hole should be located 9" to 10" (22.9–25.4 cm) above the floor. An inside perch, which could be made from one half of the entrance hole wood, should be screwed 3" (7.6 cm) below the bottom of the entrance hole. *(Leave this perch off when building for owls, however.)* When you cut the entrance hole, be sure to take into account that the floor must be recessed ¼" (.6 cm) to create a drip edge. Cut ⅝" (1.6 cm) off each of the four corners of the floor to create drainage holes. Alternatively, drill four or five ¼" (.6 cm) drainage holes in the floor. Drill three ⅜" (1 cm) holes near the top of the nonpivoting side for ventilation.

The back edge of the roof and the top edge of the front will fit better if you bevel-cut them at 5 degrees. Or you can nail or screw a ½" (1.3 cm) maple dowel where the roof and back meet to keep rain from seeping in (see page 155).

> **NOTE:** *Cedar may split, so predrill nail holes.*

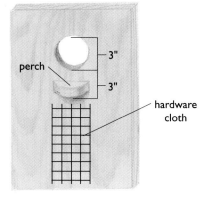

inside view of *front*

Cutting Diagram

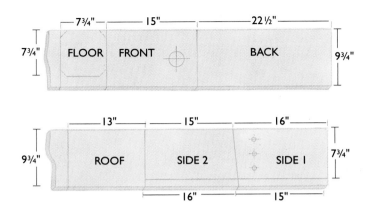

Assembly

1. Screw or nail *side 1* to the *back* of the box. (*Side 2* will be hinged at the top with two finishing nails later.)

2. Make sure that the hardware cloth strip and inside perch (the latter only for kestrels) have been fastened below the entrance hole. Then screw or nail the *front* to the *side*.

3. Attach the *floor*, being careful to recess it ¼" (.6 cm) from the bottom.

4. Now attach *side 2*, using two pivot nails near the top. Note that the pivot nails must be lined up exactly opposite each other, and that this side is ¼" (.6 cm) shorter than the other, to allow it to swing open properly. Predrill a centered ⅛" (.313 cm) guide hole, then use the pan-head screw and a washer to fasten the bottom of this *side* to the *floor*.

5. Screw or nail on the *roof*.

6. If you have not bevel-cut the back edge of the top, nail or screw the ½" (1.3 cm) *dowel* where the top meets the back.

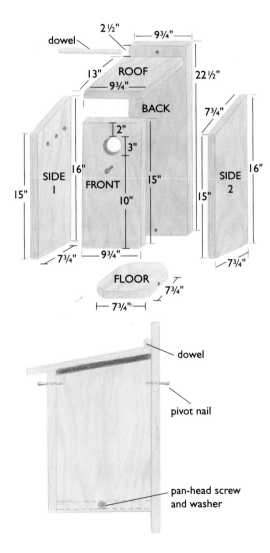

Painting/Staining

You do not need to paint cedar boxes. Pine boxes will last longer if you do, but untreated pine boxes may last approximately 10 years. Be sure to use light-colored exterior latex house paint, and treat only the outside. For owls, boxes can be painted or stained dark brown on the outside only. Do not use paints or stains that contain lead or toxic wood preservatives.

Location

For kestrels, mount the box at least 10 feet (3.1 m) high, and preferably 12 to 20 feet (3.7–6.1 m) up, in open country — farmland, meadows, and abandoned fields. Locate the box 15 to 30 feet (4.6–9.2 m) from a snag, or a tree with dead limbs. Males use such sites as prey "plucking posts." Face the box away from prevailing storms, usually south or east. Space boxes about 1 mile (1.6 km) apart, and no closer than ½ mile (.8 km). Kestrels require a minimum of 1 acre (.4 ha) per pair.

Screech-owls generally prefer open woodland. Locate boxes in shaded areas of open city and rural parks, small woodlots, and apple orchards from 15 to 50 feet (4.6–15.4 m) up in a tree in the woods. Place boxes on straight trunks that have diameters larger than those of the nestboxes. Boxes should be 100 feet (30.5 m) apart. Make sure that there is an unobstructed flying area near the box.

Northern Saw-whet Owls also tend to nest rather high, so mount the box 14 feet (4.3 m) off the ground, or higher in deciduous, evergreen, or mixed forests, woodlots, and swamps. Place the box in a mature, live tree, preferably near water.

Mounting

Boxes may be attached to metal or wooden poles or large dead trees (of sound wood) with bolts or lag screws. Be sure to wrap a 30-inch (76 cm) wide sleeve of aluminum around wooden poles or dead trees, to prevent predators from reaching the nestbox. Boxes can also be placed on silos, barns, windmills, or even on the backs of highway signs (be sure to obtain permission from the proper agency first). Where the use of lag screws or bolts is not possible, wrap stainless steel or galvanized metal banding material around the top and bottom portions of the backboard (but do not try this where climbing snakes are a threat). For mounting alternatives, see pages 161–164.

It may be wise to make your mounting pole of two telescoping sections, bolted together. This way you can lower it for cleaning and repair without a ladder.

Place only 1 inch (2.5 cm) of wood shavings (not cedar) in the bottom of the box as nesting material for kestrels; 2 to 3 inches (5.1–7.6 cm) for screech-owls and Northern Saw-whet Owls. Do not use sawdust, because it may irritate the nostrils and eyes of the nestlings.

For information about the fabrication and installation of predator guards, see pages 164–167.

Great Crested Flycatcher/Ash-throated Flycatcher Nestbox

This box is basically a larger version of the standard slant-roof, side-opening bluebird nestbox, but with a 2-inch (5.1 cm) diameter entrance hole. A 1¾-inch (4.4 cm) diameter entrance hole may be sufficient to permit entry by these flycatchers, but most authors recommend the larger size, especially for the Great Crested Flycatcher.

The box has a 6 × 6 inch (15.2 cm × 15.2 cm) interior floor size. It is 11⅞ inches (30.1 cm) deep at the back, and 8 inches (20.3 cm) from the bottom rim of the entrance hole to the floor. It may be advantageous to add ¾ inch to 2 inches (1.9–5.1 cm) of wood chips (not cedar, which can irritate nestlings) to the bottom of this box prior to the nesting season.

Materials

- ⅞" x 9¾" x 6' (2.2 cm x 24.8 cm x 1.8 m) rough-cut (unplaned) grade 3 cedar. Rough-cut or planed pine may be substituted, but has a shorter life span.
- ½" x 9¼" (1.3 cm x 23.5 cm) maple dowel (optional)
- Twenty 1⅝" (4 cm) drywall screws or 6d (2", or 5.1 cm) galvanized ring-shank wood siding nails
- Two 4d (1½", or 3.8 cm) galvanized finishing nails
- One right-angle screw

Tools

- Table saw, saber saw, jigsaw (two bevel cuts are required), or carpenter's saw and miter box
- 2" (5.1 cm) diameter keyhole saw or expansion bit, to cut entrance hole
- ⅛" (.313 cm), ¼" (.625 cm), and ⅜" (.938 cm) drill bits
- Power or hand drill
- Claw hammer
- Tape measure or yard (meter) stick
- Carpenter's square
- Pencil
- Phillips-head screwdriver or power drill fitted with screwdriver bits (optional)
- Sandpaper (optional)
- Rasp or awl (if smooth lumber is used, the inside of the front will have to be roughened up)

Cutting and Preparation Notes

Be sure to allow for the width of the saw blade when measuring. The grain of the lumber should run lengthwise, to prevent warping and cracking. Cedar resists warping, so if you are building your box of pine, you may want to use cedar for the roof.

Cut ⅝" (1.6 cm) off each of the four corners of the floor to create drainage holes. Alternatively, drill four or five ¼" (.6 cm) drainage holes in the floor. The back of the roof and the top of the front must be beveled at 5 degrees for a better fit. This amounts to cutting ⅛" (.3 cm) off the edges of both.

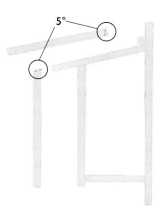

NOTE: *Cedar may split, so predrill nail holes. Make sure seams are tight. If unable to make angle cut to roof, attach dowel.*

Cutting Diagram

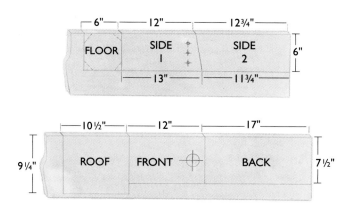

Assembly

1. Nail or screw *side 1* to the *floor*, being sure to leave a ¼" (.6 cm) drip edge below the bottom of the floor (which already has ⅝", or 1.6 cm, cut off the corners, or four ¼", .6 cm, drainage holes drilled through it). The side should have three ⅜" (1 cm) vent holes drilled horizontally near the top.

2. Nail or screw the *back* to the joined *side* and *floor*, maintaining the ¼" (.6 cm) drip edge. You may want to drill a ⅛" (.3 cm) hole in the center of both the projecting portions of the backboard (above and below) prior to assembly; this can also be done just prior to mounting.

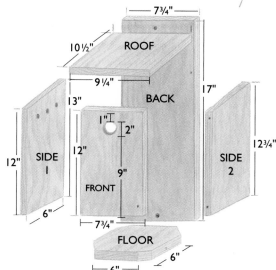

3. Attach the *front,* making sure that it is flush with *side 1* (the center of the 2", or 5.1 cm, diameter entrance hole should be located 2" down from the top of the front). If you are using planed lumber, you must roughen up the inside of the front, below the hole, with a rasp, awl, or other sharp implement.

4. Now fit *side 2* (the one that will swing out) in place, creating the ¼" (.6 cm) drip edge at the bottom and a ¼" gap at the top. While holding *side 2* flush with the *front*, drill two small-diameter guide holes opposite each other near the top. Insert two 4d (1½", or 3.8 cm) galvanized finishing nails into the guide holes as pivots, but do not drive them in fully. Use the right-angle screw to hold *side 2*, first drilling a small guide hole at the proper point, near the lower edge of the front.

5. Finally, make sure that the pivoting side will open properly with the roof in place, and that the roof is centered. Now drive in the two pivot nails fully, then nail or screw the *roof* to the assembled box.

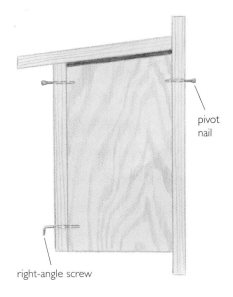

pivot nail

right-angle screw

Painting/Staining

As with other designs, wood treatment is not necessary. Indeed, flycatchers may be more likely to use unpainted nestboxes.

Location

Site boxes for Great Cresteds in open deciduous, deciduous-coniferous, or coniferous woods, or along the edges of wooded areas. Ash-throated Flycatchers prefer open woodlands of piñon-juniper, as well as chaparral and riverside groves. They also nest in oak canyons and desert washes. For both species, place boxes about 8 feet (2.4 m) above the ground, although 4½ to 20 feet (1.4–6.1 m) is acceptable. The entrance hole should be clear of obstructing vegetation.

Mounting

Attach boxes directly to tree trunks for these flycatchers. (In central Florida, boxes were successfully mounted on recently cut 6¾-inch (17.1 cm) diameter slash pines that had limb stubs left on them.) Drive two 2½-inch (6.4 cm) lag screws through the predrilled holes in the backboard. Be sure to protect the birds from predators by affixing predator guards such as a 30-inch (76 cm) wide sheet of aluminum wrapped and secured around the trunk. See pages 164–167 for more about predator guards.

Where starlings are a problem, you may want to suspend your boxes from a 16-inch (40.6 cm) length of chain or flexible wire. In areas where squirrels gnaw nestbox entrance holes, you may need to screw a metal plate with a 2-inch (5.1 cm) diameter hole over the outside of the box.

Mounting Methods and Predator Guards

Mounting your nestbox properly is almost as important as building a nestbox that meets a bird's particular needs. Remember that in northern climates, it is advantageous to drive pipes or bury posts in the ground during fall. In late winter or even early spring, the frozen earth can make this job all but impossible.

Predator guards provide an extra line of defense for birds and increase the likelihood of nesting success. Several options are described in the second part of this chapter.

Mounting Methods

Nestboxes may be attached to or hung from trees, wooden posts, metal pipes, or a variety of other supports. Some of the most often-used mounting technologies are described here.

Trees

It is generally a good idea to avoid mounting boxes on tree trunks, because these boxes are more vulnerable to predation. Exceptions include boxes meant for species that nest in wooded or forest edge habitats. In such situations, effective predator guards are imperative.

Nestboxes may be screwed, nailed, or otherwise affixed directly to dead or living trees. Before attaching the box to a dead tree, make sure that the wood is sound. Brass or galvanized wood screws or drywall screws that are 3" (7.6 cm) long are better than nails, because removing nailed-on boxes for repairs or relocation can be very difficult. When attaching boxes to live trees, do not drive the screws or nails in completely, to allow for future tree growth.

◄ Nesting material hanging from a nestbox is a telltale sign of raccoon predation. A properly mounted predator guard could have prevented this.

The easiest mounting method is to drive two screws or nails through the backboard, one above and one below the box. Use a drill or nail and hammer to create guide holes for the screws before mounting.

Wooden Posts

The majority of nestboxes are probably attached to wooden posts. Posts have an advantage over trees, of course, by being mobile; they can be relocated with relative ease.

Cedar posts 4" × 4" (10.2 cm × 10.2 cm) are perfect for most situations and can be purchased in 16' (4.9 m) lengths. Redwood and cypress posts also withstand rot extremely well. These are all quite expensive initially, but their long life spans probably make them cheaper in the long run. Pressure-treated lumber posts may also be used. They are less expensive than cedar, but impregnated with a toxic substance, chromated copper-arsenate. Pressure-treated lumber should not be used in situations requiring in-water mounting. Your last resort is using untreated lumber. Applying wood preservative to the bottom several feet prior to burying it in the ground will prolong its life.

Many boxes, especially those meant for bluebirds, are mounted directly onto wooden fence posts. Unless fitted with guards, these boxes are rather vulnerable to predators.

Use two 3" (7.6 cm) long drywall, brass, or galvanized screws to attach boxes to wooden posts; you can also use lag bolts and washers. Guide holes must be predrilled for either method. Alternatively, you can pass baling wire through two horizontal holes drilled in the backboard (both above and below the box), then twist it around the supporting metal post, to hold the box in place. Avoid using nails; removing boxes will be difficult at best.

L-bracket mount

Another way to mount wooden nestboxes on square or rectangular posts is to use four L-brackets, each fastened with four brass or galvanized wood screws (see the diagram).

Metal Pipes

Galvanized (zinc-coated iron) plumbing pipe 1" (2.5 cm) to 1½" (3.8 cm) in diameter is another popular way of supporting nestboxes, especially in open habitats. Pipe is relatively expensive, but also long lived and very sturdy. Short sections can be combined into longer lengths with a coupling.

For heavy martin houses, use 2" (5.1 cm) diameter galvanized pipe in order to provide a sturdy enough support.

It is important not to use thin-walled electrical conduit, or any pipe less than ¾" (1.9 cm) in diameter, for any type of nestbox, unless it is used in conjunction with reinforcing rod (see "Other Methods" on page 164).

Pipe-flange mount

Boxes can be attached to the top of galvanized pipe with a round pipe flange that threads onto the end of the pipe. Use four galvanized or brass flat-head screws to attach the bottom of the nestbox to the flange. Attach the flange to the bottom of the box first.

In another mounting method, you tightly screw two metal pipe clamps over the pipe into the backboard of the nestbox. Phillips-head screws are usually best, especially in areas where vandalism may occur. Be sure to drive the end of the pipe at least 2' (.6 m) deep to stabilize it.

Metal-clamp mount

Telescoping Poles

For boxes that need to be placed 8' (2.4 m) or more above the ground, you may want to construct a telescoping pole from two 5' (1.5 m) long sections of PVC plastic pipe. This will allow you to lower the nestbox or martin house to a level that enables you to monitor without a ladder. For large, heavy martin houses, a winch system is almost required for regular monitoring.

Metal pipe can be used as well as PVC, although the plastic pipe is much lighter in weight. You can also combine the two, constructing the top portion (the one that will be lowered) of plastic. Simply fit 5' (1.5) of a 1½" (3.8 cm) diameter pipe inside 5' of a 2" (5.1 cm) diameter one. Make sure that you have at least 1' (30.5 cm) of overlap. Then drill a ¼" (.6 cm) hole through both sections, 2" (5.1 cm) below the top of the lower pipe. Place a ¼" (.6 cm) diameter carriage bolt with washers at both ends through the hole and secure it with a nut. To lower the nestbox, remove the bolt and slowly slide the top section down into the lower one. Lining up the holes will be easier if you mark the smaller-diameter pipe holes with an indelible marker. *Note:* Be sure to put a pipe cap over the top end of the upper pipe, to keep birds from getting trapped in it.

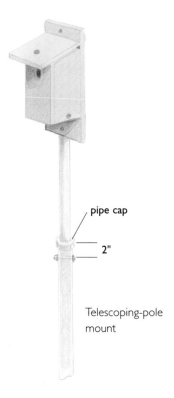

Telescoping-pole mount

Metal Fences or Signposts

Steel T fence posts, fitted at the bottom end with triangular anchor plates, are available from farm or ranch supply stores. These are extremely sturdy, but fairly heavy and expensive. They may not always be long enough to allow you to mount your boxes at a sufficient height. Use baling wire to attach the nestbox by passing it through the predrilled holes in the backboard and twisting it around the post.

T- fence-post mount

Your federal, state (provincial), or local highway department office may have used metal signposts, which you may be able to obtain for use in mounting nestboxes.

Setting the Support in the Ground

Be sure to bury the end of your pole, post, or pipe at least 2' (.6 m) into the ground; deeper for heavy nestboxes. A posthole digger is a useful tool for this task. You may wish to attach three or four 2" × 4" (5.1 cm × 10.2 cm) stabilizing boards at right angles to the bottom of the post before burying it. Alternatively, tamp gravel firmly into the hole and then backfill the remainder with soil. Or you may want to pour concrete on top of the gravel as an antivandalism measure. Mound concrete on the surface to help drain water away.

Hanging Nestboxes

For some species, such as wrens, hanging is a viable alternative. This is especially true where climbing predators take a toll on eggs and nestlings. In southern California, hanging boxes have been used by Western Bluebirds with good results.

Hang nestboxes from live trees only. Use flexible 9-gauge wire for this purpose; you can also use vinyl-coated clothes-line wire, which is quite strong and relatively easy to work with. Suspend boxes from at least a 12" (30.5 cm) length of wire. Be sure to use an eyebolt, nut, and washer attached to the roof of the box; a screw eye can loosen, causing the nestbox to fall. When you attach the wire from a tree limb, pad the top of the limb with a piece of rubber or vinyl to protect the tree.

A special tool made of PVC plastic pipe has been developed by Dick Purvis for placing and removing boxes easily and without a ladder.

Hanging nestbox

Nestbox mounting tool

Other Methods

Alternatives include the use of iron reinforcing rod (also known as "rebar"): Slip a ½" (1.3 cm) diameter section of electrical conduit over a ½" diameter section of rebar to create a sturdy support. Use pipe clamps to attach it to the back of the nestbox.

Predator Guards

The purpose of a predator guard is to keep climbing predators from reaching the nestbox. If a predator somehow surmounts this first line of defense, other guards, fitted directly onto the box, must keep it from gaining access to the nest, its contents, and the adult birds. There are four basic predator guard designs, each with variations. Patterns for the basic designs are illustrated and described here.

Baffle Block

The baffle block is the most basic and probably the least-effective type of predator guard. It does not preclude predators such as raccoons from reaching the nestbox; it only makes the task of reaching the nest contents more difficult. (An 18-pound [8.2 kg] raccoon, after all, has a 20" [50.8 cm] reach.) And a baffle is totally ineffective against snakes. Still, it does offer some measure of security, especially in combination with other baffles or with a long roof overhang.

baffle block

Making a baffle block is very easy. Simply bore an entrance hole (of the same diameter as that of the box you are mounting the guard on) into a ¾ to 1" (1.9–2.5 cm) thick block of wood. Use four brass flat-head wood screws to attach the block directly over the entrance hole. This will force predators to make a slightly longer reach.

There is some evidence that male Western Bluebirds are reluctant to enter a cavity that has a wall thickness of more than 2" (5.1 cm). Be sure not to exceed this, and remember to take into account the thickness of the box front itself. Also, Eastern Bluebirds will select narrower-walled boxes over those thicker than 1½" (3.8 cm) if given a choice. An alternative is to attach the thicker guard only after the nest is well established. Still, Tree Swallows and House Wrens will enter even boxes fitted with double blocks, each 1½" to 2" (3.8–5.1 cm) thick.

An effective variation on this design, meant to exclude raccoons and used only on the Wood Duck/Hooded Merganser nestbox, is an 8" (20.3 cm) long wooden tunnel constructed of 1" (2.5 cm) lumber mounted directly over the entrance hole and protruding out from it (see page 152).

Noel Wire Raccoon Guard

This guard is said to be the most effective deterrent to raccoon and cat predation. It is made from a 5½" (14 cm) × 18" (45.7 cm) piece of ½" (1.3 cm) galvanized wire mesh hardware cloth. The ends of the wire mesh are purposefully left projecting outward, which means that the raccoons, opossums, and house cats must reach past these wire points to get at the nestbox (see the diagram). You might even want to sharpen the points with a file. Much more effective than the baffle block, this guard creates a long, very uncomfortable reach for the predator.

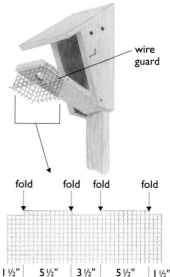

wire guard

fold   fold   fold   fold

1½" | 5½" | 3½" | 5½" | 1½"

Cone Baffle

Galvanized sheet metal (26 gauge) can be cut and fashioned into very effective baffles that thwart virtually any predator's attempt to climb the support post or pole. Draw the 36" (91.4 cm) diameter circle with a piece of string and a permanent marker, or a length of wood with two protruding nails 18" (45.7 cm) apart (see the diagram on next page). Use four small pan-head sheet metal screws to hold it together. You will need hardened drill bits to make the holes, and tin snips to cut the metal. Cones are usually mounted below the nest-box, but are also sometimes mounted above it to keep squirrels and snakes from getting in from above.

Rather than being mounted rigidly, the cone baffle should be tippy or wobbly. A stable cone is somewhat self-defeating in that it allows climbing predators to use it for support. Cones work best on small-diameter pipes and poles; they are more difficult to attach to trees. Cone baffles deter most snakes.

Variations. One variation on this design, touted as an effective snake guard, consists of attaching a 24" to 30" (61–76.2 cm) square piece of galvanized sheet metal or hardware cloth directly to the bottom of the nestbox. One monitor in Kansas has used a 24" × 27" (61 cm × 68.6 cm) piece of corru-gated roofing metal, from which 3" (7.6 cm) was cut off the corners. This baffle is mounted with baling wire just below the nestbox. Position the corrugated metal 4' (1.2 m) above the ground and in such a way that the sheet droops directly in front and back of the box. Make sure the fit around the pipe or post is a tight one so that snakes are not able to bypass the sheet at this point.

Metal or Plastic Sleeve

The metal sleeve is well suited for use on trees, poles, and (with some modification) pipes. In its simplest form it consists of a 24" to 30" (61–76.2 cm) wide sheet of alu-minum or galvanized metal wrapped around the trunk of a tree or post below the nest-box. Be sure to leave some space between the trunk and the sleeve. The bottom of the sheet should be at least 6' (1.8 m) above the ground, to prevent predators from jumping over the sleeve from the ground. You can use long galvanized pan-head screws to hold it to the tree or post and to hold it together.

Sleeve guards can also be made from two sections of 7" to 8" (17.8–20.3 cm)

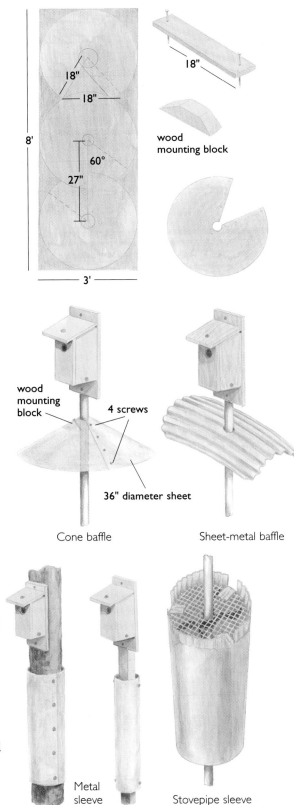

wood mounting block

Cone baffle

4 screws

36" diameter sheet

Sheet-metal baffle

Metal sleeve

Stovepipe sleeve

diameter galvanized metal stovepipe or vent pipe suitable for poles, posts, and small-diameter trees. Insert nails or screws only partway into live trees, so that you can adjust the sleeve as the tree grows. If using a stovepipe sleeve, attaching a circular piece of hardware cloth cut to fit the inside diameter of the pipe will deter snakes. Bolt two strips of plumber's hanger wire tightly to the supporting pipe (see diagram on previous page).

PVC
sleeve

   Variation. PVC plastic pipe is another variation on the basic sleeve design. Place 24" to 30" (61–76.2 cm) long sections of 4" (10.2 cm) diameter PVC pipe over the supporting pipe and attach it with carriage bolts. You will need a hardened drill bit, for drilling metal. Such a sleeve presents the predator with a smooth, slick surface that it finds impossible to climb. Spraying silicone on the exterior of the pipe, or polishing it with carnauba wax, makes it even slicker. Another variation has been tried with success in Wisconsin: 1¾" (4.4 cm) diameter PVC pipe was fitted over metal pipes from the ground up to within a few inches of the nestbox.

   Greased metal pipes generally do not work against snakes. Remember, too, that athletic cats can jump 6' (1.8 m) up, so mount your box at the appropriate height if cats are a concern.

Special Challenges

   In the southern United States, fire ants can be a major factor in nestling mortality. Simply applying grease to the mounting pole is not sufficient to deter these. One method that has succeeded involves mixing turpentine and chassis grease: Mix 1 quart (1 L) of turpentine with 5 pounds (2.3 kg) of grease, and apply this to metal pipes as needed during the nesting season. The turpentine will keep the grease soft. Cut the grass near the pole short; otherwise, tall grasses blowing in the wind against the pipe will abrade the grease. Note, too, that raccoons will lick grease off pipes.

   In many areas, squirrels enlarge entrance holes by gnawing them with their sharp incisor teeth. To combat this, attach over the front of the box a small square of sheet metal with a hole cut in its center that is the same diameter as the entrance hole. Drill four small holes in the corners with a hardened bit, and use pan-head brass or galvanized screws to hold it in place.

Additional Tips

   If one predator guard does not work for you, try another. Sometimes lengthening the roof overhang to at least 7" (17.8 cm) can make a difference. Or put long, sharp-pointed nails out through the roof and/or front of the box (from the inside out), to keep mammalian predators from getting to the entrance hole. Sometimes, changing from wooden posts to metal pipes can make the difference; raising the height of the box to 6½' to 7' (2–2.1 m) can also solve the problem. Do not be afraid to try a new approach. One martin landlord in Wisconsin mounted an inverted round white plastic garbage pail below his martin house as a predator guard. Experimentation is often the name of the game in defeating predators.

Landscaping
a Habitat

In the context of this book, *landscaping* refers to changes or enhancements that will be made to an area for the benefit of cavity-nesting birds. Before you consider making any changes to your property, take time to study the habitat needs of the birds you want to attract in the species profiles chapter (pages 17–125). Depending on the preferences of your desired species and what your property has to offer, little or no landscaping may be necessary.

Typically, bluebirds, swallows, kestrels, and flickers prefer open fields. Wrens and chickadees favor edges of forests, while titmice, owls, nuthatches, and certain woodpeckers prefer forest interiors. Practicality is an important consideration, and your budget and the size of your property will dictate the extent to which you can modify an area in order to create or enhance the desired habitat for your chosen nesters.

Be realistic — recognize that it is impossible to re-create the integrity and complexity of a natural ecosystem. Our natural surroundings have been so fragmented by development and urbanization that much of their biodiversity has been lost. If you choose to do some bird-friendly landscaping, a reasonable goal would be to add "desirable diversity" to your property, ideally with native plants. Knowing the habitat needs of a specific bird species allows you to cater your landscaping choices to benefit that species, resulting, according to Ross, in as much as a twofold increase in the number of birds visiting or inhabiting your property.

A Plan of Action

As you begin contemplating your many options, consider the following plan, which will help you approach the landscaping process with confidence and, no doubt, will make maintenance of your property more carefree.

• **Become familiar with the range and habitat needs of your desired species.** Reviewing the range maps in the profiles chapter will help you determine which birds frequent your area. Studying the habitat needs provided in the same chapter will allow you to enhance your landscape for a particular species.

- **Get to know your land.** Research what the land was like before it became a house site; read historical accounts of your area. This information can give you insights into how the land has changed over the years and may suggest ways you can improve it today.

- **Learn the difference between native and non-native vegetation.** Outfit yourself with the appropriate field guides, and start learning your plants. Native vegetation is preferred.

- **Inventory the woody vegetation and plants on your land.** Knowing what you have already will help you make wise decisions about new plantings and may inspire you to rid your land of troublesome non-native species.

- **Map your property.** A map is a handy visual reference to have and will help you consider the big picture as you plan. Include as much information as you can. Walkways, fences, trees, plants, light conditions, and drainage, among other features, should all be recorded.

- **Test your soil.** Knowing your soil quality and United States Department of Agriculture (USDA) plant hardiness zone will help you choose plants that will thrive in your locale.

- **Keep a wary eye for non-native plants.** In addition to birds, other types of wildlife spread seeds. As a result, invasive non-native species can take over your property if you aren't watchful. Rid your property of non-native species when practical. Oriental bittersweet *(Celastrus orbiculatus)*, multiflora rose *(Rosa multiflora)*, Common buckthorn *(Rhamnus cathartica)*, and Tatarian honeysuckle *(Lonicera tatarica)* are common invasive non-natives.

- **Consider reducing the size of your lawn.** Instead of high-maintenance lawn, plant trees, shrubs, ferns, and native wildflowers.

- **Develop a planting plan.** Review "Important Plants for Birds" (page 177), then consult with your local nursery or garden supply center to determine what plants will work best on your property. Remember to consider the habitat needs of your desired species when choosing plants. Using tissue-paper overlays for the map of your property, experiment with several planting scenarios.

- **Situate plants for convenience and efficient upkeep.** Keep high-maintenance areas such as vegetable and flower gardens close to the house, and plant "natural" unfettered gardens toward the edge of your property, where they will be free to grow wild.

- **Keep the edge of the lawn mowed, or cut paths through tall grass.** Ground cover is important for birds. If you choose to let your lawn grow wild for ground cover, selective maintenance can make the area look groomed rather than neglected — an important consideration if neighbors are nearby. Stone or wood-chip paths can also help establish a sense of order. Keep paths away from nestboxes. If paths are cut too close to a nestbox, they may guide predators there.

- **Shun toxic chemicals.** A relaxed acceptance of insects, leaf litter, and dead wood makes your property more desirable to birds.

- **Avoid electronic bug zappers.** They aren't effective at controlling mosquitoes and can reduce the number of insects on which birds feed. They might also inadvertently kill beneficial insects.

- **Confine all cats.** Cats are natural predators. Birds have a better chance of successfully raising their brood if cats are kept indoors.

If planning to mount nestboxes and feeders in your yard, plan also to keep your cats indoors. Cats typically inflict heavy losses on wildlife.

Preliminaries

Before you landscape a habitat, it's important to know what your land already has to offer. Take inventory of woody vegetation, map your property, and test soil quality to gather the information you need to make wise planting choices.

Inventory Woody Vegetation

Birds are instinctively drawn to trees and shrubs — they are places to hide from predators, find food, construct a nest, or simply rest. Take inventory of the area around existing nestboxes or prospective nestbox sites. Then answer these questions, suggested by Tarski:

- What types of trees and shrubs are present?
- Does the cavity nester you want to attract require open spaces? If so, do trees and shrubs need to be removed? Would such a change be practical?
- How many different types of trees are present?
- Are there any evergreens? How dense are they?
- Do the trees and shrubs have limbs and branches that could serve as perches?
- Do any of the trees or shrubs bear fruit, nuts, berries, seeds?

A variety of woody vegetation increases the likelihood of attracting a variety of bird species. For year-round winged residents, woody vegetation represents critical shelter during extremes in weather. A dense stand of evergreens can help to shield birds from bone-chilling temperatures and icy winds; in hot climates, evergreens serve as protection against heat and intense sunlight. Trees and shrubs are vital for birds during rains and storms, providing much-needed shelter. At night during the nesting season when most females are brooding their eggs or young, males roost in trees. As the young mature, both parents take up overnight residence in trees.

Map Your Property

Mapping your property provides a helpful visual reference and also alerts you to any potential unseen hazards, particularly if you're contemplating making major changes. Here is a process recommended by Johnson and Wolfe.

Using graph paper, draw a map of your property to scale. Identify as many features as possible. All buildings, sidewalks, fences, septic tank fields, wells, trees, shrubs, and patios should be indicated on your map. Contact the telephone and power companies to identify any buried cables and power lines, and be sure to include them on your map. Also, indicate those areas that tend to be low-lying and wet, are generally sunny, usually remain shaded, or are sandy. Record how much sun is available in different areas throughout the day, and note those areas of your property used by pets and for recreational purposes. Because most bird species are tolerant but fearful of humans and other mammals, it's a good idea to make bird-friendly enhancements to locations somewhat removed from high-traffic areas.

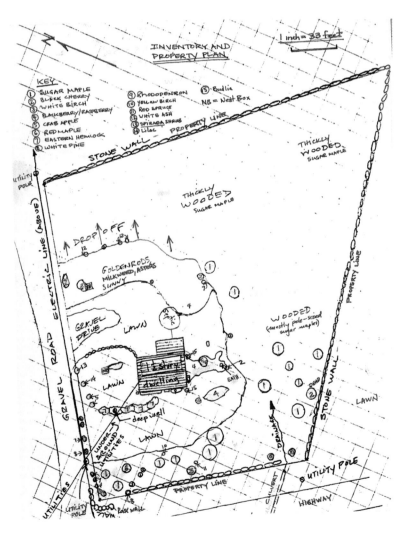

A simple scale drawing of your property is a useful tool when developing a planting plan.

Test Your Soil

Before you begin compiling a list of prospective plants for your property, test your soil. Knowing what type of soil you have and what nutrients, if any, are missing increases the likelihood of planting success. Soil type and your USDA plant hardiness zone will help you choose plants most appropriate for your property.

Soil test kits are available at your local garden center or local cooperative extension service. If the test reveals that your soil needs help, amending the soil with compost, organic fertilizers, or other additives can significantly improve its quality. Plants generally do well in rich, well-balanced soil, though some varieties thrive in less-than-ideal conditions. If you have questions about the quality of your soil, consult a representative from your local garden center or agricultural extension service.

Habitat Essentials

When considering habitat for birds, recall that the area where you locate your nestboxes should provide accessible shelter, food, and water. Always try to foster a "natural" environment, and know that the habitat you provide for birds can help them survive and thrive.

Provide Shelter

Shelter protects birds from severe weather and offers a safe haven where they can preen their feathers or just rest. Different plants provide different types of cover. For example, dense evergreens, because of their insulating properties, help birds survive the effects of strong winds, heavy rains, snow, and cold nighttime temperatures. Large trees also offer sanctuary from mammalian and avian predators. Dense shrubs and vine tangles furnish hiding places from such predators as the sharp-shinned hawk *(Accipiter striatus)*. Low shrubs and ground cover provide refuge and safety when birds are on the ground.

Generally speaking, about 8 to 12 percent of the trees you plant should be "needle-leaved" evergreens: firs, hemlocks, spruces, or pines. The broad-leaved evergreens such as rhododendrons, laurels, and American holly *(Ilex opaca)* offer effective cover, but the needle evergreens, because of their insulating properties, provide much better protection. To maximize the benefits of these trees and shrubs, they should be grown in the back, in corners, or along the sides of the property you are landscaping.

In addition to the natural shelter and cover provided by trees and shrubs, you can construct simple shelters that benefit birds. The next few sections discuss some of our favorites: brush piles.

Nestboxes do double duty for cavity nesters, providing sheltered roosts in winter and nesting sites during the breeding season.

Brush Piles. Brush piles provide cover for adult birds and fledglings, as well as for mammals like rabbits. Brush piles are easily constructed from tree and shrub clippings, and should be placed along forest edges, in forest openings, at the corners of fields, or along streams and marshes. Situating brush piles near other sources of natural cover increases the likelihood of regular use, as they add desirable diversity to the habitat. Isolated piles receive minimal use.

According to Megalos, Jones, and Turner, the largest clippings — branches approximately 6 inches (15.2 cm) in diameter — should be placed first, to give the brush pile its base. Lay the branches at right angles to each other to form a square. For the second layer, lay the branches to form an X. This sequence (square, then X) is repeated until the pile reaches the desired height. Another option is to crisscross large branches so they form a solid structure with some open spaces in the middle. Smaller branches would likewise be crisscrossed. Post-season Christmas trees, tree tops, branches, stones, or stumps can be added to the pile to add interest to the structure. The more you add to the pile, the more cover and perching spots you provide for birds. Laying evergreen boughs over the pile provides added protection from wind, rain, and snow.

Ideally, brush piles should be 4 to 8 feet (1.2–2.4 m) tall and from 10 to 20 feet (3.1–6.1 m) wide. An acre of land can hold up to four such piles. Along wooded edges, one brush pile spaced every 200 to 300 feet (61–91.5 m) will provide adequate cover for birds. A well-constructed brush pile may last up to 10 to 15 years but should be reworked every 5 to 6 years. Large brush piles are more appropriate in a rural, rather than residential, setting.

Living Brush Piles. Living brush piles are another option, suggested by Megalos, Jones, and Turner, but they may not be appropriate for all locales. (For example, in a residential setting, a living brush pile would likely conflict with the more manicured appearance of most backyards.) A living brush pile is created by making a clean, partial cut through a tree's trunk, then pushing over the top portion of the tree. Because a strip of bark and inner wood remain intact, nourishment continues to reach the fallen part of the tree, keeping it alive.

Wide-crowned trees that are 6 to 8 feet (1.8–2.4 m) tall are the best candidates for this project — red cedar *(Juniperus virginiana)* and holly *(Ilex* spp.) provide excellent cover. Trees draped with grape *(Vinus* spp.), Virginia creeper *(Parthenocissus quinquefolia)*, or native honeysuckle are also good candidates, as the vines provide additional cover, sanctuary, and nourishment for birds.

In spring, make a clean, partial cut through the tree's trunk, 3 to 4 feet (.9–1.2 m) above the ground. (The living pile will grow on the side of the tree opposite the cut, so be sure to plan carefully before you take saw to wood.) Saw just deep enough for the tree to be pushed over easily. Secure the top of the tree to the ground with a stake and tie.

Stone Piles. In rocky areas like New England, you can create inviting stone piles for birds. For a stone pile to be useful to birds, it must be stable and have open spaces. Use stones and rocks of different shapes and sizes to create inviting spaces for birds. Wrens, in particular, enjoy exploring rocky haunts.

If you turn the soil — especially if it's sandy — near a stone pile, you'll find birds using the spot regularly for dust baths.

Dead Trees. If you're lucky enough to have large dead trees on your land, by all means keep them! Dead trees are irresistible to birds such as woodpeckers. Once these primary cavity nesters are through nesting, the holes they made might very well be inhabited by secondary cavity nesters like bluebirds, titmice, chickadees, or even owls or kestrels. Dead trees also make wonderful perches, and the insects they harbor are a valuable food source for many species.

Shelter Helpers. If you live in a residential area and piles or dead trees are simply out of the question, consider providing birds with a small platform or wire basket filled with nesting material. These shelter helpers can be hung from limbs of trees or shrubs, or nailed to the trunks of trees. Use an assortment of fibers of various lengths (e.g., dog hair, lint from the clothes dryer, single threads of yarn, narrow [¼" (.6 cm) or less] strips of cloth), but note that string-like materials should be no longer than 8 inches (20.3 cm). A string longer than 8 inches could cause a bird to become entangled.

Putting feathers out for nesting swallows can give you rare glimpses of nest-building activity. Here, a male Tree Swallow is en route to a nestbox.

You might also want to put out feathers for use by Tree Swallows and Violet-green Swallows. Feathers can be obtained from farmers who raise ducks, geese, or chickens. Feathers from wild birds other than the House Sparrow, European Starling, and pigeon should not be used, as it is against the law to have these feathers in one's possession. If an old quilt or pillow has seen better days, this is another good source of feathers.

Children especially enjoy placing feathers on the ground near the nestbox and watching for birds to pick them up. Feathers are used as nesting material by various cavity nesters and open nesters.

Provide Water

A water source is one of the most effective ways to enhance your property's bird habitat. The water source should be clean and reliable. Birds come to depend on the water we provide, so don't disappoint them. Always keep your water sources filled. The Georgia Wildlife Federation recommends locating a water source in a shaded, protected spot, approximately 15 feet (4.6 m) from shrubbery and 5 feet (1.5 m) or more above the ground, so as to be out of reach of the neighborhood cat and other mammalian predators. (Shrubs offer cover but can also conceal predators.)

You might choose to use a standard birdbath or something as simple as an upside-down garbage can lid as a water source. Whatever container you choose, its bottom

A steady source of clean water will enhance your property and attract many species of birds, such as this Carolina Chickadee.

should gradually slope to a depth of about 2 to 3 inches (5.1–7.6 cm). Aquarium gravel can be added to the bottom of the container to create a sloping surface and to provide birds with better footing. Placing a flat rock in the container will help anchor it and gives birds a place to shake off excess water after bathing.

Birds find dripping water especially appealing. One of the simplest ways to provide this is with a 10 to 12 quart (9–11 L) wooden bucket or metal pail. Drill a small hole at the lower edge of the bucket, so that only an occasional drop of water seeps out. Suspend the bucket about 2 feet (.6 m) above the birdbath. (If the container is suspended any higher, the wind might carry the water drops away from the birdbath.) To keep birds happy, be sure that the water is clean and ever-present.

During periods of high use, baths should be cleaned frequently and scrubbed periodically to keep algae in check. A 10 percent solution of bleach (1 part bleach to 9 parts water) is best. Remember to rinse thoroughly before refilling.

Provide Food

Trees and shrubs provide berries and seeds that are an important source of food, particularly for those migrants, such as bluebirds, that return to an area early in the season. The timing of the birds' return may not coincide with the emergence of insect populations, so early migrants are especially dependent on these plants for food. Having such a food source near the nestbox could entice the bird to use it for nesting.

For most cavity nesters, insects are the principal source of nourishment for adults and young. Because of this, the use of bug zappers is strongly discouraged. They can reduce the number of insects on which birds feed, and they might also kill insects that are beneficial. The Wise Plant Choices chart on page 184 includes several trees that harbor insects. Any one of these, and even a dead tree, would be much appreciated by birds. (See individual species profiles for more on food preferences.)

Important Plants for Birds

Now that we have considered the elements all birds need in a habitat, it's time to consider what plants we can use to make our property most desirable to birds. Before we discuss the particulars, though, it's essential to understand why native plants are so vital.

Return of the Native

Our native species of birds and plants have co-evolved through time. Alien birds and plants have been introduced by humans and are foreign members of our ecosystems. Because their relationships with native animals have not yet been established, alien plants rarely benefit native species of wildlife. A good example of an invasive alien species is purple loosestrife *(Lythrum salicaria)*. Though each plant produces millions of tiny seeds, the seeds are not used by our indigenous wildlife, nor do their magenta flowers provide nectar and pollen for many native insects.

Generally speaking, when compared to non-native species, native plants need less fertilizer and water to thrive, and require less human effort to control pests. According to the National Wildlife Federation, native plants may support 10 to 50 times more species of wildlife than non-native plants, such as Oriental bittersweet, which spread rapidly and can take over fields and woodlands, thereby diminishing biodiversity. Non-native plants compete with native plants for resources, and their spread and competition is akin to that of the House Sparrow and European Starling with native cavity nesters.

Therefore, using native plants for landscaping is best. Check with your local college or university botany or horticulture department or with your state or province's Natural Heritage Program for a list of trees, shrubs, and wildflowers native to your area. Your local garden center or local agricultural extension service is also a good resource. Consider your list of native plants the starting point for your landscaping plan. Native species are naturally adapted to local conditions and are a good long-term investment. They are beautiful for landscaping purposes and are excellent for birds and other wildlife. (If you must include non-native plants in your plan, be sure that they are not considered "invasive pests" by horticultural experts.)

Planting Recommendations by Category

On a broad scale, your geographic location, or USDA plant hardiness zone, will determine the type of habitat you will be able to achieve. More specifically, the size of your property, quality of soil, and availability of sun and shade will determine what native plants will do best in your locale. Fortunately, most local nurseries and garden centers carry only plants that do well in that particular area, so it would behoove you to shop for plants locally.

Important plants for improving bird habitats fall into five broad categories, according to Ross:

I. Conifers. Pines, spruces, hemlocks, firs, arborvitae, junipers, cedars, and yews provide cover and shelter for cavity nesters. In addition, some conifers provide sap, buds, and seeds that can be eaten by cavity nesters. Though these tree products might not be used during the nesting season, birds returning in spring find them an important source of nourishment.

Fruit-bearing trees and shrubs, like this summer-ripening, non-native red mulberry, will lure birds, including American robins, to your garden.

2. Grasses and legumes. These plants provide needed cover,* particularly when cavity nesters are on the ground. They also harbor the insect prey that many nestbox occupants pursue as food for themselves and their young.

3. Summer fruiting plants. These plants produce fruit and berries from May through August. Plants such as cherry (*Prunus* spp.), chokecherry (*Prunus* spp.), honeysuckle (*Lonicera* spp.), raspberry (*Rubus* spp.), serviceberry (also known as juneberry or shad) (*Amelanchier* spp.), blackberry (*Rubus* spp.), blueberry (*Vaccinium* spp.), grape (*Vitis* spp.), mulberry (*Morus* spp.), plum (*Prunus* spp.), and elderberry (*Sambucus* spp.) are important food sources, particularly during wet, rainy summers when birds have a difficult time finding insects. In times of fair weather, fruiting trees and shrubs are havens for caterpillars and nectaring adult insects, both important food sources for birds.

4. Autumnal fruiting plants. These plants retain their fruit long after it first ripens in the fall. Many such fruits are not palatable to birds until they have frozen and thawed numerous times. Such plants include the glossy black chokecherry *(Prunus virginianna)*, Siberian and 'Red Splendor' crabapple, snowberry *(Symphoricarpos albus)*, sumacs (*Rhus* spp.), American highbush cranberry *(Viburnum trilobum)*, Eastern and

*Excellent native candidates for ground cover, other than grasses and legumes, include partridge-berry *(Mitchella repens)*, bearberry *(Artostaphylos uva-ursi)*, and wintergreen *(Gaultheria procumbens)*. Recommended non-natives include English ivy *(Hedera helix)* and Japanese spurge *(Pachysandra terminalis)*. Japanese honeysuckle *(Lonicera japonica)* should not be used because it is a vigorous climbing vine that will overrun anything in its path.

European wahoo (*Euonymus* spp.), and Virginia creeper *(Parthenocissus quinquefolia).* These fruits are especially important for returning migrants in early spring, before insect populations have emerged.

5. Nut and acorn plants. Oak (*Quercus* spp.), hickory (*Carya* spp.), buckeye *(Aesculus glabra)*, chestnut *(Castanea dentata)*, butternut *(Juglans cinera)*, walnut (*Juglans* spp.), and hazel (*Corglus* spp.) trees offer two food sources: the meat of the nut or acorn and insect larvae that they frequently harbor. Chickadees are particularly adept at extracting over-wintering larvae from nuts and acorns.

Keep in mind that your goal is to attain "desirable diversity," so plant an assortment of trees, shrubs, and flowers that will attract and benefit the birds in which you are most interested. If you plan carefully, this process can be inexpensive and fun.

If you still aren't sure what birds frequent your area, talk to friends and neighbors. Attend a local bird club meeting, and ask local birders how they attract birds to their yards. Get tips from other bird enthusiasts.

Develop a Planting Plan

Armed with the information you've gathered to this point, you now should be ready to start developing a planting plan. One last time, scrutinize your property. Study the map that you created earlier. Do you have plants that will attract your desired nestbox occupants? If not, what native plants will be most appropriate, given the size of your property and the quality of your soil? Will you need to make changes to provide shelter, water, or food? Develop a wish list of plants, drawing from the five categories important for birds, and then start planning.

The Edge Effect

Edges are important because they represent transitions between two or more habitats. Birds that inhabit this area are usually different from those that reside in either of the bordering habitats. Therefore, edges create diversity and encourage a greater variety of birds to take up residence.

Edges are found along fields or agricultural land, and in forests, where fire, wind, or insects have had a hand, or where soil characteristics change abruptly. Most edges are the result of human activities, according to Karriker, Jones, and Megalos. However, too much edge can be detrimental, particularly to interior forest nesting birds such as thrushes. Increased edge provides predators, such as raccoons and cowbirds, easier access to ground-nesting birds. Balance is key.

Many fruit- and berry-producing trees and shrubs flourish along edges. Because these plants need full sunlight to thrive, they cannot compete successfully or survive in the shade of mature forests. Neither can they endure the disturbance associated with cultivated areas and grazing. Some of these trees and shrubs include plum *(Prunus americana)*, persimmon (*Diospyros* spp.), mulberry (*Morus* spp.), crabapple (*Malus* spp.), mountain ash (*Sorbus* spp.), dogwood (*Cornus* spp.), red bud (*Cercis* spp.), blackberry, wax myrtle or bayberry *(Myrica pensylvanica)*, elderberry (*Sambucus* spp.), sumac (*Rhus* spp.), and blueberry (*Vaccinium* spp.).

Dead trees, such as the one just past the shrubs, are important sources of insect food and nest sites for cavity-nesting birds. They should be allowed to stand whenever possible.

Ensure Abundant Fruit

Many species of tree, such as hollies, have separate male and female plants. In order to ensure maximum blossom, seeds, and fruit, plant male and female trees within reasonable proximity to each other — that is, close enough so the male pollen can fertilize the female flower.

If you are considering adding fruit trees to your property, you might want to keep female plants away from walkways or patios. Some seeds and fruits leave stains that can permanently discolor sidewalks and decks, not to mention clothing. When you plant fruit trees and berry bushes, remember that birds enjoy them as much as we do. Share your harvest whenever possible.

Experiment with Different Layouts

To help you visualize the changes you want to make to your property, place a piece of tracing paper over the map of your property (see page 172) and begin sketching. On the overlay, sketch the exact placement of trees, shrubs, vines, and flowers you want to add. Consider the value of edges and how to ensure abundant fruit, if you want to add fruit trees. Try several different options on separate pieces of tracing paper.

Plan so trees and shrubs are graduated from the tallest at the back and sides of your property to the smallest in the center. The more varied a habitat you offer, the more species you will attract. If you are able to plan for year-round cover and food, all the better. The birds will thank you with their presence.

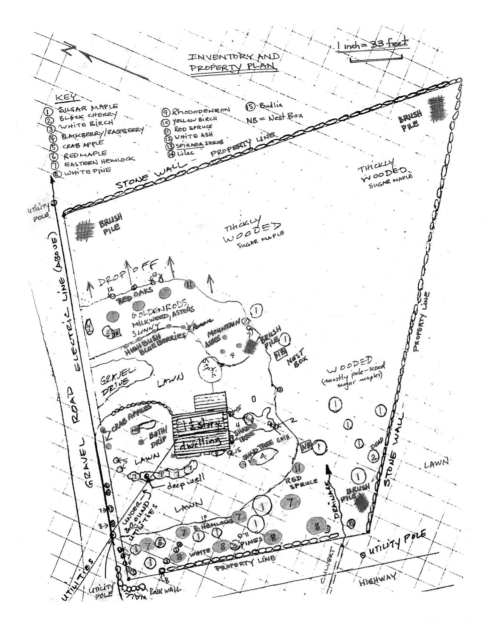

Adding tracing paper overlays to the sketch of your property is a convenient way of "testing" a variety of planting scenarios.

Make your sketches on the overlays as realistic as possible. Draw trees to a scale three-fourths of their mature width, and show shrubs at their mature width. Remember that the plants you place today will grow larger.

Space your plantings appropriately on the overlay: Consider the distance from structures and buildings as well as the distance between plants. Spacing is determined by the mature height of your plants. Generally, large trees should be spaced apart to one-third of their maximum height, and small trees and shrubs to one-half or one-third their maximum height. For example, if a tree grows to be 75 feet (22.9 m) tall, plant two trees of the same species no closer than 25 feet (7.6 m) apart. A smaller tree that reaches only 30 feet (9.2 m) should be planted 15 to 20 feet (4.6–6.1 m) from its nearest neighbor. Spacing trees and shrubs correctly will allow them to develop properly as they grow.

And don't forget to consider the location of power lines, the proximity of trees to your house, and your neighbors. All might be negatively affected years later by an ill-placed tree.

Implement Your Plan

At last, once you've tallied up your wish list and purchased your plants, you're ready to start planting. But before you begin, refer to your property map and design overlay one last time. Note where the plants should be placed in order to grow best. Enlist the help of family members and then get started.

Use color-coded stakes — one color for trees, another for shrubs — and lay out your design in the intended area. Use rope to define group plantings, and be sure to leave some open spaces. In sunny spots, flowers and shrubs will thrive. When your layout is clear, start planting. Record your plantings on paper and photographically. If period-ically take photos from the same vantage point, you'll be able to track the growth of your plants and how they change over time.

Keep your new trees, shrubs, and flowers adequately watered. Strategically placed landscaping film, wood chips, or shredded bark mulch will keep unwanted plants or weeds in check. Resist the urge to trim out undergrowth and bottoms of shrubs. These are the spots favored by certain birds.

Remember that plants need time to grow and flourish. A reasonable timeline for a landscaping project of this sort is about five years.

Wise Plant Choices*

Plant	Benefit
Grasses	Shelter, food
Trees (mature and dead)	Food, nesting sites
Oak (*Quercus* spp.)	Food: insects (known to host about 300 different species), seeds (Wood Ducks eat acorns)
Alder (*Alnus* spp.)	Food
Beech (*Fagus* spp.)	Food
Willow (*Salix* spp.)	Food: insects (known to host about 250 different species), seeds
Poplar (*Populus* spp.)	Food: insects (known to host about 100 different species)
Birch (*Betula* spp.)	Food: insects (known to host about 250 different species), seeds
Shrubs	
Holly (*Ilex* spp.)	Excellent escape cover and roosting; food (berries)
Juniper (*Juniperus* spp.)	Shelter, food
Scarlet Firethorn (*Pyracantha* spp.)	Good ground cover, food
Bearberry *(Arctostaphylos uva-ursi)*	Good ground cover, food
Cranberry *(Vaccinium macrocarpon* and *V. oxycoccus)*	Good ground cover, food

Spreading varieties — Good ground cover, food
- Elderberry (*Sambucus* spp.)
- Ivy (*Hedera* spp.)
- Rose (*Rosa* spp.) (avoid invasive Multiflora Rose)
- Honeysuckle (*Lonicera* spp.) (avoid invasive Tatarian and Japanese)
- Hawthorn (*Crataegus* spp.)
- Dogwood (*Cornus* spp.)
- Flowering Japanese Quince *(Chaenomeles speciosa)*

Flowers — Food: insects, seeds
- Forget-me-not (*Myosotis* spp.)
- Sunflower (*Helianthus* spp.)
- Poppy (*Papaver* spp.)
- Cosmos *(Cosmos bipinnatus)*
- Asters (*Aster* spp.)
- Evening primrose (*Oenothera* spp.)
- Thistle (*Cirsium* spp.)
- Nettle (*Urtica* spp.)
- Petunia *(Ruellia humilis)*
- Thyme *(Thymus)*
- Lobelia (*Lobelia* spp.)
- Marjoram (*Origanum* spp.)
- Foxglove *(Digitalis purpurea)*
- Lavender (*Lavandula* spp.)

*Acquire your plants from native seed sources and local nurseries. Do not remove plants from public lands or from private property without the landowner's consent.

Prime habitat for birds and other wildlife includes safe sources of food and water, as well as shelter and nesting sites, as at this location.

References

Backyard Wildlife Habitat Planning Guide. Georgia Wildlife Federation, 1996.
http://www.gwf.org/library/hab_byh.htm

"Creating a habitat: Problems associated with traditional landscaping." National
Wildlife Federation, 1997.
http://www.nwf.org/mwf/habitats/creating/greener/traditional.html

Dennis, J. V. *The Wildlife in Your Life.* Washington, DC: Defenders of Wildlife/Rachel
Carson Memorial Wildlife Education Fund, 1976.

"Grow Natives." National Wildlife Federation, 1997.
http://www.nwf.org/nwf/habitats/greenerold/natives/index.html

Johnson, R. J., and C. W. Wolfe. "Backyard Wildlife Planting for Habitat."
Cooperative Extension, Institute of Agriculture and Natural Resources, University of
Nebraska—Lincoln. (G84-671; revised December 1994)
http://birding.miningco.com

Karriker, K. S., E. J. Jones, and M. A. Megalos. "Managing Edges for Wildlife." North
Carolina State University Cooperative Extension Office, North Carolina A & T
University, U.S. Department of Agriculture.
http://www.ces.ncsu.edu/nreos/forest/steward/www15.html

"Landscaping for Birds." Lincoln, MA: Massachusetts Audubon Society.

"Landscaping for Wildlife." Wildones — Natural Landscapers, Ltd., and Great Lakes
National Program Office.
http://www.epa.gov/glnpo/greenacres/wildones/wo24-25.htm

Megalos, M. A., E. J. Jones, and J. C. Turner. "Low-Cost Habitat Improvements."
North Carolina State University Cooperative Extension Office, North Carolina A & T
University, U.S. Department of Agriculture.
http://www.ces.ncsu.edu/nreos/forest/steward/www18.html

Rappaport, B. "How to Naturally Landscape without Aggravating Neighbors and
Village Officials." Wildones — Natural Landscapers, Ltd., and Great Lakes National
Program Office.
http://www.epa.gov/glnpo/greenacres/wildones/wo10.htm

Ross, T., ed. "Landscaping to Attract Birds." In *Homes for Birds.* U.S. Fish &
Wildlife Service.
http://www.bcpl.lib.md.us/~tross/by/attract.html

Tarski, C. "Attracting Birds Using Trees and Shrubs." General Internet Inc., 1998.
http://birding.miningco.com

Conservation Projects

Putting up and monitoring nestboxes can be a wonderful project for a variety of interest groups. Scout groups might try it with adult supervision; families might choose to construct, erect, and monitor nestboxes as fun weekend projects; church groups and school environmental clubs could use their properly made nestboxes for fund raisers; and schools could work cooperatively with their woodshop departments in the construction and monitoring of nestboxes as an interdisciplinary project.

Where to Place Boxes

Whether you want to work alone or as a member of an organized group, you can easily expand your birding horizons beyond your backyard or garden by establishing a nestbox trail, or a series of nestboxes. Good places for trails include golf courses (but beware of pesticide and herbicide use), cemeteries, fencerows along cultivated fields, church properties, nursing homes, community gardens, hospitals, and businesses with landscaped areas.

Opportunities abound, so think creatively. A few years ago a friend of ours, after obtaining permission from his employer, established a series of bluebird boxes on the grounds of his company. Simon checked the boxes regularly during his lunch period and garnered the interest of many coworkers. Gardeners at community garden sites typically welcome nestboxes, as potential nesters will consume some of the insects that might bother their crops. Reviewing topographic maps of your region might suggest new or unexpected areas that could serve as possible nestbox sites.

Bluebird Trails

◄ Bluebird trails, such as this one maintained by the State University of New York College of Agriculture and Technology at Cobleskill, have resulted in an increase in Eastern Bluebird populations as well as shedding light on nestbox-style preferences.

First advocated by T. E. Musselman in 1934, bluebird trails were erected across the United States and Canada starting in the 1960s. They have been very successful and have resulted in an increased bluebird population. Contact the North American Bluebird Society (see the appendix) or a local wildlife sanctuary to find out about bluebird groups in your area or how to start your own bluebird trails.

Before erecting any nestbox, obtain permission from the landowner. Explain what you would like to do, why you are doing it, what species might be attracted, and your monitoring procedure. Inquire as to the use of herbicides and pesticides. If these are used, politely decline the opportunity to establish a trail and seek alternate sites. The use of these chemicals may hurt the birds and work against your goals for putting up nestboxes.

Boxes should also be placed in areas of minimal traffic, both human and vehicular. Also be aware of vandalism. If you spot evidence of this in the vicinity, chances are that the boxes you establish won't be around for long.

School environmental clubs, scout troops, and other organized groups, under the leadership of a knowledgeable adviser or with the assistance of a local wildlife agency, could establish and maintain trails as part of the group's activities. This would give valuable insight to members not only into the life histories of their local birds but also insight into scientific fieldwork and research.

Kestrel Nestbox Program

One interesting project for kestrels began in Iowa and now has expanded to other areas and other species: the placement of nestboxes on the backs of highway signs. This could open new habitats to cavity-nesting birds. Contact your state or provincial highway department. If you would like to support a kestrel nesting program, contact the Hawk Mountain Sanctuary and inquire about its Adopt a Kestrel Nestbox Program (see the appendix).

Volunteer Opportunities

Any nature center or bird club that maintains nestboxes usually needs help in nestbox record keeping. Volunteering for a few hours each month could be very rewarding and educational. It could even be a good opportunity to find out more about whether birds like to use boxes with old nesting material. Contact the Cornell Laboratory of Ornithology (see the appendix) for more information not only on nestboxes and record cards but on other projects this facility is conducting as well.

With the rapid increase in technology, many organizations are seeking volunteers to enter information into computer databases. This work could give you insights into the kinds of research being conducted and the information that is being collected, as well as some of the implications of this data — it might also improve your typing skills.

If, on the other hand, you enjoy the outdoors and observing birds during late spring and early summer, volunteer to participate in a Breeding Bird Survey. This requires you to be in the field by sunrise. You will help map, identify, and record singing males. From this, you will be able to determine the species breeding in a given area and their